Sex Crime and the Media

In memory of my father – the greatest teacher ever.

Sex Crime and the Media:
sex offending and the press in a divided society

Chris Greer

WP
WILLAN
PUBLISHING

Published by

Willan Publishing
Culmcott House
Mill Street, Uffculme
Cullompton, Devon
EX15 3AT, UK
Tel: +44(0)1884 840337
Fax: +44(0)1884 840251
e-mail: info@willanpublishing.co.uk
website: www.willanpublishing.co.uk

Published simultaneously in the USA and Canada by

Willan Publishing
c/o ISBS, 5824 N.E. Hassalo St,
Portland, Oregon 97213-3644, USA
Tel: +001(0)503 287 3093
Fax: +001(0)503 280 8832
e-mail: info@isbs.com
website: www.isbs.com

First published 2003

ISBN 1-84392-004-2 (hardback)

British Library Cataloguing-in-Publication Data
A catalogue record for this book is available from the British Library

Project management by Deer Park Productions
Typeset by GCS, Leighton Buzzard, Beds
Printed and bound by T.J. International, Padstow, Cornwall

Contents

List of figures

Acknowledgements

I owe a considerable debt to the many people who have provided support from the start to finish of this book. Some have provided intellectual support. Some have provided emotional support (sharing through every lift, dip, loop and turn in the roller coaster ride that has been the last eighteen months). Many have provided both.

First, I am grateful to all those who participated in this study and without whom it would not have been possible. Special thanks must go to the survivors who gave up their time and spoke candidly about difficult issues. This can't have been easy, and your contributions have greatly enriched this project. I am also grateful to Brian Willan for his encouragement and his patience.

To Kieran McEvoy, thanks for your guidance, insight and humour, and for your dreadful impersonation of Benny from Abba. To Mike Brogden, Kevin Stenson, Jamie Thompson and colleagues at the Queen's University of Belfast, Buckinghamshire Chilterns University College and Northumbria University, our conversations have helped enormously in crystallising and articulating the ideas presented here. John Morison, Keith Soothill and Robert Reiner all scrutinised the research on which this book is based and provided helpful advice. Keith Soothill, Peter Francis and Yvonne Jewkes read drafts of the full manuscript and offered perceptive criticisms, timely encouragement, and were helpful in many other ways. Thanks especially Peter for your warmth and friendship.

Thank you Sandra for the inspiration you gave me. And finally my family and friends, among whom I am fortunate enough to include many of those mentioned already. Mum, Kieran, Kelley, Mike (and gremlins), Hannah and Steve (and Noah), Splant and Ella, Wills, Al and Helen, Dax and Catherine, Clare and Dean, Colin, Gar, Caroline, Esther and Neil, Gordy and Cat, Debs, Jade, Roge and Jo, Suzanne and Adam, Peter, Jamie, Vanessa and Nathaniel, Sean and Connie, and others not mentioned here (sorry!); though you may not know it, you have contributed enormously to the completion of this book. Without you I would be lost.

Chris Greer
April 2003

Chapter 1

Introduction

Introduction

This is a book about the representation of sex crime in the newsprint media in Northern Ireland. It is about the nature of press narratives, the messages they ultimately impart and the implications of these for public perceptions and social responses to sexual offending in contemporary society. It is about the complex inter-relationships between the influences, pressures, demands, incentives and sensibilities that shape the construction of this major source of fear and anxiety. While the focus is press representations in Northern Ireland, many of the issues addressed are relevant to any investigation of newsprint media discourse in liberal capitalist societies.

The problem of sexual offending, in its many different forms, has in recent decades taken on an unprecedented significance in the public imagination, both in Northern Ireland and elsewhere (Jenkins 1992; West 1996). Over this period, in a climate of heightened awareness which frequently borders on mass panic (West 2000a; Wilson and Silverman 2002), there has emerged a range of groups and organisations espousing values, beliefs, interests and ideologies that find consensus on some issues, but conflict on others. These groups engage in an ongoing and, at times, quite venomous struggle for definitional superiority, social credibility and political power. The press constitute a major site on which this contest is played out.

This throws up a number of interesting and important questions: what are the key areas of consensus and dispute? Who commands the greatest definitional power? What are practitioners' and journalists' key concerns and complaints – about each other, about the nature of press representations, about their consumption by news readers, about the cultural climate within which the problem of sex crime is constructed, about public sensibilities? And what, if anything, do they think should be done about it?

This book, then, is an exercise in contextualisation, in situating the construction of sex crime within its wider contexts in order to offer some idea as to why the problem of sexual offending has become so prevalent in media discourses. It examines the extent to which representations of sex crime have changed in recent years, how and why these changes have taken place, and what the implications of all this may be for the production, transmission and reception of images of sex crime in the press.

The Research Literature on Sex Crime and the Media

The book builds on an already substantial literature on media representations of sexual deviance. Most of the criminological research exploring this type of crime has been conducted over the last fifteen years (but see Soothill and Jack 1975; Chibnall 1977). Relevant texts, scholars and studies in the areas of sex crime, crime and the media and media studies more generally are referred to extensively throughout the study and, for that reason, I will not engage in an exhaustive review here. On the literature specifically on sex crime and the media, however, it is important to establish a few points at this early stage.

The sociological analysis of sex crime in the media has, with few exceptions (Paglia 1992; Kitzinger and Skidmore 1995; Young 1998), really meant the sociological analysis of sex crime in the press. Studies exploring images of sexual violence against women have variously concentrated on specific offences like date rape (Lees 1995), rape, sexual assault and sex murder (Cameron and Frazer 1987; Soothill and Walby 1991; Benedict 1992; Jenkins 1992, 1994; Grover and Soothill 1995; Soothill, 1995) and violence (including sexual violence) against women more generally (Meyers, 1997; Howe 1998). Research on images of child sexual abuse has considered offending in statutory care environments (Campbell 1988; Nava 1988; Franklin and Parton 1991), by members of the clergy (Jenkins 1996), by predatory strangers (Best 1990; Kitzinger 1999b; Websdale 1999) or across a range of forms (Jenkins 1992; Kitzinger and Skidmore 1995; Soothill *et al* 1998). Representations of the sexual abuse of children within the home are notable for their absence rather than their prevalence in media discourses (Kitzinger 1996; Greer, 2001a, 2003).

The theory and methods used in these studies have varied considerably. There has been a clear leaning towards feminist scholarship (Benedict 1992; Kitzinger and Skidmore 1996; Meyers 1997; Howe 1998), but studies have drawn from a diversity of theoretical perspectives. The constructionist paradigm for social problems research, with its emphasis on 'claims-making' and the 'framing' of events in popular consciousness (Jenkins 1992, 1996; see also Best 1995; Loseke 1999) and the related and emerging field of cultural criminology (Websdale 1999; see also Ferrell and Sanders 1995; Ferrell 1999; Presdee 2000), are two notable examples which bear a direct relevance to the analysis conducted here. As with the literature on crime news production more generally (Reiner *et al* 2000a, 2000b), many studies have considered representations of sex crime over a single, relatively short period of time (Benedict 1992; Meyers 1997; Howe 1998). Some, however, have explored changes and continuities over longer periods (Soothill and Walby 1991; Jenkins 1992; Kitzinger and Skidmore 1995).

Limitations of Existing Research

Much of the existing research investigating media representations of sex crime is partial in nature. That is, scholars have focused – sometimes in considerable detail – on particular aspects of the representation of sex crime, but this has generally been at the expense of considering others. For example, some studies have concentrated on only a few high-profile and particularly sensational cases (Benedict 1992), and then advanced general conclusions on that basis. As Soothill (1995) points out, the extent to which a few examples can be said to represent the 'norm' of media reportage is debatable.

Some scholars have cast the net wider (Soothill and Walby 1991), investigating the nature and extent of press representations of a broader range of sex crimes, but given little consideration to the influences which shape them. Soothill and Walby's (1991) *Sex Crime in the News* was the pioneering study in the area and remains one of the most frequently cited in the academic literature. But again the analysis in this research is partial because it overlooks crucial aspects of the news production process and is thus limited in its capacity to contextualise the 'construction' of the problem of sex crime.

Others have concentrated on the external 'social and economic contexts' which shape media representations (Jenkins 1992, 1996), but paid virtually no attention to the equally important influences that occur internally, within newsrooms. Understanding the competitive and highly politicised activities of different 'claims-making' groups is vital, but it is just as important to understand how these activities are shaped and influenced by the organisational constraints and commercial exigencies of news production, the routinisation of journalist–source interactions, and the unequal distribution of power both within newsrooms and between dominant and marginalised source organisations.

Some recent studies have provided more comprehensive accounts of the news production process and the representation of a wide range of criminally violent behaviours (Meyers 1997). And the development of increasingly sophisticated research methods has increased knowledge of how media images (of child sex abuse) are received, interpreted and, ultimately, understood by news audiences (Kitzinger and Skidmore 1995). Yet these studies, too, have paid only limited attention to the relevance of, for example, commercial shifts in the information marketplace and wider cultural shifts in late capitalist societies. Thus, though the existing research collectively has advanced our understanding of specific aspects of the representation of sex crime, no single contribution has presented a complete analysis of all those forces and influences – internal and external – that shape its construction in the press.

Press Representations of Sex Crime in Northern Ireland

This book presents an analysis of press representations of the full spectrum of sex offences, including: adult sex murder, child sex murder, offences against children and young persons, incest offences, indecency offences, consensual homosexual offences, offences against the mentally impaired, prostitution, pornography offences, rape, sexual assault, and sexual harassment.[1] Using illustrative examples throughout, it seeks to elucidate both the nature of the news product and the complex processes through which that product comes to be formed, framed and textured in Northern Ireland newsprint media discourse. To achieve this, it is necessary to examine the influences on news production (social, political, organisational, cultural, economic); the nature and significance of relationships between journalists and sources (professional and personal); the images of sex crime that ultimately constitute press narratives; and, crucially, the relevance and impact of wider change in late modernity. The analysis is situated in a deeply divided society, in a climate of ongoing social and political flux. Some of the issues I have addressed are peculiar to Northern Ireland. But many, as noted above, are generic, and I have sought to provide a more holistic account of what has thus far been explained only partially.

Empirical evidence has been sampled from two main sources. Long hours spent in a Belfast newspaper library with an unreliable laptop and yellowing fingers resulted in an archive of around 500 items, articles, letters and reports which relate directly in some way to the issue of sex crime. The quantitative and qualitative information yielded by this archive was supplemented with 37 in-depth interviews with key players in the construction of sex crime as news – journalists and editors, police officers, probation workers, sex crime counsellors, survivors of sex crime and others. As will become increasingly apparent throughout this book, and in line with the findings of others (Pfohl 1977; Jenkins 1992; Thomas 2000), sex crime is a highly contested terrain.

The Northern Ireland Conflict

The political and civil unrest in Northern Ireland has been well documented (Bowyer Bell 1993; McGarry and O'Leary 1995; Bew *et al* 1996; Ruane and Todd 1996). To offer a brief overview here, the two prevailing political doctrines are Nationalism and Unionism. Supporters of Unionism, who are largely Protestant, regard themselves as British and wish to remain part of the UK (Rees 1998). Supporters of Nationalism, who are largely Catholic, regard themselves as Irish and wish to actualise their 'Irishness' by breaking the Union between Great Britain and Northern Ireland and establishing a United Ireland, comprising both North and South, subject to the executive powers of an all-Irish government (*ibid*).

The Unionist and Nationalist ideologies have supporters who would advocate peaceful means for achieving political progress and conflict resolution, and those (called Loyalist and Republican, respectively) who believe that violence is a necessary evil in the struggle to achieve a lasting solution (McGarry and O'Leary 1995). Both sides, including associated paramilitary organisations, are officially represented by political parties that together form the Northern Ireland body politic. The party structure is dominated by the constitutional issue. Not all Protestants are Unionists and not all Catholics are Nationalists and, further, not all Unionists balk at the idea of a United Ireland and not all Nationalists recoil at the possibility of remaining part of the UK. Nevertheless, the majority of supporters of each ideology have strong beliefs about their cultural heritage and political future.

Locating the 'Troubles' within Northern Irish society is more complex than is often suggested. A diversity of communities are distinguishable, not just on religious and political grounds, but also geographically and economically. Almost half the population of around 1.6 million people lives in the Greater Belfast area. The remainder mainly inhabit small towns and rural communities, although there are notable concentrations in the smaller cities of (London-)Derry and Armagh.

The Northern Ireland Communities Crime Survey (NICCS) demonstrates the previously understated importance of social class and urbanisation in community experience and attitudes to crime and social control (O'Mahony *et al* 2000). When asked about their concerns regarding their children's safety from being bullied, run over or sexually molested, parents in urban areas showed significantly higher levels of concern than their rural counterparts, particularly in working-class communities (O'Mahony *et al* 2000). This reinforces the view that social and cultural settings significantly influence how individuals interpret the world around them. People make meaning out of whatever 'ideational resources' are most accessible as a consequence of living within a particular social milieu (Gamson *et al* 1992; Gubrium 1993; Sasson 1995). Among the most accessible of these resources, of course, are the media. How media represent social phenomena is central to how we, as consumers with limited first-hand experience, make sense of them and their 'place' in our everyday lives. This book considers the role of the press, within this context of deep division, as just such an ideational resource (or, perhaps better, as a collection of often conflicting ideational resources) used by news consumers to help 'make sense' of sex crime. Next, then, a word on the Northern Ireland press.

The Northern Ireland Press

The regional press in Northern Ireland comprise three daily newspapers (the *Belfast Telegraph*, the *Irish News* and the *Belfast News Letter* – henceforth the *News Letter*) and two Sunday newspapers (the *Sunday Life* and the *Sunday World Northern Edition* – henceforth the *Sunday World*). The *Sunday World* is frequently referred to as Dublin based, though the Northern Edition, considered here, is produced almost entirely in Northern Ireland. To increase the sample size, one further title – the *Irish Times* – was also considered. This newspaper is essentially Dublin based, but it too maintains offices and a substantial circulation and readership in Northern Ireland.

Each newspaper subscribes to a more or less Unionist or Nationalist agenda. Briefly, of the four dailies, the *Belfast Telegraph* (broadsheet) and the *News Letter* (tabloid) are Unionist, and the *Irish News* and *Irish Times* (both broadsheets) are Nationalist.[2] Of the two Sunday newspapers (both tabloid), the *Sunday Life* is, in the words of one journalist, 'fairly neutral' politically, while the *Sunday World*, though it also claims no position on the constitutional issue, tends more towards Nationalism than Unionism. These classifications are admittedly crude, and the range of ownership structures and the precise organisational and ideological differences between the newspapers are discussed in later chapters. The point here is simply to offer some indication of the types of newspapers examined in this book and the spread of ideological opinion represented in the Northern Ireland press.

The regional press constitute a market which is distinct from others in certain crucial respects. In reporting the conflict for the past thirty years, newspapers in Northern Ireland have developed a rich social and political heritage and established important levels of integrity and credibility with their audiences. As such, they play a key role both in reflecting and reaffirming the cultural identities of their readerships. Indeed, these newspapers, some of which are centuries old, may take on an almost unique importance in this regard.

In a small jurisdiction like Northern Ireland, where political culture is a defining characteristic of everyday life, a newspaper's ideological orientation and consequent editorial line can determine its readership almost entirely. Crucially for this research, it can influence profoundly the representation of the British state and its apparatuses of control. It is common knowledge, for example, that some titles will be more likely to carry stories that are critical of the police and the judiciary than will others. Correspondingly, it is widely acknowledged by journalists that a newspaper's coverage of the constitutional issue and, in particular, issues of law and order can affect profoundly its working relations with the key criminal justice agencies.

Given the oppositional and highly politicised nature of public debate in Northern Ireland, the regional press are prone to producing deeply partisan coverage (Rolston 1991a; Bromley 1997). Yet not all issues are easily appropriated by party politics; not all debates are wrenched into a Unionist or Nationalist groove. Some are so emotionally charged that they resonate with equal intensity across cultures and transcend the party politics that underpins so many discourses in that jurisdiction. One such issue is the problem of sex crime. For this reason, the press representation of sex crime in a divided society – Northern Ireland – is of special relevance, and special sociological interest.

The Structure of the Book

The remainder of this chapter is concerned with describing the structure of the book and, then, providing a critical overview of the dominant theoretical approaches – the liberal pluralist and radical readings – which have traditionally underpinned the sociological analysis of news production. Each reading has its strengths and its weaknesses, depending on the context in which it is applied. It is with this in mind that Chapter 2 situates the analysis more precisely within Northern Ireland. It seeks to abstract, distil and refine those elements of the radical and liberal pluralist interpretations which can be applied best to explain the construction of sex crime in the regional press. The aim is to synthesise the strengths and address the weaknesses as they apply specifically to this research. Chapter 3 completes the formative theoretical discussion by outlining and evaluating the criteria which inform news selection and production, generally, and the representation of sex crime, specifically. The key questions here are: 'what is it that makes sex crimes so eminently reportable?', 'why are some sex crimes so much more newsworthy than others?' and 'how are the various behaviours that attract the label sex crime perceived by journalists and practitioners?'

Chapter 4 proceeds with an empirical analysis of regional press representations of sex crime in Northern Ireland between 1985 and 1997. Drawing from archival and interview material, it examines the way in which sex offences were constructed throughout this period, highlighting in particular major changes and continuities in the amount, nature and style of reporting. Chapter 5 seeks to explain those changes by situating the construction of sex crime within its wider social, political, cultural, ideological and commercial contexts. It is proposed that it is only through consideration of the wider environment within which press representations of sex crime are produced that one can begin to unpack and understand why they take on the form and flavour that they do.

For many, the form and flavour of sex crime coverage are highly problematic. Chapter 6, therefore, explores practitioners' views and concerns about the representation of sex crime in the press. There is no consensus in Northern Ireland (or elsewhere) regarding the right or wrong way to deal with sex crime. Nor is there unanimity regarding the 'proper' way for sex crimes to be reported. Rather, competing values, interests and beliefs continually jostle for superiority. This chapter establishes the key areas of consensus and controversy relating to the representation of sex crime in the press. Chapter 7 seeks to resolve some of the tensions by locating journalists' and practitioners' often conflicting views within an empirical framework.

Chapter 8 advances the discussion further by drawing together theoretical and empirical considerations and moving towards a more holistic analysis of the press construction of sex crime. It considers the role that relevant parties feel they can, do and should play in the press construction of sex crime, systematically identifying and exploring those factors that promote or constrain the representation of what is known of the social reality of sex crime in Northern Ireland. Finally, Chapter 9 sets out the conclusions of the book and offers some tentative suggestions as to how press representations of sex crime might be expected to develop in the future, should they continue to follow current trajectories.

The Sociological Analysis of News Production

Crucial to any investigation of the representation of crime, deviance and control is a clear and well-substantiated explication of the role played by journalists and sources in that process and, bearing in mind cautions against media-centric analyses (Schlesinger 1990), a solid conception of the power relations between them (Manning 2001). That is, in order to understand the anatomy and dynamics of the construction of sex crime in the press it is critical to understand the anatomy and dynamics of news production in Northern Ireland.

Two principal interpretations – the liberal pluralist reading (with variants referred to as 'market' 'commercial', 'laissez-faire', 'competitive' or 'subversive') and the radical reading (with variants called '(mass) manipulative', 'structural-culturalist', 'dominance' or 'hegemonic') – have in a variety of forms framed much of the research in this area since its emergence proper in the 1970s. There is no single author whose work encapsulates the complete radical or liberal pluralist picture. Rather, in what follows I abstract from a range of variations a number of general themes which represent the commonalities or general lines of argument shared by those approaching media analyses from either a liberal pluralist or a radical perspective. I then make some suggestions regarding how each approach might be used to explain and understand the construction of sex crime in the press. The key characteristics of each reading can be outlined as follows.

The liberal pluralist reading of news production

From a liberal pluralist perspective, newsworthiness is determined largely by public interests and consumer demand (Koss 1984). Journalists are tasked accordingly with meeting those interests by collecting news and providing consumers with objective and realistic information about the world (Whale 1977; Grabosky and Wilson 1989). Reporters insist upon, indeed pride themselves upon maintaining high levels of professional autonomy and are actively encouraged in this pursuit by colleagues who share the same system of values (Gans 1980). The emphasis on professionalism 'includes a strong commitment to detachment and objectivity, and a belief in the importance of ensuring that the public is adequately informed' (Curran 1998: 82).

Journalistic autonomy, it is argued, is reinforced on two levels – organisational and individual. At the individual level, any pressures by editors or advertisers to follow a particular line, apply a particular 'spin', suppress a particular piece of information or in some other way distort the 'truth status' of the news product will be forcefully resisted. To comply with such pressures would conflict with a reporter's professional values (Hetherington 1985). At the organisational level, the private economic ownership of most modern media agencies brings financial (and thus to a significant extent ideological) independence from the state. And the diversity of ownership within a given capitalist economy ensures 'genuine competition' between a plurality of ideas (McNair 1998). In this view, reporters are 'free' to act as watchdogs over the actions of the powerful, exposing when necessary abuses of power and holding those responsible to account. Journalism here is viewed as a key mechanism for safeguarding the democratic process.

News sources actively compete for media access and influence, but 'free competition for media space and political power ensure that a variety of voices are heard' (Miller 1998: 66; see also Blumler and Gurevitch 1995). This interpretation is thus underpinned by the insistence that there is equal competition between groups to promote their respective social, political and ideological views. The media's role is to provide a public platform for resolving ideological differences through the 'facilitation and organisation of public debate' in which all parties have a say (McNair 1998: 19). It is the diversity of the myriad groups rivalling for attention and influence in an open market which is stressed, rather than any notion of inequality in terms of structured dominance and subordination (see, for example, Hansen 1991). In short, media discourse is seen to take place on an ideological playing field which is, more or less, level.

There is little room, then, for notions of hegemonic ideological domination in the liberal conception of news production. In fact, it is held that advanced capitalist societies can be broadly defined in terms of social harmony rather than ideological contest. In an essentially functionalist view of social cohesion in the midst of ongoing change, members of a given social order are bound through socialisation by a shared system of core values and beliefs. This 'cultural consensus', it is argued, both frames and is reflected in journalistic accounts and judgements. By protecting the public interest, journalists' reportage serves to legitimate and reinforce the cultural consensus and the normative framework to which it gives rise. Through their role as public watchdog and as representatives of those members of society who do not themselves command a public voice journalists empower the masses. They play a central role in ensuring the transparency and democratic integrity of the political process. Curran (1998: 83) summaries the liberal pluralist reading as follows:

> News media can be seen as being shaped by consumer demand, the professional concerns of media workers, pluralistic source networks, and the collective values of society. While the liberal tradition is not agreed about the relative weight that should be accorded different influences, it has in common a tendency to see the media as serving the public.

This interpretation is frequently adhered to by journalists themselves, and has found support to varying degrees in a range of academic studies (Tunstall 1971; Gans 1980; Hetherington 1985; Hansen 1991). It tends also to be favoured by those who command economic and political power – that is, by those, as McNair observes, 'for whom the kind of capitalist society we live in today is, if not the best of all possible worlds, very nearly the best we can reasonably expect' (1998: 21). The criticism this reading most frequently attracts is that it oversimplifies what is in fact a much more complex process. It overstates the liberating powers of commercialisation and the fluidity of competition, at the same time understating the constraining effects of the organisational realities of news production. Securing access and exposure in the media and influencing public debate are seldom as free and easy as liberal pluralist commentators suggest.

The radical reading of news production

Advocates of the radical reading draw from critical social theory, foregrounding in particular Marxist and Gramscian conceptions of social inequality and hegemonic class rule. Here, the material selected and constructed as news is determined not by the wider public interest, but by the interests of those who own and/or control the news agencies – the political, cultural and economic elites that constitute the dominant groups in advanced capitalist societies.

In this reading, 'the information media are viewed, like other cultural institutions in a class society, as producers of ideology, representing the interests of an elite minority to the subordinate majority' (McNair 1999: 22). Different accounts have stressed different pressures, demands, constraints and expectations to explain – to varying degrees – how this is achieved, variously fitting into social-organisational (Rock 1973; Molotch and Lester 1974; Gitlin 1980; Hallin 1986) structural-culturalist (Hall *et al* 1978; Tuchman 1978) and political-economic (Murdock 1974; Herman and Chomsky 1994; McChesney 1997; cf. Golding and Murdock, 2000) models of news production. For explanatory purposes here, radical interpretations of the influences on journalistic production can be grouped into four (inter-related and overlapping) categories – political, economic, social-organisational and cultural.

First, the nature of the political system in advanced capitalist societies helps safeguard the reproduction of elite-establishment views. Governments, it is argued, have considerable regulatory, censorial, legislative and intimidatory powers directly to influence what media agencies say and do. They may use the various tools at their disposal to foster alliances with key sectors of the journalistic media or to silence dissident media voices (Chadwick 1989; Garnham 1998). Though journalists may challenge dominant groups and institutional structures on various issues, they are effectively limited to criticising the administration of the system, rather than the system itself (Miliband 1973; Herman and Chomsky 1994).

Secondly, economic conditions contribute to the perpetuation of elite values and interests. In recent decades, more and more owners have diversified from concentration on one medium (for example, newspapers) to several (newspapers, magazines, television). Diversification has been accompanied by a shift towards oligopoly (Murdock 1990; Barwise and Gordon 1998) which, in turn, has resulted in a small number of individuals building up massive media empires that command considerable economic, political and cultural power (Bagdikian 1997; Curran and Seaton 1997; Curran 2000). Rather than using their power to facilitate genuine debate, however, radical critics argue that media owners are more interested in maintaining the cultural conditions and socio-political systems that will nourish the continued generation of profit (Murdock 2000); a concern shared by other elite members, such as major advertisers and representatives of government and big business (Kellner 1990). Proprietors may exercise significant influence in their newsrooms to ensure that elite values and interests are reproduced in media discourse (Golding and Murdock 2000). This influence can be direct, but is most often exercised through the appointment of like-minded editors (McNair 1999).[3] Rather than being coercive, a reward structure based on conformity taps into journalists' desire for advancement and tends to foster compliance through self-censorship (Breed 1980).

Thirdly, those in powerful and privileged positions – the political and economic elite – maintain a structural advantage or 'privileged access' in the media. Journalists rely on a narrow range of powerful groups and institutions for routine access to newsworthy material. This is partly attributable to the organisational constraints of news production (most obviously, limitations of time and space). But more than this, elite sources are recognised as accredited providers of credible and authoritative information (Schlesinger and Tumber 1994). They carry the cultural status of 'authorised knowers' (Ericson *et al* 1989) and, as such, are granted privileged access in the media almost as of right (Hall *et al* 1978). The information these sources provide, it is argued, is pre-formulated in a way that advances the interests of dominant groups. Journalists may appear to be 'free' to report with impartiality, objectivity and balance, but due to their reliance on dominant groups and the biased nature of the information they receive, they are in fact structurally, organisationally and culturally constrained to reproduce the values and beliefs of the powerful.

And, fourthly, news production (as in the liberal pluralist reading) is characterised by the notion of a 'cultural consensus'. In liberal pluralist interpretations, the media reflect the cultural values of a socially harmonious society. For radical scholars, by contrast, the media reflect the cultural values specifically of those at the top of the social hierarchy. Media discourse not only reproduces elite values and interests, it also contributes to their wider naturalisation and acceptance (Hartley 1982). It legitimates the conditions of class dominance and subordination created by capitalism, ensuring that the interests of the few are shared to some extent across the social system by representing them as the interests of all. Because of the elite ownership of both material and mental production, the dominant ideology comes to be objectified in major social, political and legal institutions, including the media. This ideology informs journalists' worldviews, ultimately constituting the 'interpretative frameworks' with which they 'make sense' of the social world around them. Whether they are aware of it or not, it is argued, through their reportage journalists help protect the interests of the ruling elite.

In contrast to the liberal pluralist interpretation, then, the radical reading holds that journalists are not ideologically autonomous (though they may think they are). Rather, they are subject to multiple pressures by economic elites, dominant sources and the organisation and structure of their own professional environment to represent the social world in accordance with a particular ideological line. Herman and Chomsky (1994: 298) summarise the radical reading of media production as follows:

> [T]he 'societal purpose' of the media is to inculcate and defend the economic, social and political agenda of the privileged groups that dominate the domestic society and the state. The media serve this purpose in many ways: through selection of topics, distribution of concerns, framing of issues, filtering of information, emphasis and tone, and by keeping debate within the bounds of acceptable premises.

While the liberal pluralist reading has been most popular among practitioners and policy-makers, the radical reading has been the more influential within the academy. It is most frequently challenged on the grounds that it overstates both the homogeneity of elite-establishment views and the capacity of the powerful to maintain an ideological dominance virtually unchallenged in public discourse (Schlesinger and Tumber 1994; McNair 1998; Schudson 2000). In the process, it understates the extent to which marginalised groups can enter into those discourses, sometimes with alarming success, and redefine the terms of the debate (Jenkins 1992; Miller, L. 1993). The radical interpretation has also been criticised for downplaying the relative autonomy of journalists, for placing them too far down the structural hierarchy of news production when, in fact, they can – and do – play a crucial role in the creative process of making news.

Applying Theory to the Press Representation of Sex Crime

While both perspectives retain their fair share of adherents, it is now widely accepted that neither on its own provides an adequate framework for understanding the complex process of making news. Nor, then, is either adequate for framing a sufficiently comprehensive account of the construction of sex crime in press discourse. Much of the work on media representations, criminological and otherwise, has committed too readily to one or other of these models and paid too little attention to the possibility of establishing a middle ground. The result has been the development of a somewhat polarised research literature where, at one extreme, news media are seen as empowering the people and, at the other, they are seen as controlling them.

Recent accounts suggest that a fruitful way to proceed may be to draw on elements from both the radical and liberal pluralist readings in order to develop a more inclusive approach which navigates a path between the 'diametrically opposed viewpoints of many leading analysts' (Curran 1998: 81). That the liberal pluralist and radical perspectives are in many ways diametrically opposed is significant because, in certain crucial respects, the evaluation of one simultaneously facilitates the evaluation of the other. With respect to journalists, the question is whether they are in fact autonomous and free to report objectively, or the mouthpieces of the powerful. And regarding sources, the question is whether there is equal competition for access and influence in the media and, consequently, genuine competition between a plurality of ideas, or whether certain powerful organisations can secure ideological closure around key issues of public concern. Tackling each of these questions is central to understanding the complex and varied processes that influence the construction of sex crime in the press. By way of illustration, it is useful here to suggest what advocates of the liberal pluralist and radical perspectives might expect to find if they set about exploring the construction of sex crime, on the basis of their preferred interpretations of the news production process.

In terms of journalistic autonomy, for example, the liberal pluralist reading maintains that proprietorial intervention (whether applied directly or channelled through editors) does not feature as a major influence on journalists' activities. Nor, then, should it feature as a major influence on the way in which sex crimes are represented. Rather, liberal pluralist scholars would expect journalists to be left largely alone to report sex crimes in the manner dictated by their professional journalistic values which, from this perspective, are held to be fiercely guarded. Any efforts to impose restrictions on journalists' reportage which undermine the integrity of the news they produce – for example, overly sensationalist coverage or the distortion of the issue through case selection, language and the types of information included and omitted – may be met with forceful and collective resistance.

The radical reading, by contrast, insists that journalistic autonomy is routinely and fundamentally constrained by proprietorial and editorial intervention in the interests of commercial success and the maintenance of a preferred political or ideological line. From a radical viewpoint, then, it would be expected that the construction of sex crime narratives, like other news forms, will be carefully supervised by proprietors and editors and shaped in a way designed to maximise profits rather than safeguard the integrity or quality of the information being provided. Given the radical emphasis on commercial success, representations of sex crime might be expected to prioritise audience-seeking sensationalism and the detailed description of dramatic events over informed and serious discussion around key issues like causes, risk and prevention.

In terms of source activities and the facilitation of open democratic debate, the liberal pluralist reading acknowledges that sources compete for access and influence in the media. However, the nature of media ownership, free competition for influence and political power and the sheer number and diversity of groups vying to have their voices heard ensures that a wide range of views and interests is represented. From this perspective, then, one would expect sex crime narratives to include opinion and comment from a wide range of sources representing a diversity of values, interests and beliefs. In line with this insistence on open competition and source diversity, the use of sources should not be restricted to powerful, socially instituted groups and organisations which command considerable resources (and in many cases employ dedicated PR representatives). It should also accommodate less powerful or marginalised groups which are, comparatively speaking, resource-poor. It would be inconsistent with this reading, therefore, if reportage drew from a narrow range of powerful sources and was consistently characterised by, say, an especially punitive (or, for that matter, rehabilitative) stance with regard to the treatment of convicted sex offenders. Rather, a more balanced, objective presentation of a range of positions would be anticipated.

The radical picture again differs considerably. In this view, news production is dominated precisely by those groups and institutions specifically at the top of the social and political hierarchy – authorised knowers who are seen to command legitimacy and credibility in both political and cultural terms. In radical interpretations of news production, press discourse represents the views and interests, not of society as a whole, but of the powerful elite. In the construction of sex crime narratives, then, it would be expected that powerful source organisations – for example, the police and the judiciary – will dominate, setting the agenda and framing the terms of the debate. Groups with more marginal views, by contrast, will be subordinated to lesser positions, maintaining lower profiles and commanding lesser influence in press discourse and the public arena.

Finally, both the radical and liberal pluralist readings suggest that news is constructed on the basis of an assumed consensus, indicative of a society in which certain core values and beliefs are shared in common. Their difference lies in the question over precisely whose interests those values and beliefs reflect. Both positions encounter serious problems when applied to news production in Northern Ireland. From a liberal pluralist standpoint, the notion of Northern Ireland as a consensual society in even the broadest terms seems untenable. Yet the radical claim of some unified dominant elite or ruling class alliance is equally implausible. Northern Ireland is characterised by conflict, not consensus; there is no unified political or cultural elite. Indeed, it is in the role of political culture in the news production process and the cultural role of news that Northern Ireland differs most significantly from other, comparatively stable, social orders. In this climate of ongoing flux, as noted, press representations of sex crime take on a special relevance. Establishing the cultural relevance of sex crime in Northern Ireland, and how this intersects with radical and liberal pluralist interpretations of news production and the construction of law and order, is one of the central aims of this book.

Conclusions

In recent years the problem of sex crime has emerged as a key issue in political and criminal justice policy debate, and a staple of media discourse. At the same time, it has become a major source of public fear and anxiety. Understanding and explaining the construction of sex crime in the press are central to understanding its resonance in contemporary social life. Much of the existing research has provided a partial account of the media representation of sex crime. This book takes the analysis further by examining more fully the diversity of social, political, cultural, organisational and economic forces that shape its construction in newsprint media discourse.

The aims in this chapter have been threefold. The first has been to introduce and contextualise this study of the representation of sex crime in the Northern Ireland press. I have offered a brief overview of the existing research literature, identified what appear to me to be important gaps and suggested how in the course of this study I will try to fill them. The second aim has been to map out the structure of the book to in order to give the reader a clear vision of what follows. The third has been to outline the dominant theoretical paradigms which have traditionally informed sociological analyses of the media. It is the further consideration of these dominant theoretical approaches and their application to the production of news in a divided society that forms the basis of discussion the following chapter.

In Chapter 2 I argue that both the radical and liberal pluralist readings are too deterministic and inflexible when located within the context of news production in Northern Ireland. I have attempted to develop a theoretical middle ground, a critical framework which synthesises elements from both readings, but seeks to address the inconsistencies and weaknesses clearly contained in each. I am not suggesting that the framework outlined in this book is applicable in all social contexts – it is not. Indeed, one of the key failings of previous research has been the attempt to generalise models, to assume they can be imported between social orders that differ significantly in political, economic and cultural terms. Nevertheless, despite the uniqueness of Northern Ireland in a number of respects, the information marketplace in that jurisdiction has been subject to the same transformations and pressures experienced by many others. On this basis, it seems reasonable to suggest that the explanatory framework presented here may help to elucidate the complexities of news production in other advanced capitalist societies.

Notes

1 For full definitions, see Appendix I.
2 Though *The Irish Times* claims to have no position on the constitutional issue, it is widely viewed as sympathising with Nationalism.
3 In the English market, highly interventionist media moguls including the late Robert Maxwell and Rupert Murdoch, have openly announced that they routinely use(d) their outlets to advance their own political and economic interests. Robert Maxwell famously boasted that his newspapers were a 'megaphone' with which he could 'raise issues effectively' (Curran and Seaton 1997: 76; see also McNair 1999: 53). And former News International editor for *The Sunday Times*, Andrew Neil, recalled Rupert Murdoch's editorial omnipresence, his talent for 'being there even when he is not'. Murdoch would regularly impose his right-wing view of the world on his staff and, subsequently, on his media's content, and frequently spike stories that might have incurred negative consequences for his business holdings outside publishing (Neil 1996, cited in Curran 1998: 87). Indeed, few media owners would 'bother to deny that they use their media interests not just to make money but to influence public opinion and the political environment' (McNair 1999: 54).

Chapter 2

Theory and context

Introduction

This chapter seeks to develop a framework for analysis which draws on both the radical and liberal pluralist readings of news production, while recognising the weaknesses in each. The objective is to establish a suitable theoretical foundation on which to structure the examination of sex crime in the Northern Ireland press. This requires the investigation of a number of inter-related spheres of influences which impact directly on the news production process, namely economic, social-organisational and political-cultural. Of key interest here are how these influences serve to promote or constrain journalistic autonomy, access to media exposure, and the generation of open debate and the genuine competition between ideas.

What follows is not intended to be a full investigation of all aspects of the radical and liberal pluralist readings. Such an undertaking lies outside the scope of this book. Rather, the aim is to highlight the particular strengths and limitations which relate directly to the press representation of sex crime. For example, the regulatory and legislative powers of government to manipulate journalistic output, while of considerable interest in general terms, have limited bearing on this analysis. More important is the role of the wider political culture, the subtler ideological influences from owners, editorial staff and news audiences and how these serve either to constrain or enhance journalists' autonomy and shape the news they produce. For this reason, political influence is discussed in relation to its intersection with the economic, social-organisational and cultural spheres. I will begin by considering the effects of the economic environment on news production in Northern Ireland.

Economic Determinants of News Production

Radical scholars argue that the ideological line of newspapers is determined by proprietorial (elite-establishment) interests, that the prevailing culture within newsrooms is perpetuated through the selective appointment of like-minded editors and that journalistic autonomy is severely limited by constant pressures to report in line with a particularly ideological stance. The liberal argument, on the other hand, maintains that a newspaper's line is determined primarily by market interests, that newsprint media discourse is played out on an ideological playing field which is more or less level, and that journalists are largely autonomous with their reportage being informed, first and foremost, by professional journalistic values. Both accounts suffer from a number of limitations, which are amplified further when situated within Northern Ireland.

Proprietorial influence

Three of the six newspapers considered in this study are owned by the same company. The *Belfast Telegraph*, its sister publication the *Sunday Life* (printed in the same building, but within separate offices and under different editorial, reporting and managerial staff) and the *Sunday World*, are all produced by Independent News and Media, chaired by Irish businessman Sir Tony O'Reilly.[1] Independent News and Media bought the various titles produced by Belfast Telegraph Newspapers for £300 million in March 2000 (*Belfast Telegraph* 29 March 2000). Unionist MPs were strongly opposed to the acquisition. Officially, complaints were advanced on the grounds of competition and fairness – that the transfer would give Independent News and Media too great a share of the Irish newspaper market. It is widely felt, however, that concerns more likely reflected discomfort with a Dublin-born and Catholic businessman owning a traditionally Unionist newspaper and the implications this might have for the *Belfast Telegraph*'s editorial line. This in spite of the fact that the company's titles in the Republic of Ireland – the *Irish Independent* and the *Sunday Independent* – have traditionally been pro-Unionist.

Several journalists insisted, however, that Unionist concerns over the acquisition were misplaced. Since Independent News and Media bought the *Belfast Telegraph* its editorial policy has not changed. Indeed if anything, they suggested, the new proprietor has taken a distinctly 'hands-off' approach to its running. There are a number of factors which may serve to constrain proprietorial intervention in this and other newspapers.

Most obviously, as a result of his many and varied business interests, Tony O'Reilly spends much of his time abroad. This has clear logistical implications, in the most straightforward sense, for the maintenance of any significant level of direct proprietorial intervention on a daily basis. More importantly, the *Belfast Telegraph* is an extremely profitable enterprise. Proprietors need to be wary of possible staff resistance to intervention. But they must also consider how any planned changes to the accepted *and expected* form and flavour of their titles' reportage will be received by the target audience. As *Irish News* editor Noel Doran cautioned, 'we would get a revolt from our readers if we deviated too far from what they expect'. A newspaper's market success may restrict proprietorial intervention as much as facilitate it.

The *News Letter* has been owned by the Mirror Group (now Trinity–Mirror plc) since 1996. The company owns a wide range of other titles throughout the UK, including the Northern Irish *Derry Journal*. The *News Letter* (printed in Belfast) supports a Unionist political agenda and the *Derry Journal* (printed in (London)Derry) is Nationalist. There is no ideological unity or elite consensus collectively reinforced by these newspapers.[2] In fact, they differ fundamentally on their position on the constitutional issue. Should any members of the Trinity–Mirror consortium wish ideologically to realign one of the titles, they would be faced not only with possible resistance from other consortium members, but also with the immediate and obvious possibility of 'audience revolt'. As the *News Letter*'s editor Geoff Martin put it, 'If somebody became a major influence in Trinity–Mirror and decreed that all its newspapers must follow a particular line, that would be disastrous commercially for the company, not to mention the integrity of journalism'. Ownership structure, then, may also serve to constrain proprietorial influence.

By contrast, the *Irish News* is owned by local businessman Jim Fitzpatrick, an ex-solicitor who also maintains property holdings in Belfast. Mr Fitzpatrick is permanently resident in Northern Ireland and keeps an office in the *Irish News* buildings. It seems reasonable to suggest that it would be easier, at least logistically, for this proprietor to intervene if he wished to do so. Indeed, Jim Fitzpatrick was responsible for a clear shift in the newspaper's editorial policy which appeared to go against the grain of commercial interests. Before his acquisition of the *Irish News* in the mid-1980s, it had traditionally carried IRA death notices.[3] These obituaries reported the deaths of IRA staff who had been 'killed in active service'. The new owner banned the notices and, in so doing, brought the paper into conflict with its substantial Republican readership. Here, then, personal ideological convictions would appear to have taken precedence over commercial concerns. It is worth bearing in mind, however, that sales of the *Irish News* have increased substantially since the mid-1980s, while circulation for its main competitors – the *Belfast Telegraph* and the *News Letter* – has fallen.[4] This success may be due in part to the newspaper's alignment with a more moderate Nationalist position. A certain level of foresight and commercial savvy should not, therefore, be ruled out. But the evidence of direct intervention in this newspaper is clear.

All this suggests that proprietorial influence is more complex than the radical reading suggests. The research literature in a diversity of social orders illustrates that certain media owners can and do play a proactive – and sometimes coercive – role in influencing policy and content. But it is important to avoid the kind of reductionism which assumes that they are all cast in the same highly interventionist mould. Even if the inclination is there, proprietorial influence is constrained by a range of countervailing factors including market forces, logistics, ownership structure and professional culture. Of course, the radical reading does not restrict its conceptualisation of proprietorial influence to direct intervention. Its advocates contend that influence is most often sustained by the appointment of like-minded editors. In the Northern Irish regional market, however, this notion too garners little support from the available evidence.

Proprietorial influence through editorial appointments

The ownership of several Northern Ireland regional newspapers has changed more than once in recent years. Yet despite these proprietorial changes, all have maintained consistent ideological lines and, importantly, the same editors have remained in post throughout. The *Belfast Telegraph* and the *Sunday Life* were administered under three different proprietors between 1993 and 2001. During that time, both their editorial policies and their editors stayed the same. The *News Letter* has been administered under two different consortia since Geoff Martin became editor in 1990, but its Unionist editorial line and Geoff Martin's position have remained constant. Perhaps most significantly, International News and Media and Trinity–Mirror produce newspapers which espouse both Nationalist and Unionist views. Given this straddling of the political divide, it is far from obvious what the ideological convictions of a like-minded editor would be.

It is not the ideological predilections of media owners but the established predilections of the audiences at whom the news product is targeted that takes precedence in determining editorial policy in Northern Ireland. The *Belfast Telegraph*'s Chris Thornton suggested that 'the nature of the papers when they started defined their readerships, but the readerships define those papers now'. If a new proprietor is to maximise or even maintain sales for the recently acquired outlet, he or she must be careful not to deviate too far from that title's recognised and expected line, thus invoking the circulation-threatening displeasure of the assumed audience. The *News Letter*'s editor, Geoff Martin, put it as follows:

> Newspapers have their standing in society, built up over decades, if not centuries. In many ways, in Northern Ireland the readers feel they own the newspapers [laughs]. Anything which our regular or long-standing readers would see as a betrayal of the newspaper's position is likely to cause problems.

In Northern Ireland, then, it seems that market forces (underpinned by and inextricably linked to long-established political traditions) and the attendant risk of a negative audience reaction to ideological change seem sufficient to safeguard the maintenance of a consistent editorial policy, regardless of what the predilections of those who 'own' the titles might be. In this sense, liberal conceptions of news production seem nearer the mark. The daily running of the regional press in Northern Ireland appears to be left largely to the editors who, on the basis of audience expectations and sales performance, seem more concerned with maintaining ideological consistency than with occasioning change. Next, we consider the extent to which editorial influence is brought to bear on journalists' routine activities.

Editorial influence

The *Belfast Telegraph*'s Security Correspondent, Chris Thornton, suggested that journalistic autonomy increases as a function of seniority within a given newspaper:

> I mean, I would have more autonomy than someone who is new in the game, just because I've been around longer. Probably the news desk would be less inclined to change a story of mine or, at least, talk to me before changing it. But just, I mean, in a general scenario, you write a story, it goes to your news editor who may make some minor style changes, may even send the whole thing back to you.

This was a frequently stated view: because senior journalists have usually been around longer, their skills are considered to be more developed (hence the position of seniority) and they are more likely to be capable of producing appropriate copy without the need for editorial supervision. Experience, then, would seem to be the key issue. But it is not experience as related to the enhancement of journalistic skills in the technical sense (as suggested by most journalists) that is of greatest significance here. Rather, it is the effect of experience on a journalist's recipe knowledge and routine practices that is crucial.

Reporters who have been working at a title for longer will be more sensitised to the newsroom culture than more recent recruits. They will be more likely *automatically* or *habitually* to produce news stories that are structured within the expected ideological framework. Less senior reporters, by contrast (or those who have been around for less time), will be less familiar with 'the way things are done' and may therefore need more guidance from editorial staff to ensure that the copy they produce is not only of a sufficiently high standard, but also that it reflects the 'right' values and beliefs. It is because of higher levels of 'occupational socialisation' (Ericson *et al* 1987: 125) rather than increased technical ability (though this is also clearly a factor) that they will need less direction – in the form of editorial guidance or copy alteration – to produce work in keeping with that title: 'It is a matter of learning by experience and precedent on the job … arising in daily transactions among reporters, sources, editors and news texts' (Ericson *et al* 1987: 133; see also White 1950; Schudson 2000; cf. Gieber 1964). The following story, recounted by a journalist who worked for both the Nationalist *Irish News* and the Unionist *News Letter*, illustrates this point.

At the *Irish News*, there was policy relating to security coverage called 'know your enemy'. It involved conducting interviews with Loyalist as well as Republican paramilitaries and presenting the material side by side in the report. Linked to the journalistic imperatives of objectivity and impartiality (Chibnall 1977; Palmer 1998), the clear aim is to maximise credibility by presenting both sides of the story (Tuchman 1978). After moving to the *News Letter*, attempts to apply a similar approach were met with subtle but certain resistance. At the editorial level, the journalist recalled, 'Perhaps the sub-editors, although the decision may have come from higher', stories were restructured, rewritten and, in some instances, cut altogether. 'Inappropriate' material was placed further down the story – reflecting the inverted pyramid technique of presentation (Weaver 1975; Hallin 1986) – decreasing the likelihood that it would be read. Stories that were included 'were buried way in there, in a small article near the back somewhere'. 'After that had happened a few times', it was explained, 'I realised that it was just a waste of time to include interviews of that nature and so I stopped doing them, you know. It was just a waste of my time.' Future coverage conformed more closely to the style and content designated by the editorial staff.

Thus, editorial intervention can be straightforward and explicit, but it can also be more subtle. The combined impact is to encourage journalists to adopt, internalise and habitually reproduce a style that reflects and promotes the values, interests and beliefs of the newspaper for which they write. In this way, those values and interests – whether or not they are shared personally – are inculcated into that journalists' professional recipe knowledge (Epstein 1973). They come to constitute the 'vocabulary of precedents' which informs (often implicitly and un-programmatically, without any need for conscious articulation) the manufacture of news within that working environment (Ericson *et al* 1987: 133–8). The *Belfast Telegraph*'s Chris Thornton, with a certain unease, did not deny this possibility. 'I'd like to think that's not the case', he said, 'but I'm open to argument.'

That is not to suggest that journalists cannot and do not bring their own experiences to bear on their reportage (Goldenberg 1975; Lichter *et al* 1986;). The point is that there is only limited space within which those experiences can breathe. Editorial influence (Gitlin 1980; Hallin 1986), occupational socialisation and professional adaptation (Ericson *et al* 1987), and the journalistic imperatives of objectivity and impartiality (Chibnall 1977; Tuchman 1978) all militate against personal – or, perhaps better, non-conformist – views percolating through to news coverage. These influences do much to safeguard the reproduction of the expected form and flavour and, where relevant, the normative ideological contours of that title. As one reporter pointed out, though the statement is in no way unique to Northern Ireland, 'in the culture of Belfast journalism it is implicitly accepted that you adapt to the editorial line of the newspaper'.

Economic determinants and the representation of sex crime

The forces that shape the editorial line of the Northern Ireland press – market-based demands and the expectations of the established readership, rather than the views of the proprietor – more closely reflect the liberal pluralist interpretation of news production. Yet the clear constraints on journalistic autonomy as they go about 'making news' more closely reflect radical concerns. Though journalists' freedom may appear to increase with experience, it is in fact conditional upon compliance and the reproduction of a predetermined style and ideological line, to the point that non-conformist copy may be edited, sent back or cut completely. Editors are the key players here, but not, as radical scholars have suggested, as safeguards for the self-serving political preferences of media proprietors. Editorial influence is both commercially and ideologically geared to maintain, or ideally augment, the newspaper's readership in a highly competitive market, irrespective of what the owner's personal preferences may be. This has important implications for the representation of sex crime.

The following chapters illustrate that it is less a question of how journalists believe the problem of sex crime should be reported – though many have clear views on that matter. Rather, it is a question of how their seniors within the newsroom (most notably editors), influenced by wider commercial concerns and, in particular, the nature of the market, directly or indirectly shape journalists' reportage. A number of questions follow from this: what is the prevailing style and content of sex crime coverage in the regional press? What messages are imparted? Are there major differences between markets and between individual newspapers? How does this tally or conflict with journalists' and practitioners' views on how sex crimes should be represented? Each of these key questions is answered in the pages that follow. Next, though, the social-organisational determinants of news production and the implications of these for the construction of sex crime narratives are explored.

Social-organisational Determinants of News Production

In the liberal pluralist reading of news production, there is said to be parity of access and influence in the media and equal competition between ideas. The radical interpretation proposes that the ideology of the powerful is perpetually constructed and reconstructed in the media as a result of, among other things, the virtual monopoly of certain 'privileged' elite sources; those who are seen collectively to represent and command institutional power. In one reading, then, news media empower the masses by giving marginal groups a public voice and, where necessary, holding the powerful to account. In the other, news production is bound by structural-organisational and cultural constraints to reproduce and legitimate the existing power structures in a class society. Again, both readings suffer from limitations and, again, these are usefully highlighted when located within the context of news production in Northern Ireland.

Organisational constraints and the routinisation of news production

The production of news is restricted by a wide range of organisational constraints. Principal among these are the limitation of resources (human, financial, technological) and the requirement to routinise news-making, so that what is essentially a 'commodity' may be systematically and efficiently manufactured. The version of reality ultimately portrayed in the media is shaped in part by journalists' selective but – due to these constraints – restricted use of sources (Sigal 1973). In order to cope with deadlines and demands, reporters are forced to rely to a significant extent on dominant social and political institutions – the elite-establishment groups in society – for routine access to a significant volume of reportable information. As a result, organisations that are seen to represent institutional power will generally enjoy greater levels of media access and maintain an advantage in setting the agenda for debate. Subsequently, they will preserve a certain level of influence over the form, if not necessarily the flavour, of the news product (Fishman 1980; Miller, D. 1993; Reiner 2000b). The *Irish News* editor, Noel Doran, described the agenda-setting powers of one dominant source organisation which is of central importance in this study – the police:

> I mean, you can't take the initiative. You can't ring up an individual police officer and say … well you can try but it's not likely you can get very far. You normally have to go through the normal channels which would involve the police press office, so if you want to speak to someone … say an officer who is in charge of a particular case, you will probably have to approach them through the press office and they may or may not speak to you. You could pursue it and keep trying, if it was a case that you were particularly interested in you could try and set the agenda, but in general it's much more common that they would set the agenda.

Yet the fact that journalists have only a limited capacity to set the agenda does not mean that they are powerless to challenge the views of powerful sources. Nor does it signify that they cannot critically counterpose one set of claims against another and make an informed assessment which may or may not support the elite-establishment position (Ericson *et al* 1989). Often it is not the most politically instituted, but the most socially credible groups that succeed in securing definitional ownership of a given issue. And political power is not necessarily synonymous with social credibility (Schlesinger and Tumber 1994). Once an issue has been framed in public discourse, whether by official experts or otherwise, emergent groups may challenge the 'primary definition' (Hall *et al* 1978) and, if the challenge is portrayed and consequently perceived as sufficiently credible, undermine the definitional advantage of previously dominant authorities (Jenkins 1992; Miller, D. 1993). The autonomy of the newsprint media, understated by much of the research conducted from the radical perspective, can be crucial in this process. Indeed, the *Irish News* editor went on to explain that his newspaper's Nationalist line and its subsequent inclination to challenge on issues of policy and practice have engendered levels of tension with the police which are not experienced by other news agencies:

> There would be a certain amount of tension with the police. Certainly, when I worked at the [*Belfast*] *Telegraph* ... there would have been a reasonably friendly, cordial relationship between the police press office and the paper. There would be more tension here, and one of the reasons for that would be that we would have to go to the police much more often than other news outlets would with stories which might have negative consequences for them, because people who have complaints about the police would be much more likely to come to the *Irish News*. There is, to an extent, a shooting the messenger tendency ... 'What are they going on about now?' kind of thing.

Such tensions would not arise if journalists were constrained to 'faithfully and impartially reproduce symbolically the existing structures of power' (Hall *et al* 1978: 58), still less 'accept the presuppositions of the state without question' (Chomsky 1989: 162). Structured access does not guarantee strategic definitional advantage.

As D. Miller (1993) points out, for example, the IRA bombing campaign in Britain in the early 1970s caused widespread media and public outcry and demands for action to be taken. This led directly to the introduction of the Prevention of Terrorism Act 1974, the implementation of which resulted in the arrest and subsequent conviction of, among others, the Guildford Four and the Birmingham Six for their alleged involvement in the bombings. However, the quashing of these sentences and eventual release the Guildford Four and Birmingham Six were also orchestrated, at least in part, by a concerted media effort to expose the convictions as unsafe (Greenslade 1997; Reiner 2000b). The same media outlets which had so vehemently backed the government in their efforts to find and convict the bombers now played a leading role in implanting marginal Republican and Left counter-discourses on the issue into the central debate, shifting them from the periphery to the mainstream (Murdock 1991).

What is needed, then, is a less deterministic account of journalist–source power relations which can accommodate the clear but not uncontested dominance of certain institutional organisations, the sometimes highly successful activities of marginal groups and the active-interpretative rather than passive-absorptive role of the press in representing the social world.

Journalist–source power dynamics and organisational interdependence

Numerous factors may affect the willingness of potential sources – powerful or otherwise – to co-operate with news agencies. The editorial line of a given newspaper, prior experience of that title's coverage and even individual perceptions of the particular journalist seeking information may all have an impact. It stands to reason, then, that if a source feels that a newspaper has portrayed a given issue with undue criticism, or treated information in an irresponsible or abusive manner in the past, it will be less willing to provide information in the future.

At the same time, however, the media are of fundamental importance to any group or organisation wishing to have their views, values and beliefs widely disseminated. Certainly, the press are but one of many channels through which social actors can engage in public discourse and endeavour to influence popular consciousness. But they are a crucial, even indispensable communicative tool for reaching large sections of society at once (Kavanagh 2000; Sparks 2000). Because of this, even (perhaps especially) the most powerful and socially instituted organisations need to secure and maintain access in the press for the purposes of legitimation and self-promotion.

So in order to ensure a significant level of media access and influence, it is in the best interests of source organisations at least to foster the appearance of good working relations with the media. News agencies are limited in their powers to determine or control the information provided by sources. But sources are limited in their powers to determine or control how this information is interpreted and, ultimately, constructed as news. News production is thus characterised by an organisational interdependence – news agencies and sources are tied together symbiotically. The dialectical nature of this relationship is understated in the radical reading of news production, while the liberal pluralist reading is unrealistic in assuming an equal distribution of power between dominant and marginalised sources, and the journalists with whom they interact.

Policing knowledge and the politics of disclosure

Several journalists claimed that the police press office may co-operate less with Nationalist than Unionist newspapers. The police's Chief Information Officer, perhaps not surprisingly, strongly contested this suggestion. Referring specifically to the *Irish News*, he insisted: 'I think that on a professional level it is perfectly straightforward. You will not find somebody saying, "I'm not talking to you because you come from a particular newspaper". I think that we have very good relations with the *Irish News* on a professional level.' This argument also found support from a number of reporters. Before securing his present position as Security Correspondent for the *Belfast Telegraph*, Chris Thornton worked at both the Nationalist *Irish News* and the Unionist *News Letter*:

> When I was with the *Irish News* and the *News Letter* I would have thought that the RUC press office favours the *Telegraph* over anybody else because of the way the *Telegraph* gets stories and that sort of thing. But inside the *Telegraph* I don't find that the case. They are quite professional in the information they hand out.

A key distinction needs to be made here between the different levels on which journalist–source relations operate. These statements focus on disclosures at the official level; that is, on those knowledge transactions which are administered bureaucratically by dedicated source representatives empowered to speak on behalf of the particular organisation. It is equally important, however, to consider journalist–source relations at the unofficial level (Schlesinger 1990). Stephen Dempster, news editor for the *News Letter*, explained that 'A good reporter won't just be relying on the press office, they will be relying on contacts within the police who will give them the wider picture'.

At the official level, the police are both professionally (in the sense that they are a public service) and organisationally (in the sense that they need to maintain a favourable public profile) obliged to co-operate – to an extent at least – with the press, regardless of the particular newspaper's editorial policy. Indeed, for all powerful institutions parity of treatment is a crucial perception to engender, particularly in Northern Ireland. Consequently, there is only limited room for discretion in the official disclosure of information.[5] At the unofficial level, however, disclosures are made on a voluntary basis and may be entirely discretionary in nature. Because they are not regulated by the formal structures and procedures of information management, the ultimate decision to provide or withhold information can be based solely on subjective perceptions and judgements. It is in this context, in their efforts to establish informal police–press relations, outside the bureaucratic control of the press office, that *Irish News* journalists experience the greatest difficulties.

Editor Noel Doran explained: 'It would certainly be harder here … Some reporters might be in contact with police officers outside the police press office but it would probably happen less here than in other news organisations.' By contrast, Chris Thornton, Security Correspondent for the *Belfast Telegraph*, acknowledged that this newspaper's reputation for traditionally sympathetic portrayals of the police has yielded significant benefits in terms of gaining unofficial access: '[W]here there's a difference I think is in relationships with individual police officers … unofficial sources, and I think the *Telegraph* has a history of being generally supportive of the police and that's returned in the police's attitude towards us.' In addition to the agenda-setting powers of dominant sources, then, there are further pressures to portray powerful organisations in a favourable light. Any desire to censure critical news agencies at the official-professional level is countered by the need to create the impression of impartiality in dealings with the press. At the unofficial-personal level, however, sources may selectively disclose information at will and, as a result, journalists associated with routinely critical news agencies may be disadvantaged in the ongoing struggle to secure 'exclusive' stories and 'scoop' the competition. The assertion of journalistic independence and the right to challenge is fundamental, but it comes at a price. For a newspaper which derives its legitimacy and political credibility precisely from its inclination to question the state and state agencies of control – as the *Irish News* does – it is clearly a price worth paying. The alternative, a loss of credibility with the established audience and the implications this would have for sales performance, would be worse.

Trust, confidence and individual journalist–source relations

The importance of establishing personal relationships is not limited to journalists' dealings with the police. Several writers have pointed to confidence and trust as the keystones around which the most enduring, productive and reciprocal journalist–source relations are built (see, for example, Reiss 1984; Ericson *et al* 1989; Schlesinger and Tumber 1994). Their centrality – especially in the construction of an issue as sensitive and potentially distressing as sex crime – was noted by all those groups and organisations interviewed in this study. The Director of the Northern Ireland Probation Service (PBNI), Oliver Brannigan, suggested that 'Northern Ireland is that small that it's not about papers, it's about people'. He went on to explain his familiarity with local journalists and how this affects his handling of press inquiries:

> There are journalists in this town, and I won't name names, but when that phone goes and I am told that Joe Bloggs would like to talk to me I am totally and absolutely confident about talking to them. But other journalists phone up and I wonder, 'Well what the hell's his angle, I am going to have to be careful here'.

And Eileen Calder, spokesperson for the Belfast Rape Crisis Centre (the most resource-poor organisation considered here), explained her approach when dealing proactively with the press:

> I suppose it comes down a lot to the personality of the individual journalist and their ability to understand and be sympathetic to whatever the survivor's position is, or whatever the centre's position is, and so when I ring a newspaper, or when I am thinking of wanting publicity for something, I wouldn't necessarily be thinking in terms of which newspaper it is, but more which journalist it is and how much priority they are likely to give it.

These descriptions focus on the interpersonal rather than the organisational dynamics of journalist-source relations. Even more so for resource-poor organisations, which lack the funding to employ dedicated press officers, the development of personal relationships with journalists is crucial. There is an important interface between the individual personalities of key actors in a small jurisdiction like Northern Ireland and the broader ideological, cultural and political forces at work. In this context, the development of superior journalist–source relations is to a significant extent a matter between individuals. This point, as will become clear as this analysis develops, is central in understanding the full range of influences that shape the construction of sex crime in the press.

Social-organisational determinants and the representation of sex crime

While powerful source organisations enjoy an undeniable advantage in having their values and beliefs reproduced in the media, their definitional power is neither immutable, as the radical reading suggests, nor is it inconsequential, as the liberal pluralist reading suggests. News production is a dialectical process, and achieving definitional superiority depends on a complex of forces and influences – resourcing, access and availability, perceived credibility and legitimacy, political power – which constantly interact with one another and change over time. I have suggested already that sex crime is a contested terrain on which a diversity of groups, interests and ideologies compete for influence. A key influence on sources' success in advancing their interests in press discourse is the nature of their relationships with journalists.

In exploring the construction of sex crime narratives, therefore, a central task is to establish the nature of the relationships between journalists and those sources that can or could contribute meaningfully to the news production process. The journalistic dependence on certain, generally well resourced, sources for a steady supply of reportable information is not without consequence. With respect to sex crime, the most powerful organisations considered here are the police, the courts and, to a lesser extent, the probation service. However, it is not always the most powerful sources that win the struggle for definitional superiority. Comparatively resource-poor sources, for example voluntary counselling organisations, can counter journalists' organisational reliance on powerful institutions through additional, and sometimes highly inventive, efforts to redress this power imbalance. One key mechanism of achieving this is the development of productive and reciprocal relationships with individual journalists. How journalists and newspapers are approached or received can influence profoundly a source's success in securing access and influence in the press.

One more (inter-related and overlapping) area of influence requires consideration here – the influence of culture and, in particular, political culture on news production in Northern Ireland.

Political-cultural Determinants of News Production

One key assumption underpinning both radical and liberal pluralist interpretations of news production is that of the 'consensual' nature of society. In this view it is assumed that members of a society share a common stock of cultural knowledge and, therefore, broadly use the same frames of reference to make sense of the world. For liberal pluralist analysts, the consensus reflects core values and beliefs which are collectively shared and accepted by individuals, binding them to the social order (Thompson 1990). For radical scholars, notions of consensus are not (necessarily) analogous with the organic existence of consensus throughout society. Rather, 'consent' is something which is synthesised as a result of popular consciousness being shaped by the powerful (Hall *et al* 1978; Hartley 1982; Herman and Chomsky 1994).

Law and order and the manufacture of consent

Much of our understanding of crime, deviance and control comes from what we see, hear or read about in the media. The news media, then, provide those who command definitional power with a forum, an opportunity to advance 'an ongoing articulation of the proper bounds to behaviour in all organised spheres of life' (Ericson *et al* 1987: 3). Advocates of the radical reading propose that this articulation takes on a form and a flavour that reproduce dominant ideological meanings within that society. Crime and deviance, it is suggested, are constructed and framed by the powerful so that those frames will be reproduced in the media. If successful, these 'preferred' social definitions are planted in public discourse, where they take root and grow within popular consciousness, ultimately constituting the frames of reference used by news readers to make sense of social problems in their everyday lives. Once the social definitions of the powerful have won popular consent, support may also be won for the measures of control and containment they entail.

Furthermore, media representations of law and order can be a vital resource for doing the 'ideological work' needed to restore consensus should it come under threat. Hall *et al* (1978) argue that, faced with a 'crisis in hegemony' in the 1970s, the British state (the police, media and judiciary) generated a moral panic around the phenomenon of 'mugging'. The panic, it is suggested, was orchestrated to deflect attention away from intensifying class conflict in an affluent but destabilised society, and on to the unifying issues of crime, youth and race. The image of the 'black mugger', cast in the central role, tapped into and reinforced concerns over lawlessness, national identity and the perceived crisis in authority, providing a focal point for social anxieties. The ensuing war against crime ultimately transcended class differences and stimulated national unity and social cohesion in the struggle against a common threat. It helped to win popular consent for the shift towards the 'exceptional state', ever more inclined to use coercive, but (with the consent of the masses) 'legitimate force' against perceived threats to the social order (Hall *et al* 1978: 218). The media were thus central in justifying the authoritarian measures used in 'policing the crisis', re-legitimating the state and reconstructing hegemonic ideological domination *on the basis of consent*.

Hall *et al*'s work has been criticised both conceptually and empirically

(Waddington 1986; Sparks 1992; Downes and Rock 1998; Reiner 2000b), but it remains one of the most sophisticated analyses of the politics of representation and the manufacture of consent around issues of law and order. With respect to the latter, this was possible because the state's adoption of an increasingly authoritarian posture appeared reasonable, even necessary. The coercion against the few was perceived as being 'on behalf of and in defence of the majority' (Hall *et al* 1978: 321–2). For the powerful successfully to manufacture a popular consensus around their elite 'ideas', however, those ideas must be sufficiently 'credible', first for the media, and then for society to be convinced. Media content is now so 'diverse and multisourced that no ideology can be truly "dominant" for any length of time if it does not correspond on some level with what ordinary people feel to be, and experience as, true' (McNair 1998: 29; see also Schudson 2000; Manning 2001). If the power structures within a given social order are consistently and, more importantly, visibly in flux; if competing elites are propounding conflicting ideologies with comparable success; if none is exercising hegemony, then the construction of consensus around a particular ideological stance, and the subsequent legitimation of that group's position and actions, may be fundamentally undermined.

Law and order, social conflict and consensus in Northern Ireland

In Northern Ireland, the challenge to the state's political leadership and cultural authority has been characterised by bloody conflict lasting more than three decades. The Nationalist ideology commands levels of support within the political arena and broader social structures sufficiently high to pose a tangible threat to the increasingly precarious constitutional dominance of Unionism. Radical critiques of the media tend to envisage an essentially unified and coherent ruling elite whose views and interests – generally held to be equally unified and coherent – are reproduced in media discourse and naturalised throughout society. Northern Ireland, however, is better thought of as accommodating two co-existing elites – Unionist and Nationalist, hegemonic and counter-hegemonic – each espousing political and cultural (though not necessarily economic) doctrines which often differ fundamentally, and each adhering to ideological viewpoints which are diametrically opposed on their defining issues (Bowyer Bell 1993; McGarry and O'Leary 1995). Many Unionists and Nationalists observe distinct cultural and political traditions and recall conflicting interpretations of their social history. Consequently, certain core values, concerns and interests are derived from opposing viewpoints espousing contrary maxims, folk wisdoms, values and interests and, as such, are not shared in common. In this context, radical notions of consensus building around elite ideas become problematic in the extreme.

Hall *et al* (1978) demonstrate how consensus was mobilised around the shift to law and order in the face of an apparent crime wave. In this case it is the application of an authoritarian, law and order framework through state agencies of control that in the end 'rescues' hegemony from crisis and results in its re-establishment through consent. In this sense, the state's use of coercive control was a source of consensus. In Northern Ireland, however, the state and its mechanisms of control – the criminal law, the judiciary and the police especially – are seen as illegitimate by significant sections of the Nationalist/Republican community (Ruane and Todd 1996), and indeed by sections of the Loyalist community (McVeigh 1995), and command neither credibility nor social authority. In this context of social and political flux, rather than being a source of consensus, issues of law and order and the state apparatuses of control are more frequently a direct source of conflict.

This is a key difference between perceptions of crime, deviance and control in Northern Ireland and those in comparatively stable social orders, like the USA, England and Wales, or Scotland. The English press, for example, may differ dramatically in terms of their support for Labour or Conservative politics. And they may criticise the government, the opposition, the police force, the prison service or the judiciary, sometimes harshly, on a range of issues. But news journalism, whether it ultimately reflects the interests of a dominant elite or not, is based on the assumption of a stable and broadly consensual society. Most importantly, this assumption is realistic; it is 'credible' and so too, therefore, is its manifestation in press discourse. When agencies of crime control fall under public scrutiny and attract criticism, it is on the basis of a consensual notion that they may be flawed but, fundamentally, they are legitimate.[6] It is everybody's police, everybody's judiciary, everybody's criminal law. They should be adapted and reformed, perhaps, but not dismantled and replaced.

In Northern Ireland, however, a substantial proportion of the population does not feel represented by the state or its agencies of crime control. It is not everybody's criminal law, it is not everybody's judiciary, it is not everybody's police. For many, the answer is not to adapt and reform, but precisely to dismantle and replace. Indeed, the future of the police and the wider concept of policing in Northern Ireland have become a major point of negotiation in the search for lasting peace under the Good Friday Agreement (see Beirne and Greer 1999; Patten 1999; *Policing and Society*, special issue on Northern Ireland 2001). The representation of crime, deviance and control in the press in Northern Ireland represents a field of fierce contestation. Efforts to mobilise consent around issues of law and order can be met with forceful resistance.

The constitutional issue, the press and popular consent

The conflict is a staple of everyday news coverage in Northern Ireland. It is constantly reported, debated and analysed in stories, features, opinion columns, letters pages and editorials. What is most striking, is that a substantial proportion of news coverage focuses on the issues over which that society is most deeply divided. There is a constant stream of ideologically loaded material – sometimes implicit, sometimes not – which does not focus, as most crime narratives do, on the deviance of the few in order to promote consensus and social cohesion among the many. It actively accentuates the conflict and division among the many. Law and order routinely forms the basis of a wider discourse in which local politicians, supported by explicitly Nationalist and Unionist newspapers, engage in political one-upmanship.

In Gramsci's conceptualisation of hegemony, 'ideas are virtually used as weapons whose important role is the part they play in the struggle to change society. Relative to this role, worries about their objectivity and truth are incidental' (Cuff *et al* 1990: 189). The 'idea' of legitimate crime control and the right to use coercive force are continually used as an ideological 'weapon' in the struggle for hegemony in Northern Ireland. The forces that would mobilise consensus around issues of crime and control, thus seeking to legitimate the state and its criminal justice apparatuses, are met with equal but opposite forces which achieve comparable success in mobilising consent around their rejection.

Because of the partisan nature of newsprint journalism in Northern Ireland, and the state of prolonged conflict throughout wider society, those areas around which some form of consensus can be established become pivotal. They are vital both in terms of promoting social cohesion, and in the state's wider struggle for legitimacy and acceptance. The issue of law and order has been central in the ongoing contest for definitional superiority, ideological dominance and political legitimacy. More often than not it has been the source of conflict, not consensus. Yet there are exceptions, and one such exception, the subject of this book, is the problem of sex crime.

Political-cultural determinants and the representation of sex crime

In 1995 the liberal Unionist *Belfast Telegraph* printed a front-page story headlined 'ADAMS "CHILD ABUSE ADVICE" CONDEMNED' berating Sinn Fein president Gerry Adams for publicly advising families not to report cases of child sex abuse to the RUC (*Belfast Telegraph* 26 January 1995: front page). Mr Adams had claimed that the police were 'unacceptable' and that they were exploiting the issue 'for their own militaristic ends'. He recommended instead that Republicans report any cases of child sex abuse to local Sinn Fein councillors. Unionist politicians and police sources complained that the recommendation amounted to a call for Republicans to bypass the official services and go instead to local paramilitaries. In support of police involvement, childcare experts were quoted at length declaring their 'total support for RUC efforts against child molesters'.

The story expressed outrage at the Sinn Fein leader's use of such a serious and sensitive issue to score political points against the op-

Adams 'child abuse advice' condemned

By Martin Hill

SINN Fein president Gerry Adams was condemned today for telling families not to report child sex abuse to the police.

Mr Adams was criticised after he accused the RUC of "exploiting" child and drug abuse for its own ends.

He told a public meeting in Belfast that the police were "unacceptable" and allegations of abuse should be made to counsellors instead.

But politicians and childcare experts reacted angrily, pledging total support

■ Families 'should not tell police'

for RUC efforts against child molesters.

West Belfast MP Joe Hendron said: "As a general practitioner, I've had long experience of the victims of child sex abuse.

Skilled

"I'm 100 per cent behind the RUC on this. Anyone with information about child abuse should report it immediately to the police, not to the paramilitaries."

The Department of Health said any allegations of abuse should be made to the police, health boards or the NSPCC.

The Sinn Fein leader said: "There are bona fide and skilled counsellors who can advise on matters like child abuse, drug abuse and other issues.

"The RUC are not acceptable and, indeed, are exploiting these issues for their own militaristic ends."

He was speaking to around 200 republicans at the Star Club in Ardoyne last night.

An RUC spokesman said: "Mr Adams' remarks do nothing to help what is a very serious matter."

Printed courtesy of the *Belfast Telegraph*

position. The clear message was that Sinn Fein were insensitive and opportunistic and had sought to advance their own political agenda at the expense of their constituents' welfare. Of course, from a Unionist perspective, the advantage to be gained from advancing these claims to a mass readership – crucially backed up by 'neutral' and therefore 'credible' expert sources – is not insignificant. That the opportunity to undermine Mr Adams' credibility made the front page in the *Belfast Telegraph* and did not appear at all in the Nationalist *Irish News* is no great surprise. What is interesting, however, is that it was not reported in any of the other sample newspapers. In fact, from an archive of just under 500 sex crime items, this was the only story in which party politics superseded the focus on sex crime, and in which statements from Unionists/Loyalists and Nationalists/Republicans were presented in a directly oppositional manner. In a press defined by party politics and the promotion of adversarial positions on law and order and policing, this is significant.

The apolitical representation of sex crime in the press illustrates that, while Northern Ireland may be characterised by conflict rather than consensus, certain issues resonate with equal intensity across communities, regardless of politics and religion. Even the highly contested and frequently criticised police force receives sympathetic coverage of its policing of sex crime. In this respect, press representations of sex crime differ from representations of other law-and-order issues. As *Irish News* editor Noel Doran explained: 'In security terms politicians on both sides of the divide would occasionally criticise the police over their reaction to security things, clearing up murders and things, but in terms of clearing up and resolving sex cases, that would be fairly unusual.' Around this one issue, consensus can be mobilised largely uncontested. This is due to the fact that the emphasis in sex crime narratives is not placed on politics or culture. It is placed on 'universal moral rules or apolitical ethics … which really do command considerable assent from a majority of the population' (Sumner 1997: 502). It is placed on collective sentiments which surpass ideological differences and constitute the foundations for a consensus that is distinctly moral in nature.

At times of rapid social change the collective denunciation of society's deviants performs two important functions, as Durkheim (1964) pointed out. It consolidates moral boundaries by clearly distinguishing the 'good' from the 'bad' and, in so doing, it promotes social solidarity. The representation – and condemnation – of sex offenders in Northern Ireland serves to establish a common enemy against which all 'decent' people can unite. It denotes a criminal type that is wholly distinct from respectable society. The collective demonisation of sex offenders provides a space for moral consensus to flourish amidst deep-seated division.

Crucially, the assumption of a moral consensus is realistic; it is credible because it seems to reflect what people actually experience to be true. The emotional intensity with which sex crime, and the sexual victimisation of children in particular, is constructed and received is not something which is easily appropriated by party politics. Yet the promotion of a morally consensual, and broadly undifferentiated, fear and loathing of sex offenders is not without cost. The representation of the sex offender as 'absolute other' has important consequences. A number of practitioners voiced their concern that the narrow and highly emotive coverage of sex crime in the press identifies the wrong areas of risk. As a result, they suggested, it may actually undermine measures taken by those trying to ensure the safety of children in their care and increase the likelihood of sexual victimisation.

Conclusions

This chapter has forwarded an explanatory framework for explaining the construction of sex crime in the Northern Ireland regional press. It identifies some of the key limitations of both the radical and liberal pluralist readings of news production as they are situated within the context of this research. It also develops alternative ways of conceptualising the influences that either enhance or constrain journalist and source activities, the competition for media access and influence, and the promotion of open democratic debate.

Journalistic autonomy is constrained by internal and external forces. Internally, the most significant influence is from editors. A hierarchical system of explicit and implicit editorial 'guidance' safeguards the reproduction of that title's preferred style and ideological line, reflecting radical conceptions of news production. Editorial policy, however, is determined not by the ideological preferences of media owners, but by the established predilections and expectations of the target audience – reflecting the liberal pluralist reading. As journalists gain experience and seniority, editorial intervention diminishes. Rather than indicating an actual increase in professional freedom, however, decreasing levels of guidance correspond more closely with increasing levels of professional adaptation and occupational socialisation into the newsroom culture, thus reducing the need for further intervention. Externally, and in line with radical concerns, journalists' reliance on dominant institutional sources does present undeniable opportunities for powerful groups to frame issues in ways that reflect and reinforce their own values and beliefs. Yet reporters, especially in Northern Ireland, can and do challenge the establishment and its authority, questioning not just the administration of the system, but the very legitimacy of the system itself. This echoes liberal pluralist contentions.

Journalist–source power relations work on different levels which, paradoxically, can serve both to reinforce and constrain journalists' freedom to challenge and be critical. Organisational interdependence between sources and news agencies counters any desire, even within the most powerful groups, to censure too harshly critical journalists at the official-professional level. This safeguarding of the press's role as public watchdogs supports a liberal pluralist interpretation. However, in a small jurisdiction like Northern Ireland, the most productive journalist–source relations are those based on mutual trust established over time. It is in the development of interpersonal relationships that journalists perceived as unduly critical or troublesome may find themselves disadvantaged. There are, then, in keeping with the radical reading, clear incentives to portray powerful groups in a favourable light, but these incentives are countervailed, in line with the liberal pluralist reading, by journalists' professional values and the need to maintain credibility with news audiences. With respect to source competition, the radical claim that powerful groups maintain a clear advantage in securing media access and influence is beyond doubt. But less powerful groups, often with the support of the press, can successfully foreground marginal viewpoints and redefine the terms of a given debate. The competition for media exposure is unequal, but there is no single group (or elite constellation) in Northern Ireland that commands immutable definitional control. This is significant when considering radical and liberal pluralist notions of consensus-building, particularly around issues of law and order.

In certain contexts, under certain conditions, and at certain times, the powerful may effectively mobilise consent around crime, deviance and control, underpinned by an elite-defined notion of the 'national interest' (Herman and Chomsky 1994). In Northern Ireland, however, rather than acting as a source of consensus, issues of law and order are more often a source of conflict. But not all issues of law and order reflect and reinforce this division. The problem of sex crime – especially where the victims are children – provides the foundations for moral consensus amidst social conflict. In their representation of sex crime, journalists articulate the collective values of the community as a whole. In the construction and unequivocal denunciation of an enemy of all 'decent' people, press representations transcend party politics.

Chapters 5–8 are concerned with illustrating in greater detail how the economic, social-organisational and political-cultural spheres of influence impact directly on the construction of sex crime in the press. First, however, it is useful to consider a more straightforward, but fundamental question: What is it that makes sex crimes so newsworthy? This is the concern of Chapter 3.

Notes

1 Independent News and Media is a global company which manages media outlets in the UK, Ireland, South Africa, New Zealand and Australia, and has substantial media shareholdings in Portugal. Dr O'Reilly is also Chief Executive of US multinational H.J. Heinz and Co. and maintains a range of other non-publishing interests, including substantial property holdings in the Republic of Ireland and the USA.

2 The editor for the *News Letter* also pointed out that Mirror–Trinity owns newspapers in England 'that would operate in Tory heartlands and papers in England that would operate in Labour heartlands and papers that straddle both'.

3 The *Belfast Telegraph* and *The Irish Times* carried Loyalist and Republican (respectively) death notices throughout the 1970s (Dillon 1989).

4 See Appendix III.

5 There are, of course, grounds for legitimately declining to provide information. In terms of police–press relations, if a particular case is *sub judice*, a range of restrictions limits the amount and type of information that can be released by the press office and printed by news agencies (Hall *et al* 1978: 67). Or in the case of an ongoing investigation it may be judged that media exposure would jeopardise the success or safety of police operations (Schlesinger and Tumber 1994: 166). But barring certain exceptions, since the very purpose of these structures is the management of information, and because censorship, moderation and control require disclosure as well as denial, news agencies can expect, if not demand, a certain level of co-operation when they make inquiries.

6 Reiner (2000b: 9) remarks: 'for policing to be accepted as legitimate it is not necessary that all groups or individuals within a society agree with the substantive content or direction of specific policing operations. It means at minimum only that the broad mass of the population, as possibly even some of those who are policed against, accept the authority, the lawful right, of the police to act as they do, even if disagreeing with or regretting some specific actions.' This is a fundamental difference between perceptions of the police in relatively stable and broadly consensual social orders, and perceptions of the police in Northern Ireland.

Chapter 3

News values, newsworthiness and the construction of sex crime

Introduction

This chapter discusses the 'newsworthiness' of sex crime and, in particular, the various qualities that make sex crimes so eminently reportable in the press. Of key interest here are 'news values': '[N]ews values provide the criteria ... which enable editors, journalists and newsmen to decide routinely and regularly which stories are "newsworthy", and which are not, which stories are major lead stories and which are relatively insignificant, which stories to run and which to drop' (Hall *et al* 1978: 54). Most studies have explicitly or (more often) implicitly indicated that 'seriousness' or 'novelty' – or some combination thereof – are the primary or 'cardinal' determinants of crime newsworthiness. I argue here, more closely in line with the non-criminological literature, that while both these qualities are fundamental, their ultimate impact – and the impact of all other news values – is mediated by the notion of 'proximity'.

Though this book focuses in places on specific types of sex crime, it considers the representation of the full spectrum of sex offending, from consensual adult homosexual offences and under-age sex between consenting teenagers, to serial rape and sex murder. This wide range of behaviours is representative of vastly differing levels of criminality to journalists and practitioners, and the construction of these offences as press narratives varies significantly depending on the reaction they are supposed to elicit from audiences.

Crime as News

Crime news will always be 'prime news' (McGregor 1993). 'Crime narratives and representations are, and always have been, a prominent part of the content of all mass media' (Reiner 2002: 380). A multitude of researchers have explored this prominence, both quantitatively and qualitatively, in terms of content analysis (Roshier 1973, Dominick 1978; Ditton and Duffy 1983; Smith 1984; Marsh 1991; Soothill and Walby 1991), the effects of media representations of crime and deviance on society (Hearold 1986; Entman 1989; Williams and Dickinson 1993; Hagell and Newburn 1994; O'Connell and Whelan 1996; Cumberbatch 1998; Kitzinger 1999a; Barker and Petley 2001),[1] the origins and production methods of these representations (Chibnall 1977; Hall *et al* 1978; Tuchman 1978; Schlesinger 1990; Schlesinger and Tumber 1994; Skidmore 1995) or, to varying degrees, some combination of the three (Ericson *et al* 1987, 1989, 1991; Meyers 1997; Surette 1998; Reiner *et al* 2000a, 2000b).

Studies have concentrated on different media formats, such as television (Epstein 1973; Gerbner and Gross 1976; Schlesinger *et al* 1983; Sparks 1992), radio (Quinney, 1973), the print media (see, *inter alia*, Hauge 1965; Roshier 1973; Chibnall 1977; Hall *et al* 1978; Sherizen 1978; Soothill and Walby 1991; Jenkins 1992; Lees 1995; Skidmore 1995; Stephenson-Burton 1995; McEvoy 1996; Rolston and Miller 1996) or all three (Cumberbatch *et al* 1995). In short, the social investigation of media representations of crime, deviance and control has generated a vast body of literature which approaches a wide variety of issues from a diversity of research perspectives.

In the wake of this expansive literature, it has become platitudinous to suggest that the newsprint media do more than merely 'reflect' social reality. They can be central to the creation of moral panics (Cohen 1980; Pearson 1983; Jenkins 1992; Ben-Yehuda 1994; Maguire 1997; Thompson 1998; Wilczynski 1999), they can be key mechanisms in the construction of ideology (Fishman 1978; Cohen and Young 1981; Herman and Chomsky 1994; Rolston and Miller 1996; Schudson 2000) and they can influence profoundly the social and political responses to issues of law and order (Hall *et al* 1978; Miller, D. 1993; Beckett 1994). As Maguire neatly summarises (1997: 140–1; see also Jenkins 1992: 123):

> Whatever the source of the initial attention, if public and media interest in a particular form of activity reaches a sufficient level the result is likely to be some sort of 'deviancy amplification' or 'moral panic' ... In other words, as interest mounts, journalists discover

> and highlight new examples of the activity, heightened awareness of it among the public leads more people to report instances to the police (and perhaps more people to engage in it themselves), researchers begin to seek grants to investigate its 'scale' in a more systematic way, policy makers ask agencies to keep new kinds of records, and politicians call for government action to respond to what is now judged to be a mounting problem.

Media images have been found routinely to exaggerate both the levels of violent crime in society and the risk of being offended against (Graber 1980; Marsh 1991; Surette 1998; Reiner *et al* 2000a, 2000b; Reiner 2000b). Ditton and Duffy, for example, in an examination of Scottish newspapers over a one-month period, argue that 'crimes involving violence and crimes involving sex together constituted 2.4 per cent of real incidence, yet 45.8 per cent of newspaper coverage' (1983: 164). Marsh (1991: 75), in his international critique of content analysis studies investigating crime in the newsprint media between 1965 and 1987, finds that 'newspapers in the United States and elsewhere tended to overemphasise violent crimes against the person (murder, rape, robbery assault) and understate property crimes'. He goes on to argue that the newspapers sampled from around the world 'provided little if any information regarding the causes of crime or how to avoid victimisation'. And further that this can result in 'increased levels of fear of victimisation on the part of certain segments of society' (1991: 75).

Ericson (1991) is bemused by the surprise that such findings customarily generate, querying why anyone would expect the cultural products of mass media to reflect the social reality of crime. By way of explanation, he points out that police statistics themselves 'do not mirror the reality of crime, but are cultural, legal and social constructs produced by the police for organisational purposes' (1991: 220; see also Maguire 1997; Zedner 2002). Therefore, studies that consider media representations of crime in relation to official statistics, including a number of those cited above, compare one symbolically constructed reality with another. The problem is that neither of these realities – socially constructed and culturally and organisationally dependent – reflects the social reality of crime. The question, then, is not why media organisations over-represent certain crimes, but why they focus on particular events and, still further, why they prioritise particular classifications of those events (Ericson 1991).

There is little doubt that media images have an influence over popular consciousness about crime (Young 1981; Sparks 1992; Presdee 2000; Reiner *et al* 2000a). Indeed, my own findings strongly suggest that media representations of sex crime can significantly influence the number of survivors contacting the police and, in particular, seeking help from counselling services. Exactly who is affected, by how much and for how long, still remains a matter for debate (Cumberbatch, 1989, 1998; Philo 1999). In the context of this book, however, how media images affect popular consciousness is of secondary concern to the processes through which they are initially constructed. Central to the construction of crime narratives are the various factors that determine newsworthiness.

News Values and the Notion of 'Newsworthiness'

In what is generally credited as the first sociological investigation of crime journalism in Britain (Kidd-Hewitt 1995), Chibnall (1977: 23) identifies 'at least eight professional imperatives which act as implicit guides to the construction of news stories'. These are (in no particular order):

- Immediacy (speed/currency).
- Dramatisation (drama and action).
- Structured access (experts, authority).
- Novelty (angle/speculation/twist).
- Titillation (revealing the forbidden/voyeurism).
- Conventionalism (hegemonic ideology).
- Personalisation (culture of personality/celebrity).
- Simplification (elimination of shades of grey).

In terms of crime news, Chibnall (1977) highlights five further imperatives that inform journalists' reporting of violence. These are (still in no particular order):

- Visible and spectacular acts.
- Graphic presentation.
- Deterrence and repression.
- Sexual and political connotations.
- Individual pathology.

Cavender and Mulcahy (1998: 699) echo many of these themes when they propose that 'stories should be dramatic and sensational, should focus on notable individuals, and should feature conflict, even wrongdoing'. Ericson *et al* (1991: 4) begin the final stage of their complex tripartite analysis with the straightforward proposition that 'deviance, equivocality, and unpredictability' are the major determining factors in news selection. For Hall *et al* (1978: 54) the dominant news values include unexpected and dramatic events, negative consequences, human tragedies, elite persons and recurrent themes. They insist, however, that these news values operate together as 'supplementary sources of newsworthiness' and that the 'cardinal' news value is 'novelty' (p. 74). And in a general summary of the research, Surette (1998: 61) reiterates the earlier findings of Roshier (1973), arguing that the principal determinants of newsworthiness are 'the seriousness of the event, whimsical circumstances, sentimental or dramatic elements, and the involvement of high-status persons'. He goes on to suggest with respect to crime news that 'seriousness is the primary factor' and that the 'criterion for seriousness is harm to individuals rather than overall social harm' (1998: 61).

Most accounts, then, have reflected similar themes and categories of newsworthiness in relation to crime news production. But despite their broad similarities, different scholars have elevated different news values to 'primary' or 'cardinal' status. These differences are important. In Hall *et al*'s (1978) view, for example, it is the 'novelty' of a criminal event or phenomenon (in their case mugging) that ultimately determines its newsworthiness. In Surette's (1998) view it is its 'seriousness'. I have reservations about both these claims. The proposition, for example, that 'novelty' is *the* primary determinant of newsworthiness requires qualification. All newsworthy events may be in some sense novel, but not all novel events are newsworthy. There is something else, over and above the newness, rarity or extraordinary nature of an event – and over and above its perceived seriousness – that makes it eminently reportable. It must be relevant or meaningful to the news reader, and that meaningfulness is determined by the notion of 'proximity' (see also Galtung and Ruge 1970; Sparks 1992).

Newsworthiness and 'Proximity'

The news value of 'proximity' has both spatial and cultural dynamics. Spatial proximity is the 'nearness' of an event to the news reader in simple geographical terms. In short, events happening close by will be more newsworthy than those happening far away, all other things being equal. This quality is especially relevant in a small jurisdiction like Northern Ireland, where it might be argued that all news is, in a sense, 'local'. Cultural proximity, which closely intertwines with the spatial dimension, is the 'nearness' of an event to the news reader in cultural terms. It can be thought of as the extent to which a given event resonates within a news reader's existing framework of values, interests, beliefs and concerns; the extent to which it is culturally meaningful in the most simple sense.

Both these factors are reflected in the journalistic axiom known as McLurg's Law, which establishes a ratio between the size of an event and its distance from (or relevance to) the news audience (Schlesinger 1987; Palmer 1998). It holds that the threshold for newsworthiness – in terms of the level of individual news values required to pass from news invisibility to news visibility – increases with spatial and cultural distance from the news reader. For example, a relatively small car accident in the UK might receive some local press coverage. And if someone was killed or somebody famous was involved, it might attract national attention. A car accident in the USA, however, would have to be much bigger – for example, involving multiple fatalities – to attract the same level of interest in Britain, and a car accident in India (a non-Western and therefore more distant culture) would have to be more dramatic still.

Discussions of the importance of proximity as a key determinant of newsworthiness have featured in journalistic guides dating back several decades (see, for example, MacDougall 1968), and within a range of studies in the sociology of journalism (Galtung and Ruge 1970; Gans 1980; McNair 1998). In the literature on news making around crime and deviance, however, this news value tends to be subsumed within other categories of newsworthiness (Ericson *et al* 1987), or ignored altogether (Kidd-Hewitt 1995; Surette 1998; Reiner, 2002). As a result, the centrality of proximity in determining the newsworthiness of a given criminal event has been consistently understated.[2] In the remainder of this chapter I want to explore the issue of newsworthiness specifically as it relates to the construction of sex crime in the Northern Ireland press, using examples and interview material where appropriate to substantiate my arguments. I am seeking to redress the imbalance in the research literature by establishing precisely how the news value of 'proximity' intersects with other key determinants of newsworthiness – including novelty – and plays a fundamental role in the selection and production of sex crime as news.

Seriousness, Newsworthiness and 'Novelty'

The proposition that seriousness is the primary determinant of newsworthiness in crime news production, as noted above, is problematic. Journalists who participated in this research suggested that certain types of sexual offence, in news terms at least, are 'trivial'. It could be argued, of course, that there is no such thing as a 'trivial' offence. As Young (1988) has pointed out, people's responses to the same act of criminal victimisation – in his case 'a punch' – may vary enormously. But it seems reasonable to suggest, in line with the views of journalists and practitioners interviewed in this study and the wider legal definitions of offences, that certain forms of sex crime are more harmful than others. Soliciting and prostitution, were generally regarded as minor forms of sexual offending. Sexual harassment, which can represent a wide variety of behaviours and levels of physical contact, was also considered to be relatively minor. And indecency offences such as flashing or nuisance calling, while they may cause considerable trauma for those involved, were not viewed by most journalists as particularly 'serious'. Paul Connelly, News Editor for the *Belfast Telegraph*, equated the coverage of these types of sex crime to a waste of resources: 'Newspapers have limited resources, so you target what you throw your resources at, and you do not throw your resources at trivial offences.'

However, while these 'trivial' offences were virtually negligible in terms of their overall representation in the archive, they provided the basis for a series of front-page stories, carried by a range of newspapers and sometimes attracting sustained interest over several days. These offences were not reported because of the nature of the criminal act. Their perceived seriousness was not a primary (or perhaps even a secondary) consideration. They invariably possessed an additional quality or qualities that superseded the relatively minor nature of the crime itself; each demonstrated some element of 'novelty'. As Hall *et al* (1978: 71) rightly point out, 'most stories seem to require some novel element in order to lift them into news visibility in the first instance'. In this straightforward sense, 'novelty' is clearly a weightier determinant of newsworthiness than 'seriousness'. In those trivial cases that received high levels of press attention, the element of 'novelty' was constituted primarily by the news values of 'personalisation' and 'dramatisation'.

Personalisation, Dramatisation and Celebrity

'Personalisation', as conjured through the involvement of 'notable individuals' (Cavender and Mulcahy 1998) of 'high status' (Ericson *et al* 1991), is a powerful determinant of newsworthiness. 'Notable' and 'high status' in this context can be defined in terms of a number of factors including fame and deviance or, better still, the famous being deviant. If a suitable personality is not readily available, journalists may construct one – a practice that is evident in the coverage of sexual offences perpetrated by unknown offenders, where, in the absence of any tangible evidence, images of sex fiends and sex beasts (Soothill and Walby 1991), vicious predators (Websdale 1999) who may be mentally ill (Kitzinger and Skidmore 1995; Websdale 1999), or deranged Satanists (Best 1990; West 1996; Jenkins 1992) have variously proliferated. Our main concern here, however, is with those individuals who can be identified.

The attribution and individualisation of responsibility to an offender whose 'individual pathology' (Chibnall 1977) marks him or her out as distinct from the rest of society are central to the news value of 'personalisation'. The more clearly and unambiguously the deviant personality can be defined (thus reducing uncertainty and intersecting with the news value of 'simplification') and, most importantly, located within a context that will be culturally meaningful to the news reader ('proximity'), the greater the overall newsworthiness of the story.

For this reason 'personalisation' is most easily conjured in cases of (sex) crime involving celebrities with whom audiences are already likely to be familiar. In cultural terms, stories about famous personalities are immediately relevant because they resonate within existing frames of reference. With notable individuals of this kind, as with anyone else, the seriousness of the offence is a crucial factor in determining the newsworthiness of the resulting story. But with celebrities who are already widely known, the level of deviance required to attract media attention is significantly lower than for offences committed by 'regular people'. Put another way, relatively minor acts, in terms of harm done, will have greater news appeal because of the already meaningful identity of the perpetrator. There will be greater potential for 'dramatisation' because of the high levels of 'personalisation' already embodied within the story.

Narratives detailing the sexual deviance of the famous are rare. Their 'novelty' in this regard accounts in part for the sometimes extraordinarily high levels of media attention they receive when uncovered. Recent examples which attracted massive levels of media coverage include the 1998 case against pop star George Michael for indecent behaviour in a Beverly Hills public lavatory and the 1997 charges against Hugh Grant for 'lewd conduct' with a prostitute in LA. A further, and more serious, example of celebrity sex crime is the rape case against Mike Tyson, for which he was subsequently convicted and sentenced to imprisonment. Had the alleged offenders not been celebrities, it is debatable as to how much, if any, media interest they would have attracted.

Only two sex crime stories involving international celebrities appeared in the archive – one involving Olympic gold medallist Ed Moses, and the other, US President Bill Clinton. Both detailed so-called 'trivial' offences – prostitution and sexual harassment respectively. Yet both were constructed as front-page narratives in at least one of the sample newspapers, and picked up on the inside pages in a range of others.[3] In each case the seriousness of the offence was almost ancillary to the celebrity context of the story; it was a supplementary rather than a cardinal news value. A *celebrity* had committed a *crime* involving *sex*, and that was enough. It was the conflation of sex and crime with the notion of celebrity, rather than the nature of the act itself, that merited press coverage. Here, the news values of 'personalisation', 'dramatisation', 'novelty' and 'titillation' were sufficiently strong to overshadow the relatively minor nature of offences that would otherwise have almost certainly been ignored.

The Intersection of Personalisation and Proximity

Hall *et al* (1978: 72) find in their analysis of mugging reports that 'the news value of "elite or famous persons" does not appear to play, in our sample anyway, an augmenting role'. Their definition of 'elite or famous', however, appears to be narrow and literal and, therefore, is somewhat limiting as a heuristic device. 'Personalisation' is not solely dependent upon celebrity stardom on a global scale. The notion of elite or notable individuals and corresponding conceptions of high status, as intimated above, work on a number of levels of which international stardom is only one. Most importantly, they are closely intertwined with the notion of 'proximity'. Stephen Dempster, News Editor for the *News Letter*, offered an example to illustrate the dynamic nature of the relationship between 'celebrity' and 'proximity', and their bearing on the selection and production of particular events as news:

> If David Beckham was shot in London tomorrow and an RUC [Royal Ulster Constabulary][4] man was shot outside the [Belfast] City Hall it's going to be the RUC man that makes the front page. So it doesn't matter that David Beckham's, you know, a world superstar. The more important thing is what's happening on your doorstep, you know, and that's what it's all about. Proximity is

> obvious when you think about it. Proximity is probably the one overriding factor.

It was perhaps with this in mind that when Paul Connelly, News Editor for the *Belfast Telegraph*, explained that 'trivial' offences are generally of little interest to daily newspapers, he added the caveat: '… unless they happen to involve some public interest like the person was an MP, or in a position of authority over children, like a teacher or something like that.' The images conjured here are not of pop stars or world leaders, famous on a global stage – though this may be preferred – but of MPs and school teachers, little if at all known outside their own constituencies. These are notable individuals who command high status in a different way. 'Personalisation' in this kind of narrative describes people who command high status at the local level. They might exercise direct authority over others, in the case of school teachers, priests, youth leaders and so on, or people might appeal to their assumed authority as authorised knowers, in the case of MPs or local councillors. When these individuals commit sex crimes, their acts represent a 'betrayal of trust' (Dominelli 1989; Moore 1995), a rupture to the social fabric of the very community in which the news reader him or herself lives.

Such cases of public interest featured heavily in the archive. Sometimes the narrative described sex crimes of an extremely serious nature, for example, when teachers, youth leaders or, most frequently, members of the clergy were implicated in child sex abuse inquiries. On other occasions, however, the nature of the offence – its seriousness as defined in terms of harm done – could only be conceived of, in journalistic terms, as minor. In these latter cases the story's 'hook', its novel element, was not simply that a sex crime had been committed, but rather that a sex crime had been committed *by that individual* and *within that context*. Their 'nearness' and their 'meaningfulness' to the assumed audience made the 'dramatisation' more compelling and the 'personalisation' more culturally resonant. It was because of their spatial and cultural 'proximity' that they were considered sufficiently important and, ultimately, sufficiently newsworthy to merit coverage. Ronan Henry, Deputy News Editor for the *Belfast Telegraph*, further explained the importance of 'proximity' to the perceived newsworthiness of crime stories:

> Well, if we were to take a case from the UK or wherever, involving any sort of crime at all, because we are a local newspaper, the crime itself would have to be more shocking, it would have to be

> disproportionately big over there to be carried over here. Because people over here, people anywhere, are interested in what's going on in their own doorstep rather than … I mean … if a man gets shot on Royal Avenue [main shopping street in the centre of Belfast], you know, somebody walks up, puts a gun to his head and shoots him dead in Royal Avenue, you know, it's going to be all over the front pages of every newspaper. If it happens in Piccadilly or in Manchester, unless he's Irish, it's not going to make the front page. It's the same with anything. Unless there is something to tie it in with back home, and that just doesn't go with [sex crime], it goes with everything, you know.

In light of this statement, which is a straightforward rearticulation of McLurg's Law, it is not surprising that of the 211 cases of sex crime recorded in the archive, well over half (123 cases, or 59 per cent) described offences committed within Northern Ireland. And if *The Irish Times*, which is printed in Dublin and thus routinely reports a majority of sex crimes committed in the Republic of Ireland, is excluded, the figure increases substantially to four fifths (105 out of 132 cases, or 80 per cent).

The exceptions were those cases in which news values such as 'personalisation' and 'dramatisation' were especially strong or the overriding sense of 'novelty' was sufficiently powerful for the stories to be carried across the water. Sampled from a world forum, these narratives tended to involve high levels of violence or, in the few cases where they did not, as the above examples illustrate, they possessed some other extraordinary attributes, such as celebrity offenders or unexpected consequences. Regionally committed offences, too, frequently demonstrated high levels of violence. But many of these narratives were reported more on the basis of their public interest and their cultural resonance. Consequently, they represented a wider diversity of offence types and levels of harm.

Hence, a journalistic corollary of increasing 'proximity' is a corresponding decrease in the requisite levels of other news values – including 'novelty' – for narratives to be deemed sufficiently newsworthy to cross the threshold into news visibility. In terms of 'personalisation', the required status of either victim or offender is significantly reduced in a regional context – international celebrities in the USA, but local schoolteachers in Northern Ireland. Furthermore, because people react more strongly to events and conditions happening nearby, which may influence them directly, levels of 'dramatisation' also have a greater impact within a regional context – sex murder or serial rape in the USA but, in addition to many extremely serious offences, comparatively minor cases of indecent exposure or sexual harassment in Northern Ireland.

Seriousness is clearly a preferred theme in crime narratives, but it is not *the* defining characteristic of newsworthiness. The newsworthiness of a criminal event is determined primarily by 'novelty', which in turn is mediated by notions of cultural and spatial 'proximity' to the news audience. Next we consider the impact that these news values and the narratives into which they are incorporated are intended to have.

Crime Hierarchies and the 'Shock Factor': Novelty and Proximity

In addition to the dominant news values outlined above, there are a range of additional factors which influence the selection and production of (sex) crime narratives. These include the relative newsworthiness of other crimes and other potential news, the reporter's time and interest, the willingness of sources to provide information and the quality of information being provided. Within this framework, a hierarchy of crime news emerges (Surette 1998: 62):

> At the lowest level are crime stories that serve as space or time fillers. Next are secondary crime stories, which are potentially important depending on their characteristics and other organisational factors. Primary crime news stories are those that are given prominent space or time (front page or lead story). At the top are super-primary crime stories ... that receive an enormous amount of organisational resources and develop along many dimensions.

Soothill and Walby (1991: 145) find in their examination of English press coverage that 'most attacks are not considered to merit front-page treatment'. Schlesinger and Tumber (1994: 141) suggest that '[s]exual offences ... loom large in British news coverage', and go on to point out that they account for '20 per cent of crime-related items on the front pages of mid-market papers as well as 23 per cent of popular papers' front-page crime news'. By contrast, 'for the quality press, sexual crime constitutes less than 3 per cent of crime-related front-page news' (1994: 141). These latter figures highlight the differences in opinion between news agencies regarding what merits front-page status and add emphasis to the caution, already well rehearsed in this book, about remaining cognisant of the range of journalistic styles, forms and flavours that characterise contemporary newspaper markets.

Some 14 per cent (29 out of 211) of sex crime cases in the Northern Ireland regional press received full front-page treatment (as opposed to being mentioned on the front page and covered in full somewhere inside) in at least one newspaper.[5] In the absence of a comparison against non-sexual crimes it is impossible to say whether this figure is particularly high or not. As noted already, however, there is little doubt that the over-representation of personal crimes of sex and violence is a common characteristic of mass media output (Marsh 1991). Ronan Henry, Deputy News Editor for the *Belfast Telegraph*, explained that every story is assessed in accordance with its individual merits. Further, he went on to explain the collective impact that these individual merits – the news values conjured within the story – should ideally have on the news reader:

> It's the same for any story in any field ... the individual merits of the story. We had a former deputy editor here and he used to call it the ' "F" me factor', and you can imagine what the 'F' is for. So it is basically ... something that just astounds people, the individual merits. Not all stories are going to have it, but every single story, certainly since I have been working on the news desk, is treated on how we think our readers will react to it.

These comments conjure a wide range of possible themes: 'violence', 'celebrity', 'dramatisation', 'human interest', 'negative consequences' and so on. Most importantly, though, they conjure the underpinning news value of 'novelty'. In order to be considered sufficiently newsworthy for front-page coverage, in order to qualify as primary crime news, a (sex) crime story needs to embody an element or angle or, better still, some combination of dominant news values that strongly sets it apart from the norm. Rosie Uffindel, Social Affairs Correspondent for the *Irish News*, illustrated the importance of finding an angle that explicitly demonstrates this extraordinariness, what a number of journalists referred to as the 'shock factor', to secure a headline story in the fiercely competitive business of newsprint journalism:

> I mean all journalists are in the business of shocking, and the only time I am going to get on the front page is with a story that will shock you. As a journalist I want to be on the front page and I want to find the kind of angle that will get me on the front page, and that's just the nature of the business.

By its very definition, a 'shock factor' suggests 'novelty' – it conjures images of an event, situation or example of a phenomenon which, to recall Ericson *et al*'s terminology, is 'deviant, equivocal and unpredictable' (1991: 4). The 'nature of the business', then, dictates that sex crimes which represent the norm rather than the novel will be considered less newsworthy and, as a result, be less likely to receive even modest press coverage, still less front-page prioritisation. And yet, because of its capacity to evoke such a visceral response from the news reader, whether in delight or disgust, the news value of 'novelty' is potentially the most fragile and evanescent in nature. Hall *et al.* (1978: 72) develop this contention, recognising that 'the value of novelty is eventually expended; through repetition the extra-ordinary eventually becomes the ordinary. Indeed, in relation to any one particular news story, "novelty" clearly has the most limited life span of all the news values'. The offence of rape, for example, dominated headlines in the 1970s. Throughout the 1980s and 1990s, however, this media status has been usurped by the phenomenon of child sex abuse to the extent that, as one journalist explained, 'it's got to be quite an unusual rape to get the headlines these days'.

Thus journalists are continually under pressure to find and report the exception to the rule in order to maintain a high profile in the journalistic arena and, whenever possible, secure their by-lines on front-page stories. This pressure, in turn, militates against reporting the social reality of sex crime and, therefore, impedes the construction of sex crime narratives that promote greater understanding and awareness of the phenomenon.

Sex Crime and the Importance of the Shock Factor

The desire to 'shock' is a perennial feature of news production (Frayling 1986; Soothill and Walby 1991; Benedict 1992; Walkowitz 1992). But not all classifications of crime and not all examples of sex crime have the capacity to elicit such a response. While few would dispute that sexual offending is an extremely serious issue, it is debatable how much particular types of offending shock or, in some instances, even interest news readers.

Consensual homosexual offences make up a significant proportion of sex crime coverage in the Sunday press. But for Eileen Calder, spokesperson for the Belfast Rape Crisis centre, they are not serious examples of sexual deviance: 'I mean when we are talking about adult men in, say, a toilet or something ... in the reality of my world they are not actually committing a crime.' Ronan Henry, Deputy News Editor for the *Belfast Telegraph*, offered his view of the impact of press narratives reporting consensual homosexual offences:

> If you are talking about indecency cases in toilets and stuff like that, if a court case came into it, we might put it in, like, you know, but I don't know if there is the same sort of shock factor involved. I mean, I just don't think there is.

Clearly, then, some forms of sex crime will have a more profound impact on news readers than others. What is important to recognise is that it is precisely those cases that have the potential to elicit the most resonant ' "F" me', for whatever reason, that tend to be given the highest levels of press attention and, ultimately, receive full front-page treatment as 'primary crime stories' (Surette 1998). Stephen Dempster, News Editor for the *News Letter*, offered a more detailed description of some of the 'individual merits' that elevate some stories to primary front-page status:

> Well the 'shock factor', I mean, there's not very much that shocks people these days, but it's just something that shocks people, that horrifies people, or maybe just something that would be universally condemned. Or something that moves people. I would actually say that that's the 'Number One', anything that moves people, but there's different ways of moving people, you know.

Sunday Life Editor, Martin Lindsay, offered his view of some of the main ways:

> I think it's number one, it's the shock impact, and number two, and this is very, very important, people say, 'That could happen to me, that could happen to my daughter, that could happen to my son.' So I think that once people can actually associate with the crime and say, 'There but for the grace of God …', after the shock, comes that.

And Ronan Henry, Deputy News Editor for the *Belfast Telegraph*, went on to describe some other factors that contribute to the generation of the shock factor in the construction of sex crime narratives:

> Well violence is obviously a big strong one. There is also like a sort of warning factor, you know, like this could happen to anybody, sort of stuff, like, you know … or the fact that anyone would

> actually do that. It's just that people do terrible things to each other. It's the fact that this exists and it's anathema to most common, decent people ... and just the fact that this is happening on our streets, this is happening on your doorstep.

This description evokes a range of news values. 'Dramatisation' is conjured in the portrayal of action and violence; 'speculation' and 'immediacy' are conjured in the 'warning' that anyone could fall victim to a sex attacker who might strike (again) at any time; and 'personalisation' is conjured through the attribution and individualisation of responsibility to an offender whose 'individual pathology' sets him or her apart from the rest of normal society. But of greatest significance is the final emphasis on 'proximity'. 'Proximity' is conjured by the suggestion that those sex crimes that are most likely to possess the requisite 'shock factor' will be those committed 'on our streets' – within the community to which the news reader belongs.

Sex Crime, Proximity and Public Concern

Clear evidence of the importance of 'proximity' in this regard is found in the public reaction to news of the re-housing of sex offenders after release from prison, where all the above-mentioned news values are conjured. In the summer of 2000, in the wake of the murder of schoolgirl Sarah Payne, the *News of the World* began a campaign for the introduction of new legislation (to be called Sarah's Law) which would grant a level of public access to information regarding the whereabouts of convicted paedophiles.[6] To achieve its objective, the newspaper undertook to 'name and shame' 110,000 known paedophiles.

In two successive issues (*News of the World*, 23 July 2000, 30 July 2000), the names, addresses and photographs of fifty such individuals were printed on the front page. Members of the public formed into groups and took to the streets, sometimes campaigning outside the houses of alleged paedophiles, sometimes physically attacking them. Though the campaign won considerable support from sections of the public and other news agencies (the *Daily Mirror* publicly declared its support for the campaign in its 3 August 2000 edition), it attracted widespread criticism over concerns that paedophiles would be forced 'underground', disrupting any treatment they were undergoing and thereby increasing the risk to the community (MacVean 2000; Thomas 2000; Haug 2001; Wilson and Silverman 2002). Public hostility was not always directed at the 'right' people. On the 4 August, the *News of the*

World agreed to suspend its action after at least four men were known to have been wrongly identified and targeted by vigilante groups (*Observer*, 6 August 2000).

This illustrates how notions of 'proximity' can significantly influence the impact of crime narratives on the news-reading audience and, correspondingly, the social reaction to crime. A number of news items in the archive further demonstrate how public opposition can be translated into collective outcry and action, and may in turn result in the offender being driven out of that particular community. For example, a *Belfast Telegraph* (22 January 1997: 4) story about the experiences of a convicted sex offender who had been re-housed in Northern Ireland read, 'When the offences came to light, residents in the street were outraged and [named person] moved out of his home and went to reside elsewhere' (see also *Sunday World*, 5 January 1997: 7, 14). Occasionally, newspapers themselves took the lead, carrying out the dubious public service of 'outing' offenders. Again in the *Belfast Telegraph*, the front-page headline 'CHILD SEX OFFENDER WARNING' was followed by the statement that 'A convicted paedophile is living in Londonderry within walking distance of four primary schools, it emerged today'. That the newspaper led with this story indicates just how newsworthy it was thought to be.

Conclusions

The various factors that determine the ultimate newsworthiness of a given event are manifest and complex. This chapter has sought to provide a coherent and critical account of the most important of these and, more specifically, to establish the key determinants of newsworthiness in the selection and production of sex crime as news.

The approach adopted here differs from that of others (Ericson *et al* 1987; Kidd-Hewitt 1995; Surette 1998), and rejects in particular the suggestion that seriousness is the primary determinant of newsworthiness in (sex) crime stories. Particular emphasis has been placed on the centrality of the news value 'proximity'. The chapter has identified that other key dimensions of newsworthiness, including personalisation and celebrity, the sense of seriousness and drama, and the levels of public interest attracted by sex crime narratives are all mediated by, and may change dramatically as a function of, spatial and cultural proximity. As proximity increases, the potency of other news values or dimensions required to make an event 'newsworthy' correspondingly decreases.

Sex offences – like all criminal events – are selected and constructed as press narratives in accordance with the news reader's anticipated reaction. The aim is to shock and, accordingly, journalists are constantly on the lookout for sex crimes that contain a 'shock factor'. The shock factor may derive from a range of characteristics including the seriousness of the offence, the people involved or the possibility of further attacks. Each of these dimensions – their meaningfulness and their ultimate capacity to 'shock' – is mediated by the notion of 'proximity'. To illustrate this, Chapter 4 presents an empirical analysis of press representations of sex crime in the Northern Ireland press.

Notes

1 Livingstone (1996), summarising some of the more recent overviews of the literature in this area, includes Bailey (1993), Carey (1993) and Wartella (1995) .
2 For notable exceptions, see Schlesinger (1987), Sparks (1992) and Schlesinger and Tumber (1994).
3 *News Letter* (19/01/85: front page), *Irish Times* (13/01/97: front page), *Irish Times* (15/01/85: 4), *Belfast Telegraph* (19/01/85: 5, and 23/01/85: 13).
4 As part of the process of implementing the recommendations made by the Patten Commission on Policing in Northern Ireland (Patten 1999), the Royal Ulster Constabulary (RUC) was renamed the Police Service of Northern Ireland (PSNI) on 4 December 2001. Between 1985 and 1997, the time frame for this study, the police service was called the RUC, and for the sake of clarity that name is used throughout this book.
5 If these front-page leader or 'in brief' cases are included, the proportion rises to 22 per cent.
6 Sarah Payne's parents backed the *News of the World* campaign publicly to expose convicted sex offenders who had been re-housed in the community. They argued that until the government introduced legislation better to control offenders in the community, the public had a right to know offenders' whereabouts so that they can protect their children. Sarah's Law is modelled on Megan's Law introduced in the USA in 1994, which resulted from the rape and murder of seven-year-old Megan Kanka by a convicted paedophile living in the same street (MacVean 2000).

Chapter 4

Press representations of sex crime in Northern Ireland: an empirical analysis

Introduction

This chapter investigates the nature of press representations of sex crime in Northern Ireland between 1985 and 1997. As Ericson (1991) points out, it is important to present both an aggregate (composite view) and an individual (specific elements and case studies) account of representations of crime, deviance and control. Accordingly, my aim here is to develop a critical understanding of the press construction of sex crime by exploring both broad contours and specific aspects of representations. Of particular interest are the representation of different types of offence, the prevalence of the various stages of coverage, the differences and similarities between newspapers, the use of photographs, the range and amount of coverage across newspapers, and a variety of other factors.

Press Representations and Official Statistics

Maguire (1997) observes that any attempts to make general statements about the nature and extent of crime are beset with complications and inconsistencies. Official crime statistics can only describe those incidents that have been notified to and recorded by the police, or which have been uncovered either through 'luck' or investigation, and thus incorporated into the records as specific criminal offences. Moreover, despite the apparently precise wording of legislation, the categorisation and recording of specific criminal offences are 'highly selective and value laden, the product of complex social, political, and organisational processes' (Maguire 1997: 141; see also, Coleman and Moynihan 1996; Reiner 1996; Fattah, 1997). Criminal statistics, create not just an incomplete picture of crime, through lacking the 'dark figure' of offences not reported to – or, if reported, not recorded by – the police, but a systematically biased picture of crime. They are the product not of a neutral fact-collecting process, but of a record-keeping practice which is geared first and foremost towards organisational (primarily police) aims and needs (Maguire 1997). As such, they may tell us more about the organisation producing them than about the 'reality' they are later taken to describe.

Official crime rates are subject to fluctuation by a range of factors. For example, the number of offences 'discovered' by the police can rise or fall in accordance with varying levels of statutory attention to particular types of criminal activity. Police operations targeting specific crimes will normally result in a sharp rise in the number of offences detected and subsequent arrests made (Maguire 1997). Changes in police practice can further influence the number of offences made known and thus the number of crimes incorporated into official records. With regard to sex crime, fundamental reform to police practice has resulted in better treatment of survivors and a consequent increase in the numbers prepared to come forward and report offences (Mawby and Walklate 1994; West, 1996). Indeed, improvements in police procedure may account to a significant degree for the sharp rise in detected crimes between 1985 and 1997. As will be suggested in later chapters, the media are one vital conduit for efforts to publicise such improvements. With all this in mind, some comparison can be made between the number of sex crimes recorded by the police and the number reported in the press.

The Official Picture of Sex Crime and Press Representations in Northern Ireland

The newsprint media sample sex crimes from around the world (Soothill 1995) and an official picture of sex offending on a global scale is obviously impossible to attain. However, regional newspapers tend to focus predominantly on regional crime (Ericson *et al* 1987; Soothill and Walby 1991). Consideration of those offences committed in Northern Ireland and their coverage in the press offers some insight into the relationship between the changing official picture of sex crime and changes in its representation in press discourse. Figure 4.1 illustrates the increase in press attention to sex crime between 1985 and 1997. In 1985 a

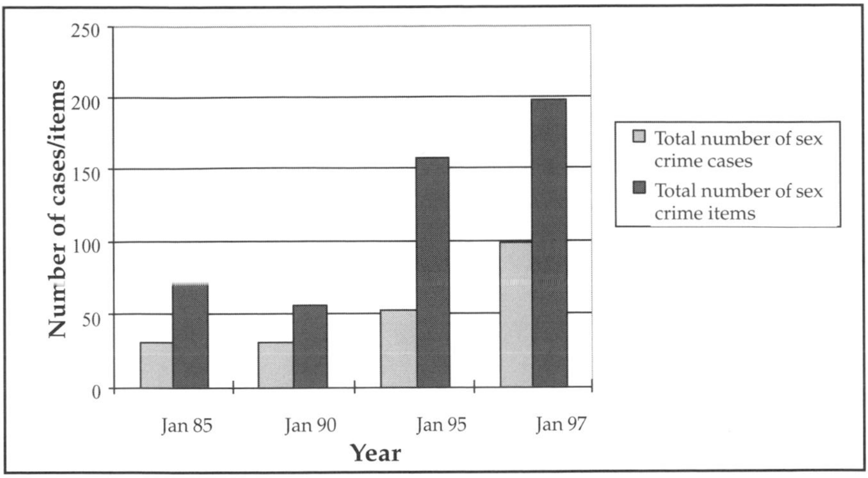

Figure 4.1 Number of sex crime cases and sex crime items reported in the press

total of 71 newspaper items reported 31 cases of sex crime. By 1997 the amount of coverage had trebled to 198 news items reporting 99 cases. There was a lull in coverage in 1990 that merits some further consideration before proceeding.

Between 1985 and 1990 the number of reported sex crime cases dropped from 31 to 30, and the number of overall items fell from 71 to 58. Over the same period the official police statistics indicate an increase in recorded sex offences of more than 111 per cent. The decline in the overall quantity of press items can perhaps be explained by the absence in 1990 of either a single major case which dominated reporting, or a specific type of offence which alone provided the focus for a substantial proportion of press attention.[1] Given the trend of the overall increase, however, it is possible that the lull in coverage in 1990 represents a chance fluctuation rather than a palpable shift in the interests and priorities of Northern Ireland news agencies.

Between 1985 and 1997, the number of sex offences recorded by the police grew by 328 per cent (from 47 to 201 in January of those years[2]), while the number of regionally committed offences reported in the press grew by 206 per cent (from 18 to 55 in January of those years). If sex crimes committed outside Northern Ireland are included, the increase rises to 216 per cent (from 31 to 98). While the number of recorded sex offences quadrupled, the number reported in the press trebled.

This is not unexpected, since only a tiny fraction of criminal events, sexual or otherwise, are deemed sufficiently newsworthy to merit press attention (Soothill and Walby 1991; Schlesinger and Tumber 1994). For a criminal event, like any event, to become news it must satisfy a range of organisational and journalistic criteria. It must fall within the news cycle of that title (Rock 1973), conjure the requisite news values (Chibnall 1977), more so than other news on the day (Surette 1998), and meet various other requirements discussed in previous chapters. Though sexual violence is generally considered more newsworthy than other types of criminality (Marsh 1991) – and this seems increasingly to be the case (Reiner *et al* 2000a) – a rise in the number of recorded sex crimes does not necessarily equate to a rise in the number that make good copy. More significant is the rate of change.

Figure 4.2 illustrates the rate of change in the number of sex offences recorded by the RUC and the number receiving coverage in the press between 1985 and 1997. It indicates that the rate of increase in press attention to sex crime (and it is worth bearing in mind that journalists receive most of their sex crime stories from the police) by far exceeds the rate of increase in offences recorded by the RUC over the same period. This is significant. In the remainder of this chapter, therefore, I want to develop an empirical analysis of the dramatic and disproportionate increase in press attention to sex crime, and the wider changes and continuities in the nature and extent of sex crime coverage between 1985 and 1997.

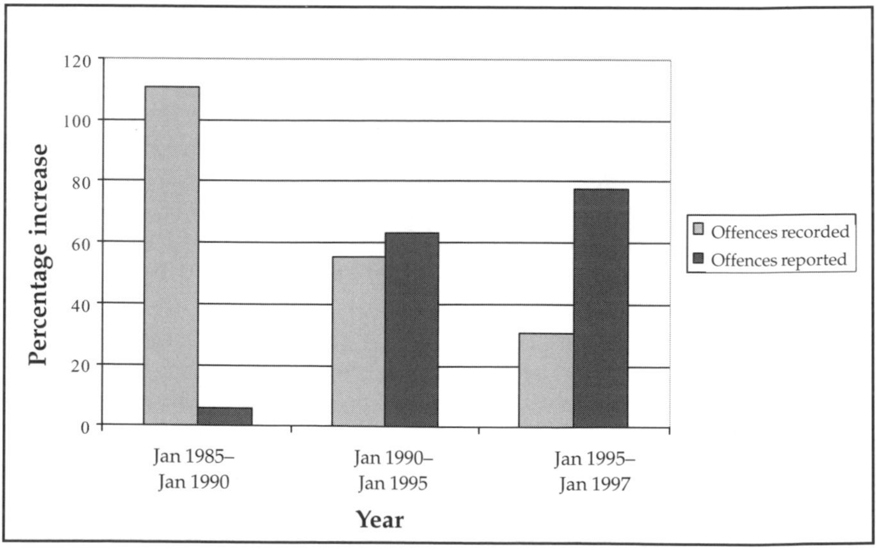

Figure 4.2 Percentage increase in the number of sex offences recorded by the RUC and the number reported in press

The Nature of Press Representations of Sex Crime

The following sections break down the growth in sex crime coverage across Northern Ireland in terms of differences between newspapers; the range of coverage; the context of representations; the offence types that featured most and least frequently; the difference stages of the social/judicial reaction at which sex crimes were reported; and the use of photographs in the construction of sex crime narratives. Specific cases are referred to where appropriate to provide illustrative examples.

The increase in press attention to sex crime by newspaper

The greatest overall amount of sex crime material appeared in *The Irish Times*, which produced a total of 79 cases of sex crime and 167 items. The *Belfast Telegraph* produced the second largest quantity of sex crime coverage (61 cases and 89 news items), followed by the *News Letter* (54 cases in 81 items) and the *Irish News* (47 cases and 73 items). Due to their frequency of publication, the Sunday newspapers naturally reported a smaller number of sex crime cases and items than the dailies. The *Sunday World* (34 cases and 53 news items) printed a substantially larger amount of sex crime material than the *Sunday Life* (11 cases and 20 news items) even after accounting for the latter's omission from the 1985 archive.[3] The comparatively small yield in the *Sunday Life* is interesting since Bromley (1997: 141) notes that 'in the first year of publication' (1989) it offered its readers 'an almost unremitting editorial diet of soaps, sex, sport, celebrities, shopping and serialisations'. Indeed, its original slogan was 'racy but responsible' (p. 141). Sex and crime may have featured heavily, but the combination of the two, it would seem, did not.

The Irish Times also demonstrated the sharpest increase in both the number of cases reported and the number of news items printed. Attention to sex crime in this newspaper escalated from six cases and 16 news items in 1985 to 44 cases and 87 news items in 1997; there were increases of more than 700 per cent and 500 per cent in the number of cases and items reported respectively. This is contrasted by the overall increase in the *News Letter* from 11 cases and 16 items in 1985 to 14 cases and 21 items in 1997. Compared with the growth in *The Irish Times*, this increase is very small. Again, the comparatively small extent of the increase in the *News Letter* is interesting because that newspaper is widely considered by journalists to be 'racier' that the other dailies.

A number of inter-related factors help to explain the extent of the increase in press attention to sex crime, both overall and within particular newspapers. Some are relatively straightforward, such as changes in the market demands of news production in Northern Ireland and the commercial potency of sex crime as a news product. Others are more complex and difficult to substantiate empirically. These latter factors include shifts in popular consciousness about sex crime, the relevance of the political situation, the impact of certain high-profile cases, the activities of various groups and organisations (and journalists themselves) and how these activities were received and represented by the press. Each of these factors is investigated in the following chapter. Next, though, a clearer picture of the empirical contours of sex crime coverage in Northern Ireland can be established through considering the range of coverage across newspapers.

The range of coverage

Four fifths (173 of the 211 cases, or 84 per cent) of sex crime cases appeared in only one newspaper. Eight per cent (16 cases) were reported in only two newspapers and 8 per cent (17 cases) received coverage in three newspapers. Only 1 per cent (3 cases) appeared in four newspapers and 1 per cent (3 cases) was mention in five. No cases appeared in all six newspapers. That means that slightly more than one in fifty cases of sex crime were reported in four or more newspapers (5 cases from 211), guaranteeing a level of exposure in the daily and Sunday press.

The context of coverage: risk, causes and prevention

The vast majority of sex crime coverage was case based. That is, most items described a single event or related series of events, rather than discussing wider issues of concern, such as risks, prevention, resources for survivors or debates around legal issues (see also Kitzinger and Skidmore 1995; Skidmore 1995; Kitzinger 1996; more generally, see Rock 1973; McNair 1999). Overall, around one in ten sex crime items (46 out of 483) included some discussion of issues of general concern (11 items in 1985, 1990 and 1995, and 13 items in 1997).

The event-based nature of reporting can be partly understood as resulting from the organisational constraints on news production. In particular, the need to produce reports according to tight deadlines contributes to their event orientation, normally at the expense of discussion of wider areas of concern (Galtung and Ruge 1970; Reiner 2000b; Schudson 2000). With respect to sex crime coverage, more specifically, the news values that inform the construction of these and other crime narratives (especially perhaps dramatisation, immediacy, personalisation, speculation and proximity) are best constituted through the portrayal of specific acts and individuals (Chibnall 1977; Skidmore

1995; Cavender and Mulcahy 1998). It is the combination of these two influences that leads to the consistent prioritisation of events over issues. A number of practitioners interviewed in the course of this study expressed their frustration at what they saw as the press's narrow interest on the details of specific cases. Oliver Brannigan, for example, Director of the Northern Ireland Probation Board, explained:

> Journalists will ring me up and ask to talk about Joe Bloggs, and I will say, 'Look, I can't talk to you about Joe Bloggs. I am more than happy to talk to you about the principles which would guide our dealing with Joe Bloggs, but I am not prepared to talk to you about Joe Bloggs'. And then they will say, 'Well then we are going to write A, B and C' and I have to say, 'Well fair enough, you are going to have to do that because I am not going to talk to you about Joe Bloggs'. And they find that unacceptable until I say to them, 'Well if you were Joe Bloggs and another newspaper phoned and asked me to talk about you, would you want me to do it?' and of course they say 'No'.

Confidentiality limits the amount of case-based information that practitioners can pass on to journalists, but it is precisely that case-based information in which journalists are most interested (see also Kitzinger and Skidmore 1995). However, while many practitioners expressed their frustration at the lack of wider debate in press discourse, some suggested that it is not the press's responsibility, or at least their priority, to address issues of wider concern. For these participants, the coverage of broader debates is secondary to the news agency's principal role of reporting up-to-date news as and when it happens. In this view, an overall proportion of one in ten sex crime items discussing wider concerns may seem quite reasonable. But journalists themselves, many of whom expressed a clear sense of pride in their perceived role within the community, contested this rather narrow conception of the place of print discourse in public life. As Rosie Uffindel, Social Affairs Correspondent for *The Irish News*, explained:

> I think that the press has an enormous responsibility. We have a responsibility to put things in context. I don't think that you can avoid going for the headline, which is the out of the ordinary stuff, and time constraints are no excuse really, but we have a responsibility to give the context about something.

What is most striking, though, is the extent to which the discussion of general issues diminished over time – from slightly more than one in six articles in 1985 (11 out of 71, or 15 per cent) to one in 15 in 1997 (13 out of 198, or 7 per cent). It is this relative decrease in attention to wider issues, in the face of a massive increase in overall press attention to sex crime, that is of greatest significance.

The discussion around issues of general concern – causes, risks, prevention, resources and so on – is not, in itself, considered by journalists to be particularly newsworthy. This explains why only a few of the 46 items that included some such discussion made this the central focus of the report. Most were in fact case based and incorporated advice specifically on personal safety and crime avoidance within the context of the particular case being described. Such advice tended to be located within the context of an ongoing investigation in which an actual offender was committing actual offences against actual victims. It was nearly always underpinned by the suggestion that the attacker could strike again – thus justifying the issuing of advice in the first place. In this way, the relatively mundane discussion of prevention and risk could be imbued with a sense of urgency and drama. The following example illustrates this point.

In 1995, the three Belfast dailies covered a series of attacks on women perpetrated by a man posing as a taxi driver. A total of five reports appeared in the three newspapers. Each gave details of the offences and a description of the attacker. The possibility of further attacks was the dominant theme throughout and the advice to women was couched in those terms. The *Belfast Telegraph* report 'WARNING OVER BOGUS TAXIS' (4 January 1995: 8) contained the investigating officer's caution

Bogus taxis spark rape warning

HALF a minute is all it takes to prevent a rape or indecent assault, police said yesterday.

RUC superintendent, Bill Lowry, warned women against using unofficial taxis as he praised two women for fighting off a possible attacker posing as a taximan.

Both women were attacked within an hour of each other on new year's day.

In both cases they got into a blue Ford Escort they thought was a taxi. When their attacker pounced the women fought back and managed to escape.

Police are looking for a man of medium build in his mid-20s with dark greasy hair, a moustache and a blackened front tooth.

Superintendent Lowry said yesterday it wasn't known how dangerous the man could be.

"The girls acted very courageously, very bravely and very correctly in screaming and getting out of the vehicle, causing as much noise as possible," he said.

"Although on this occasion the ladies weren't physically hurt they are extremely upset about what happened," he said.

The superintendent said anyone hiring a taxi should be sure it was a legal taxi. A few simple checks would make sure.

"Taxis must display on the roof a sign saying the company's name or the telephone number of the taxi.

"The drivers, if they are legal drivers, must carry identification with them from the PSV including a photograph.

"These things must be asked for and must be looked at.

"Take 30 seconds to check what you are getting into and make sure you don't put yourself in danger," he said.

Meanwhile Sinn Fein councillor and former Rape Crisis counsellor, Una Gillespie, said it was her belief that the number of attempted assaults on women and children had increased since the ceasefires.

"There have been a number of attempted abductions of children in the lower Falls before Christmas and now two attacks on women after the new year."

She said it was a trend that seemed to be increasing everywhere in the last six months.

Una Gillespie said the focus on issues has changed and that more cases are coming to light "probably because of a lot of media highlighting of child abuse. There's also more awareness now of violence against women."

She said anyone who ordered a taxi at night should not get into the car until the driver repeated the name given to the taxi firm over the phone; and they should sit in the back seat if possible.

Printed courtesy of the *Irish News*.

*Belfast Telegraph, Tuesday, January 3, 1995

Women lured in 'taxi' assaults

Plea to potential donors

HEALTH Minister Tom Sackville today urged more people to join a national computer register of potential organ donors.

Some 150,000 people had already signed up since the register was set up in October, but Mr Sackville said: "We have got to increase that rate.

"We have got to try to reduce the number of families who are unable to make that vital decision at that terrible moment in the hospital to give permission for their loved ones' organs to be transplanted."

The free phone telephone number to call for people interested in joining the register is 0800 555777. —PA

By Claire McGahan

POLICE in west Belfast are hunting for a man who assaulted two women by posing as a taxi driver early on New Year's Day.

The RUC has warned women to check taxi drivers' credentials after the attacks, which happened in less than an hour.

The first attack took place in the early hours of New Year's Day when two women out celebrating the New Year were lured into the man's blue Ford Escort on the Whiterock Road, thinking it was a taxi.

Waiting

One of the women was left home at about 1.15am, but the driver took the other 34-year-old passenger to a lane off the Falls Road, close to St Gall's GAA club, and assaulted her.

Check on credentials, warn police

The woman managed to get out and the car sped off towards Andersonstown.

Forty minutes later, the man convinced a women, who was waiting for her husband outside a Chinese takeaway, that he was a taxi driver.

She got in and he immediately drove off. When she demanded he wait for her husband, he said he was going to turn.

But instead the 24-year-old was driven to St Agnes' Court where, after a struggle, she escaped and fled screaming.

The car was later found abandoned in Andersonstown Park.

Both women described the man as being in his mid-20s, with dark, fine, greasy hair, a moustache, poor teeth and a Belfast accent.

Police say the English registered car — number C219 KGH — was stolen in the Wellington Park area of south Belfast earlier in the evening.

Anyone with information should contact police at Woodbourne — 650222.

Alone

The west Belfast assaults came less than a week after the brutal rape of a woman in the north of the city.

The 25-year-old victim accepted a lift from her attacker after he spotted her standing alone at a bus stop on the Antrim Road early last Tuesday morning.

A police spokesman said today: "We would repeat the warning that women should make sure they know exactly who they are getting into a car with."

Printed courtesy of the *Belfast Telegraph*.

that 'we don't know how dangerous this man could be', while the *News Letter*'s 'BOGUS TAXI DRIVER SPARKS RAPE ALERT' (4 January 1995: 13) urged women 'to be on their guard'. Advice was thus presented as a specific and urgent 'warning' (rather than a general discussion) and formed part of a wider, highly dramatic – and highly newsworthy – narrative of a serial sex offender at large.

Dominica McGowan, Director of the Nexus Institute for Adult Survivors of Sexual Abuse, recommended that women should 'phone for a taxi, ask who the driver is, and make sure it carries the department of the Environment registered licence' (*News Letter* 4 January 1995: 13). In another report, the police warned women to 'only use clearly marked legal taxis' (*Belfast Telegraph* 4 January 1995: 8). And in another, women were cautioned to 'check taxi driver's credentials' (*Belfast Telegraph* 3 January 1995: 3). The inclusion of direct advice from accredited sources was undoubtedly useful within the immediate context of this case. Indeed, any information that might lead to a reduction in sexual victimisation is clearly worthwhile. But there is a wider issue here, relating to the type of sex offending with which advice on crime avoidance and personal safety was most often associated.

Most sex crimes are not committed by strangers. In the vast majority of cases, the victim – whether adult or child – knows the offender (Dobash and Dobash 1979; Finkelhor and Yllo 1985; Hall 1985; Stanko 1990; Grubin 1998; Mirrlees-Black *et al* 1996, 1998). Yet discussions of risk and prevention – on the relatively few occasions on which they occurred – related to sex crime narratives featuring seemingly random predators. The association of advice on personal safety almost exclusively with these types of sex crime sends a clear message that it is strangers who pose the greatest threat.

Websdale (1999) examines the media's promotion of stranger-danger against a backdrop of patriarchal power relations. Examining the development of legislation in the USA, he argues that 'suggesting the real dangers to women and children come from freakish strangers rather than intimates or companions' may have the effect of 'counteracting the feminist push for deeper-seated reform over gender issues' (1999: 111). Soothill and Walby (1991) make a similar claim in the UK context, proposing the feminist calls for wider social reform have been resisted in favour of the promotion of an intensified law-and-order response to sexual offending. Many of those who participated in this research expressed clear views about the promotion of images of 'stranger-danger'. But here concerns tended to be of a more immediate nature. Most accorded that the disproportionate focus on stranger attacks highlights the wrong areas of risk. Some, however, went so far as to suggest that it may actually undermine preventive efforts, particularly those targeted at safeguarding children's safety. This is an extremely important contention with far-reaching implications, and it will be developed further in the following chapters.

The prevalence of offence types

Sex offences were grouped into 12 categories: adult sex murder, child sex murder, offences against children and young persons, incest offences, indecency offences, consensual homosexual offences, offences against the mentally impaired, prostitution, pornography offences, rape, sexual assault and sexual harassment.[4]

Offences against children were the most heavily reported sex crimes, accounting for 44 per cent of all cases (93 out of 211) and 48 per cent of all sex crime items (233 out of 483). At their least prevalent in 1990, child sex offences accounted for 35 per cent of the total number of cases for that period. This proportion is still substantially higher than the next most heavily reported form of sex crime, rape, which at its *most* prevalent in 1997 accounted for one quarter (23 per cent). The proportion of child sex offence items was considerably higher than the proportion of child sex offence cases in any given time period. In 1985, for example, offences against children accounted for 40 per cent of cases, but 50 per cent of news items. This disparity arises because this form of sexual deviance tended to be reported more heavily than others. Certain cases received coverage across a range of newspapers sustained for a period of several days. Other types of sex crime, depending on the news values they constituted, did occasionally receive high levels of coverage. But it was offences against children that most often attracted widespread and/or sustained attention from the press.

'Institutional abuse' involves the molestation of a victim, normally a child, by an offender in a position of professional authority – for example, a school teacher, a doctor, a priest or a scout leader. This was by some margin the most prevalent form of child sex abuse in the archive, accounting for 14 per cent (29 out of 211 cases) of the total number of sex crimes and more than one third (35 per cent, or 37 out of 93 cases) of child sex-abuse cases. Following the Kincora scandal of 1980 – which involved the systematic abuse of children in a care home in East Belfast (see Chapter 5) – charges of sex crime against care workers and others in positions of authority over children maintained a high prevalence in press discourse. These types of case featured heavily at all stages. In 1995, however, in the wake of the Father Brendan Smyth affair – convicted in 1994 of offences against children in a number of countries spanning three decades (see Chapter 5) – the proportion of these cases increased dramatically, peaking in 1997 when one quarter (24 per cent) of all sex crime coverage described incidences of institutional child sex abuse. Sex crimes involving members of the clergy were so commonplace by 1997 that the connection between priests and sexual abuse no longer needed to be made explicit. One *Belfast Telegraph* (7 January 1997: 6) headline simply read 'PRIEST IN COURT'.

Rape accounted for one fifth of sex crime cases in the archive (21 per cent, or 45 cases out of 211) and a similar proportion of items (20 per cent, or 98 items out of 483). In 1985, 1990 and 1997 this proportion remained remarkably consistent. The only significant fluctuation occurred between 1990 and 1995 when the proportion of rape cases fell from 22 per cent to 13 per cent. This may be attributable to the low overall yield for that year, rather than any shift in the press interest in cases of rape. That the proportion of rape cases closely reflects the proportion of overall rape items indicates that these offences seldom received sustained coverage either in different newspapers or spanning a range of days. In fact, only two rape cases in the entire archive were mentioned in five or more items.

The third most prevalent form of sex crime was sexual assault. These offences accounted for 15 per cent of sex crime cases (31 out of 211), but only 9 per cent of items (45 out of 483). That the proportion of items is actually smaller than the proportion of cases reflects the general tendency for sexual assaults to receive only modest coverage. Indeed, the vast majority of sexual assaults were reported in a single item, with only a few being mentioned in more than one newspaper. Despite its apparent status as less 'newsworthy' than either rape or child sex offences, sexual assault is by some margin the most prevalent type of offence in the official statistics. In 1997/1998, for example, indecent assault on a female (which is comparable to the category sexual assault used here) accounted for almost half of all sexual offences recorded by the RUC (598 out of 1,297, or 46 per cent). Rape, by comparison, accounted for less than one fifth (242 out of 1,297, or 19 per cent). It may be precisely because of this prevalence – and therefore the lack of 'novelty' in news terms – that sexual assaults are reported comparatively less frequently in the press.

Together these three types of offence – child sex offences, rape and sexual assault – accounted for three quarters of the total number of cases (74 per cent) and news items (76 per cent) in the archive. The remaining offence types – sex murder, offences against the mentally impaired, indecency offences, consensual homosexual offences and sexual harassment – accounted for the remaining quarter. The representation of these types of sex crime is discussed in the chapters that follow. The next section considers the different stages at which sex crimes were reported.

The stages of reporting

Each press item was placed into one of six categories covering the initial reporting and investigation of a sex offence; the court case; its resolution; the prison experience; the release of offenders from prison; and 'other' items that referred to sex crime but did not fall into any of the above categories. The methods of recording and classification are explained fully in Appendix II.

The initial offence and investigation

Coverage of the initial offence and the ensuing police investigation accounted for slightly less than one quarter of the archive (109 items or 23 per cent). Offences reported at this stage were frequently violent in nature and almost two thirds of these items (66 out of 109, or 61 per cent) described assaults committed by strangers. The suggestion that the attacker might strike again was a prevalent theme. This general trend is in keeping with the research findings of others. Reiner (2000b: 141), for example, observes in relation to general crime coverage that 'offences reported at the time of their occurrence are disproportionately the serious offences of interpersonal violence'. More specifically with relation to sex crime, the emphasis on stranger assaults has been identified as a prominent feature of press narratives in a range of studies – predominantly, though not exclusively, based on the English national market. Soothill and Walby (1991: 34), for example, find that the 'manifestation of the sex beast in florid form does not happen very often in the media, but the coverage is consistently geared up toward sponsoring the arrival of the sex fiend on the national scene'.

The tendency to focus disproportionately on violent stranger assaults reflects the dominant news values that shape the representation of sex crime. Among these, to recall the comments of the *Belfast Telegraph*'s Ronan Henry, are 'violence', 'the warning factor, you know, the idea that this could happen to anybody' and the sense that sex crimes are being committed 'on your doorstep'. All three elements – 'violence', 'speculation' and 'proximity' – are central to establishing the 'shock factor' and, as I have suggested already, the increasingly competitive environment in which journalists practise their craft has rendered the 'shock factor' more important than ever.

As Chapter 3 illustrated, the notion of 'proximity' is fundamental to the construction of sex crime narratives. The potential to invoke within the reader the desired reaction (generally shock) will be much greater if the unknown assailant is 'on the loose' in the same area as a substantial proportion of the readership. Accordingly, 70 per cent of items (73 out of 104) at the initial offence and investigation stage reported sex crimes committed in Northern Ireland. If the Dublin-based *Irish Times* is omitted from the count, the proportion rises to more than four fifths (69 out of 84 items, or 82 per cent). Stranger assaults invite 'personalisation' through the creation of a pathological criminal identity and 'speculation' about the possibility of further attacks. In late capitalist societies, as several scholars have pointed out, fears about crime and personal safety focus on images of 'outsiders' and 'strangers' (Hale 1996; Bauman 2000; Garland 2000). In this context, the narrative of the predatory sex attacker is especially resonant.

The court proceedings

Court reporting constituted the largest category of sex crime items. The types of offence reported at this stage varied greatly, but one conspicuous feature is the much smaller proportion of reports – one fifth – relating to stranger assaults (40 out of 226 items, or 18 per cent).[5] That is, four fifths of court reports included an explicit statement or clear indication from the nature of the charges (for example, committed over a period of weeks or months) that the victim and offender were known to each other at the time of the alleged offence(s).

Considered together, court reports accounted for almost one half of the archive (226 out of 483 items, or 47 per cent). If broken down into the different stages of the judicial process, most related to the committal or open prosecution (140 items or 29 per cent of the overall coverage). The judge's summing-up and sentencing of offenders accounted for slightly less than one fifth of the archive (18 per cent, or 86 out of 483 items). Many of the court reports were small and straightforward descriptions, perhaps taking up only a few column inches. Some merely stated that a person (or persons) had appeared in court and had been remanded until a later date. But a few – normally contested and/or particularly violent – cases attracted considerable coverage across a range of newspapers spanning several days. These high-profile cases are clearly the exception but, as Soothill and Walby (1991) point out, they are particularly important exceptions.

The general orientation towards court reporting can be understood in both cultural and organisational terms. Organisationally, it is often suggested that the 'tendency to report cases at the stage of the trial derives partly from the economy of concentrating resources at institutional settings like courts, where newsworthy events can be expected to occur regularly' (Reiner, 2000b: 142). However, each of the newspapers in the sample 'takes a service'. What this means is that a substantial amount of their court coverage is provided by freelance journalists (or 'stringers') who cover the courts on a daily basis and then sell on the most newsworthy stories to the various news agencies. High levels of court reporting in the regional press cannot, therefore, be explained by the high concentration of journalists at institutional settings. But organisational constraints may influence the levels of court reporting more indirectly.

The majority of English national broadsheets have dedicated 'home affairs' or 'legal' correspondents who, among other things, report on crime and the general operation of the criminal justice system (Schlesinger *et al* 1991). But even of these comparatively resource-rich titles, few employ full-time designated court correspondents. Indeed, recently Reiner (2000b) has described the virtual disappearance of the specialised court reporter. The regional press in Northern Ireland operate in a smaller market with a smaller staff, smaller editorial budgets and are, comparatively speaking, resource-poor. They do not have the funds to appoint full-time legal affairs correspondents, still less specialised court correspondents. They 'take a service' for court reporting precisely because they lack sufficient resources to do it comprehensively themselves. As *Irish News* Editor, Noel Doran, explained, 'We staff the Crown Court ourselves, whenever possible ... and we are quite unique in that respect. But we can't, and no news organisation can, staff every court across Northern Ireland'.

Resources are tight, and taking a service from freelance reporters – or the Press Association for cases outside Northern Ireland – frees up journalists for other tasks. Editors will, of course, send in-house reporters to cover cases that are deemed sufficiently important or newsworthy to merit individual attention. And less experienced or 'cub reporters' may be assigned to court sessions as part of their training because, as the same editor put it, it is useful for them 'to have experience of covering the courts'. But the advantages of taking a service are manifest. It maximises the number of available staff, ensures that more deadlines are met, helps in the routinisation of news production and opens up a source of regular and reliable court reports that are already journalistically formatted and largely ready to print. Organisationally, then, the high levels of court reporting in the dailies reflect the high availability of court reports. That the Belfast dailies each take a service from the same freelance journalists explains why a number of court reports appearing simultaneously in different newspapers were virtually identical in their wording.

The cultural significance of court reporting is equally important. As well as being organisationally convenient, the emphasis on court proceedings represents an appeal to the authority of the judiciary who are recognised both by journalists and throughout wider society as the guardians of 'law and order' and the administrators of justice. As Ericson *et al* point out (1987: 51; see also Hall *et al* 1978: 66–8): 'News of deviance and control function as a morality play, a conflict between good and evil people and forces. It engages the audience by being entertaining and titillating, but also by reassuring insofar as the evil element is condemned and the conflict resolved by authoritative sources.'

The 'official' denunciation of society's deviants – particularly sex offenders, who generate unparalleled levels of public fear and loathing – is nowhere more dramatically played out than in the courtroom (Garfinkel 1956; Carlen 1976). It is here that the rule of law is brought publicly to bear on those who would contravene the legal order and, in so doing, pose a threat to the wider social and moral constitution of 'respectable' society. Representations of sex crime rarely cover individual cases from beginning to end. But their cumulative content – reproducing 'micro episodes of conflict' (Ericson *et al* 1991: 11) – first illustrates how order is breached and then, through the dramatisation of the investigation, trial, sentencing and judge's admonition, how it is restored. In this sense, there is a certain circularity in press narratives of deviance and control. In the courtroom the normative boundaries of acceptable and legitimate behaviour are re-established and a sense of moral closure is found in the 'reassertion of the values of society and the limits of its tolerance' (Hall *et al* 1978: 66).

This final point is of particular significance in the context of ongoing conflict in Northern Ireland. The representation of court proceedings is one important mechanism for legitimating the powers of the state to enforce the law on behalf of the people. A significant section of the community in Northern Ireland refuses to acknowledge the legitimacy of the state and its official agencies of control. Yet, as noted previously, while the regional press defend conflicting positions on other issues of law and order, and certain papers frequently criticise the state apparatuses of control, the construction of sex crime is based on the assumption of a moral consensus in which party politics has little currency. Even the fiercely contested police service receives a broadly supportive press coverage in its efforts to address the problem of sex crime in Northern Ireland.

The activities of the judiciary are treated somewhat differently. During the trial, there is little room for journalistic interpretation in the construction of courtroom dramas. Due to legal constraints, reporters are essentially bound to convey precisely what happened, precisely how it happened. In this context, the locus of definitional power lies almost exclusively with the judiciary. After the sentence has been passed, however, and the case has finished, the press are freed from *sub judice* restrictions and may pass comment as they see fit. It is at this stage of coverage that newspapers' editorial lines become more apparent.

The prison experience

Reports on offenders in prison accounted for 22 of the 483 news items (5 per cent of the archive). All these items appeared in 1995 and were split between only two cases, each of which received a huge amount of press attention across five of the six newspapers. As Soothill and Walby (1991: 17) note, 'a few particularly notorious sex offenders will be reported in the press after imprisonment. These are the most unusual and sensational cases'. The two cases included in the archive involved the apparent suicide of a convicted serial murderer, and the experiences behind bars of a 'paedophile priest' whose legacy of abuse, once exposed, led to the collapse of the Irish government (Moore 1995; Jenkins 1996). These cases were certainly among the 'most unusual and sensational' in the archive.

Accounting for 20 items across five newspapers over a period spanning three weeks, the 1995 coverage featuring convicted child abuser Father Brendan Smyth related to photographs which had been taken during his incarceration. The fact that prison security had been breached in the first instance was newsworthy in itself. The association with the highly politicised Father Brendan Smyth affair made it even more so (see Chapter 5). The *Sunday World* was the only paper to secure access and print the photographs. Not surprisingly, then, it led on the front page with a full-page colour shot of Smyth. The photograph, which pictured Smyth in prison uniform lifting rubbish, was headlined 'PENANCE FOR A PERVERT', and the story on page two revealed how 'Evil pervert priest Father Brendan Smyth's penance is to pick up other prisoners' excrement' (*Sunday World* 22 January 1995). This newspaper printed seven reports over five pages in one edition alone, and followed this up with a further report in the next edition, all detailing the torment that Smyth was enduring from other inmates (*Sunday World* 22 January 1995, 29 January 1995).

In line with their generally more conservative approach to news production (and in the absence of any visual images), the daily press focused on the breach of prison security which had resulted in the camera being smuggled in, and the photographs to be taken and smuggled out. They also developed the legal angle through reports that interviews with Smyth relating to further allegations had been temporarily suspended until the matter had been investigated. The daily and Sunday press coverage of this were thus enormously different in terms of both content and style of presentation.

The only other prison-related incident to attract press attention was the apparent suicide of alleged Gloucester serial killer Fred West at Winson Green prison in 1995, again reported in five newspapers. This and the associated reports – mainly discussing the implications for the ongoing trial of his wife, Rose, as his accomplice – accounted for 36 items spanning a period of almost two weeks. The association of prison suicide with a convicted serial killer was prime news material. The death of such a publicly reviled figure raised obvious questions of foul play. This notion was played up by the *Irish News*' headline, 'POLICE KEEP OPEN MIND OVER DEATH' and the *News Letter*'s (2 January 1995: 3) quotation from a fellow inmate, 'every thug in the place was dying to get their hands on him'. The dailies also discussed the lapse of prison security that allowed an inmate to hang himself in his cell – thus echoing similar themes to the Father Brendan Smyth case which was being reported simultaneously.

Every newspaper that covered the incident took the opportunity to catalogue the alleged murders and more than two thirds of the items included archive photographs. Many included interviews with neighbours which fluctuated between extremes: 'JOKEY BUILDER WAS SO LIKEABLE, SAY LOCALS' (*Belfast Telegraph* 2 January 1995: 6) and a prisoner's claim that 'he was detested by fellow inmates' appeared side by side in the *Belfast Telegraph* (2 January 1995: 6). The message communicated by the *Belfast Telegraph*'s headline and a resonant, if largely implicit, theme in many of the other articles was that society's deviants are hard to spot – they cannot be picked easily out of a crowd. This view is contradicted fundamentally in other press representations, particular of child sex offenders, and is a source of concern for many practitioners.

The *Sunday World* (8 January 1995: 8) speculated that, though on trial for 12 known murders, West was in fact 'suspected of butchering as many as 60 women and girls'. This point was also made in the *News Letter* (4 January 1995: 2), but in this case it was dismissed by a senior police officer as 'without foundation'. In the *Sunday World*, the claim went unchallenged. In a feature article in the same paper, Roisin Gorman nominated Fred West as her 'prat of 1994'. The story presented a tongue-in-cheek account of his suicide and mocked the legal defence in the trial (*Sunday World* 1 January 1995: 5). Again, then, the differences between the daily and Sunday newspapers in the style and content of representations were significant.

Post-release

All reports relating to the release of sex offenders appeared in 1997. Eight news items (2 per cent of the archive) reporting three different cases appeared in four newspapers. That no press reports of released offenders appeared before 1997 is significant since the Sex Offenders Register for convicted sex offenders was introduced in September of that year. Some of the items in this time period specifically called for a register to be introduced (and in that sense pre-empted the introduction of formal legislation). Others reported that convicted paedophiles had been released from prison and were living 'at large' in Northern Ireland, frequently naming both the individual and the town. These latter cases were generally presented as scoops by the particular newspapers which variously claimed, 'The *Belfast Telegraph* can reveal …' (27 January 1997: 4) and 'You read it here first …' (*Sunday World* 5 January 1997: 14). The naming and shaming of offenders after they have been released from prison is an important and extremely current debate with serious implications for notions of freedom and control, and indeed fundamental human rights within a liberal democracy (Thomas 2000; Wilson and Silverman 2002).

The use of photographs

In three periods (1985 – 19 per cent; 1990 – 16 per cent; and 1997 – 18 per cent) less than one fifth of the items incorporated photographs. In 1995 this proportion increased to more than one third (38 per cent). The extent of this increase can be explained almost entirely by the massive press coverage of two incidents: the apparent prison suicide of convicted serial killer Fred West and the security scandal caused by the release of photographs of convicted paedophile Father Brendan Smyth in prison. Between them, these cases accounted for 38 of the 59 photographs included (64 per cent). Had they not been reported, and not replaced with any other cases, the proportion of articles incorporating photographs in 1995 would have more closely reflected the other periods, remaining at less than one fifth of the total for that year (14 per cent). However, to assume that the void caused by the absence of these cases would not have been filled with others is speculative. There is a natural journalistic tendency to include a visual image whenever possible. Photographs, the *Belfast Telegraph*'s News Editor explained, add to the visual impact of a crime story: 'Part of it is the logistics of journalism. If there are pictures … of the accused, not of the victim obviously … we would be more interested in it for design purposes. That's one criterion, pictures will give more of a show when you are designing a newspaper page.'

For Hall (1973), and others, the use of visual images extends far beyond the aesthetics of page design. In constructing a press report, he suggests, a photograph is selected not only 'in terms of impact, dramatic meaning, unusualness, controversy, the resonance of the signified event', but also in accordance with how the image 'will be treated or "angled" – that is, interpretatively coded' (1973: 232). A visual image can emphasise a point, lend a dramatic or sensational edge to an otherwise 'ordinary' piece of news, add a face to a name or establish the identity of key players in a particular scenario. But more than this, it can transmit a powerful ideological message about a given situation, set of social conditions or series of events. Photographs capture for ever a particular instant in time. They appear to be a record of the 'facts', proof of 'what really happened' and 'how things really are'. But as Hall puts it (1973: 241, emphasis in original): '[T]he choice of *this* moment of an event as against that, of *this* person rather than that, of *this* angle rather than any other, indeed the selection of this photographed incident to represent a whole complex chain of events and meaning, is a highly ideological procedure.' In short, photographs help to transmit the ideological themes woven into the text of press narratives. Reciprocally, the text of those narratives – especially the headline and caption – signifies to the reader what is being denoted in the photograph and how it should be 'read' (Barthes 1977). How a particular photograph will be interpreted, of course, can never be fully determined. Visual images are polysemic (Barthes 1977) – they are open to different interpretations depending on a range of factors. Crucially, though, the interpretation of a photograph (like the interpretation of text) is mediated by the ideological context in which it is situated and by the assumptions brought to it by its readers (Holland 1998).

Specific physical characteristics are frequently associated with popular images of sex offenders. Kitzinger and Skidmore (1995: 9), for example, have demonstrated that people often imagine child molesters to be to be 'dirty' with 'staring eyes … when you see a photo you think, oh, yeah, I can tell'. These popular stereotypes are sometimes drawn directly from the media, with particular images (such as that of Myra Hindley shortly after her arrest in the 1960s) carrying particular cultural resonance (Kitzinger and Skidmore 1995; see also West 1996). Jenkins (1992: 94) identifies precisely these same visual characteristics when he observes that in reporting a case of child sex murder in England, 'Most media accounts used the same photograph [of the offender] whose dishevelled and wild-eyed appearance epitomised popular stereotypes of the sex killer'. It is unlikely that the widespread use of this image was coincidental.

Recalling the work of Hall *et al* (1978), Jenkins (1992: 216) proposes that 'the power and resonance of a story will be augmented by the degree to which it is assimilated to an existing stereotype'. There will be more to say on this contention below. For now, though, the use of photographs, as the above example illustrates, can help with the process of assimilation. As Corner (1998: 243) points out, photographs are signifiers that are intended 'to direct and organise meaning-making, to generate sense and significance and as far as possible to cue feelings too'. In the construction of sex crime narratives the desired feeling is most often that of 'shock'. Photographs will be selected and presented in a

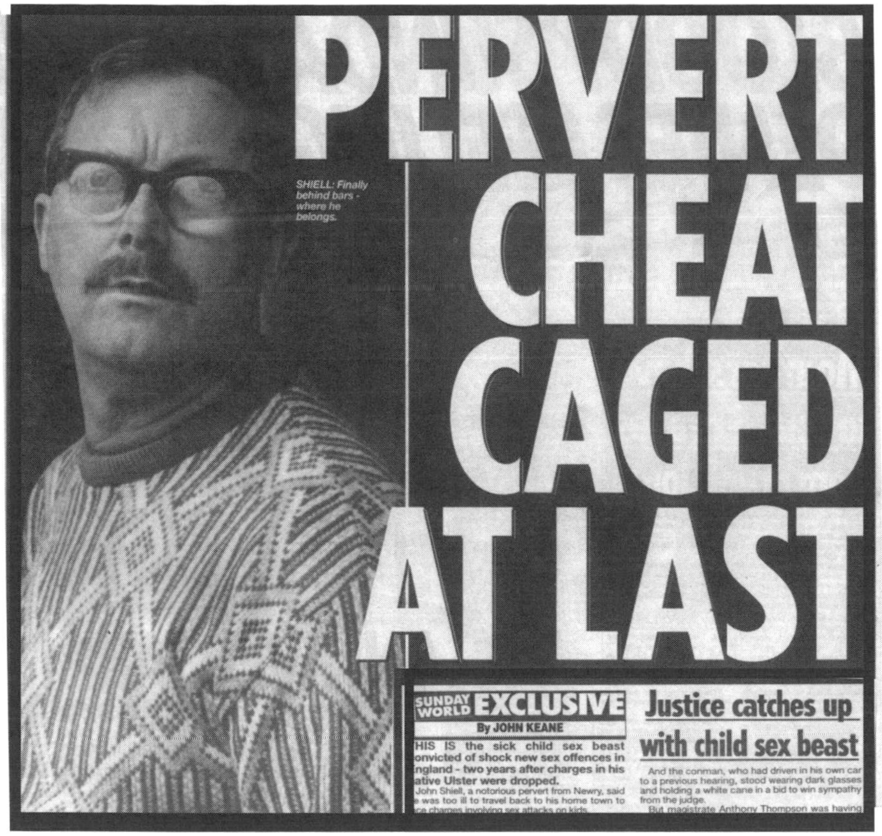

PERVERT CHEAT CAGED AT LAST

SHIELL: Finally behind bars - where he belongs.

SUNDAY WORLD EXCLUSIVE

By JOHN KEANE

HIS IS the sick child sex beast onvicted of shock new sex offences in ngland - two years after charges in his ative Ulster were dropped.

John Shiell, a notorious pervert from Newry, said e was too ill to travel back to his home town to ce charges involving sex attacks on kids.

Justice catches up with child sex beast

And the conman, who had driven in his own car to a previous hearing, stood wearing dark glasses and holding a white cane in a bid to win sympathy from the judge.

But magistrate Anthony Thompson was having

Printed courtesy of the *Sunday World*.

way that maximises the power and resonance of the story, and heightens its capacity to elicit the required response.

Correspondingly, the archive included several photographs picturing individuals who looked 'dishevelled' and 'dirty' and who seemed to have 'wild' and 'staring eyes'.[6] As such, they appeared to match the visual criteria describe above. Even so, it is hard to accept that these images on their own – no matter how stereotypical they seem – would communicate universally the very specific idea of 'sex offender' had they not been framed explicitly within that context. Regardless of how closely photographs may *appear* (especially with the wisdom of hindsight) to reflect popular stereotypes, it is the context within which they are presented that narrows ambiguity and 'makes them mean'. Located beneath headlines like 'PERVERT CHEAT CAGED AT LAST'

(*Sunday World* 26 January 1997: front page), staring eyes and a dishevelled demeanour are naturally associated with stereotypical notions of the sex offender. Indeed, in such an unambiguous and ideologically loaded context these features could scarcely be associated with anything else.

By contrast, other photographs in the archive, the majority in fact, did not reflect popular stereotypes. Most photographs of (alleged) sex offenders appeared not to have been taken in connection with the case, but rather may have been provided by family members or acquired by journalists by some other means. These photographs portrayed individuals with facial features, expressions and physical demeanours that, for all intents and purposes, seemed quite 'normal'. That is not to suggest that their capacity to shock was eliminated. Perhaps even the contrary.

What people *read into* photographs, what they purport to recognise when they say 'oh yeah, I can tell' reflects a widely shared expectation that sex offenders are markedly different from 'normal people' (Kitzinger 1999a). This expectation derives undoubtedly in part from the stereotypical representations of sex offenders in the media. But also, and more subtly, it is reflective of the social and psychological processes through which clear distinctions – including visual distinctions – are established between the 'normal' and the 'deviant', the 'righteous' and the 'wicked', the 'good' and the 'evil'. The perception of sex offenders as strangers – alien, different and unknown – is in many ways easier to sustain (Smart 1989; Kitzinger 1996, 1998). It poses no threat to the close social ties and the high levels of trust and dependency which have traditionally constituted as 'safe' the intimate social networks of family and friends.

How much more discomforting and disconcerting when the face of the sex offender is the picture of *normality*; when it jars sharply with the popular expectation – the smiling face of the school teacher, the compassionate bearing of the priest? In this latter context, it is the divergence of the image from the stereotype that might elicit the desired response – a different kind of shock perhaps, but shock none the less. Rather than reinforcing the popular stereotypes of sex offenders, these photographs actively challenge them, however unintended that may be. These images too were located under headlines and surrounded by text that clearly indicated how they should be interpreted, but here the context within which the images were presented was even more significant. What might on its own appear to be relatively innocuous or 'normal' may take on an entirely different 'meaning' and signify something completely different once located beneath the headline

'FACE OF A PERVERT' (*Sunday Life* 12 January 1997: 4). Here, then, it is the disjunction, the disconnectedness between the stereotype (what is expected) and the image (what is presented) that may produce the intended reaction within the reader.

Despite the fact that the majority of photographs of sex offenders pictured individuals who seemed to be ostensibly 'normal', it is possible that those images that reflected existing stereotypes are more potent and enduring. It may be the case that the comparatively safe and easier to sustain expectation of the sex offender as alien on some level makes news readers less resistant to images of that nature. It may be the case that images of sex offenders as visually normal, as non-identifiable, as potentially anyone, perhaps within the family, are less resonant, if not actively resisted. These propositions are suggestive rather than substantiated and too much should not be made of them here. However, support for this view can be found in Kitzinger and Skidmore's (1995) focus group research on child sex abuse, which suggests that 'images of suspicious strangers' are more potent than images of 'dangerous uncles or threats from within the family home' (Kitzinger 1999a: 9).

The Variable Form and Flavour of Sex Crime Coverage

Distinctions between the content and style of representations of crime (Hall *et al* 1978; Ditton and Duffy 1983; Ericson *et al* 1987, 1989, 1991; Schlesinger and Tumber 1994) and more specifically sex crime (Soothill and Walby 1991; Kitzinger 1996) tend to focus on the differences between broadsheet or 'quality' and tabloid or 'downmarket' outlets. In Northern Ireland, this distinction broadly translates into considering the differences between the daily and the Sunday newspapers, though there are also important organisational differences between daily and weekly titles.

With respect to the daily market, the three Belfast titles – the *Belfast Telegraph*, the *Irish News* and the *News Letter* – comprise the entire regional selection. There is of course some variation in style and content between these newspapers. For one, the *News Letter* is a tabloid in terms of size. Much of its coverage is broadsheet in nature, but its style is slightly more tabloid orientated than that of the *Belfast Telegraph* and the *Irish News*. Broadly speaking, however, these newspapers occupy a mid-market orbit, not necessarily chasing the highbrow status of the *Guardian* or *The Times*, but even less so plumbing the depths explored by much of the UK's 'yellow press'. The Dublin-based broadsheet *The Irish Times* places itself directly alongside the English broadsheets in terms of the 'quality' of journalism it purports to produce. The market orientation of the daily newspapers influences significantly the form and flavour of the news they produce.

By contrast, the two Sunday newspapers, the *Sunday World* and the *Sunday Life*, are tabloid in both form and flavour. This too is significant in terms of influencing the nature of the sex crime narratives they produce. For this reason, it is important to recognise the differences between the style and content of press representations in the daily and the Sunday press.

Sex crime in the daily press

Because of the much higher number of daily press items in the archive, the above overview in many ways constitutes an overview of sex crime coverage in the daily press also. For this reason, comment will only be made on points of particular interest or where there are significant differences between daily press coverage and the overall trends in the archive.

The daily newspapers yielded more than five times as many sex crime items as the Sunday titles (410 versus 73) and escalated from 28 cases and 66 items in 1985 to 81 cases and 167 items in 1997. The majority of coverage in the daily press was case based and reflected the overall archive both in terms of the proportion of items discussing issues of wider concern and the marked decrease in this proportion over time.[7] Child sex offences (69 cases and 179 items), rape (42 cases and 95 items) and sexual assault (28 cases and 42 items) were the three most prevalent forms of sex crime in the daily press, together accounting for four fifths of daily coverage (139 from 174 or 80 per cent of cases, and 335 from 410 or 82 per cent of items). If the offence of sex murder (involving adults) is added, the proportion of cases and items become 83 and 93 per cent respectively. Thus, the vast majority of daily press coverage concerned the most serious examples of sex crime – rapes, assaults, murders and offences against children. Most of these offences were committed in Northern Ireland.

Court reporting made up the majority of daily sex crime coverage (214 from 410 or 52 per cent, compared with 47 per cent in the overall archive). Slightly less than one fifth (18 per cent) of items reported the actual commission of the offence or the police investigation (compared with 23 per cent in the overall archive). So while there was some considerable coverage of the initial commission of sex offences, daily press coverage focused most heavily on the judicial response they elicited. Sex crimes in the daily press often seemed to be reported not because of the nature of the act, but because of the nature of the judicial reaction to it.

Sex crime in the Sunday press

The Sunday newspapers reported a smaller number of sex crime cases and items than the daily press. However, it is the style and content of these representations (as compared with the dailies) rather than the overall quantity that are of interest here. The proportion of items that included some discussion of issues of general concern was higher in the Sunday newspapers than in the dailies. In 1997, for example, one in ten items in the Sunday press included discussion of wider issues of concern compared with only one in 17 items in the dailies. This disparity is significant since, as we will see, a number of practitioners and journalists were vociferous in their complaints about what they saw as a lack of depth and context in Sunday press reporting (see Chapter 6). Like the daily press, however, the proportion of non case based items in the Sundays decreased substantially over time (40 per cent in 1985, to 33 per cent in 1990, to 17 per cent in 1995 to 10 per cent in 1997).

While the dailies concentrated on rape, sexual assault, sex murder and offences against children, the Sunday newspapers focused heavily on consensual homosexual offences and indecency, prostitution and pornography offences. These 'sex crimes' together accounted for 19 of the 45 cases (42 per cent) and 26 of the 73 sex crime items (36 per cent) in the Sundays, but only 8 per cent of cases and 4 per cent of items in the dailies. No cases were reported in both the *Sunday Life* and the *Sunday World*. So while there was a certain degree of overlap between Sunday and daily representations of sex crime, with most types of offence featuring at some time in each newspaper, the focus of press attention shifted dramatically between markets.

Representations of sex crime in the Sunday press were polarised between the most and least serious examples of sexual offending. Stories were geared either to shock, titillate or in some cases – so it seemed, at least – both shock and titillate the reader. The *Sunday World*'s Jim McDowell offered some insight into the general treatment of news material when he explained that 'as a story comes across my desk, as the editor, I will judge whether this is a story to take seriously or whether it is something to literally take the piss out of'. As this appraisal suggests, a large proportion of items in the Sunday press describe events that could be placed at the lighter end of the social, moral or political spectrum. Accordingly, a considerable amount of attention was given to those sex crimes that are generally considered to be relatively minor.

Unlike daily press reporting, Sunday sex crime coverage frequently involved situations in which it was difficult to discern clear victims and perpetrators. For example, consenting adults engaging in homosexual activities in a public toilet (*Sunday Life* 26 January 1997: 13); groups of children breaking into public grounds to drink alcohol and have under-age sex (*Sunday World* 21 January 1990: 12); and prostitutes being commended for bringing money into a seaside town (*Sunday World* 15 January 1995: 12) all formed the basis of sizeable stories. While these offences all crossed the boundary between the legally acceptable zone of personal autonomy and permissible state intervention, the actual harm inflicted was minimal.

It is different when the crime is felt to be particularly heinous, like child sex offences or violent assaults, in which an 'innocent' is violated, victimised or abused against his or her will. In the absence of a lack of consent (the defining characteristic of most sex crime) the conventional image of a 'victim' is essentially erased from the picture. The alleged offenders in these 'trivial' offences tended to be portrayed as 'kinky' rather than 'evil'; they were often treated as objects for ridicule rather than moral denunciation. These cases were reported with tongue placed firmly in cheek. In the absence of an injured party, they could be presented in a frivolous, humorous and, most often, titillating manner with little risk of offending the sensibilities of the assumed audience. Headlines were sensational and often alliterative. Typical examples included, 'BIBLE BELT SEX SHOW SHOCK' (*Sunday World* 6 January 1985: front page), 'TEEN DRINK AND SEX PARTIES SHOCK POSH PARENTS' (*Sunday World* 28 January 1990: 9) or 'KIDS GO FOR DIY SEX ORGIES' (*Sunday World* 21 January 1990: 12). The latter two stories recounted how groups of local teenagers were drinking and having consensual sex, one 'inside the secluded DIY store garden centres', one in parties organised 'in middle class homes'. Any opportunity to offer advice on teenage pregnancy or safe sex was passed over in favour of titillating images of 'naughty youngsters.'

Sunday coverage also focused on the opposite extreme of sexual offending – especially offences perpetrated by sexual predators against children. Representations of the most serious sex crimes were geared to offend fully the sensibilities of the reader and invoke the most visceral 'shock' reaction. Like the reporting of minor offences, the most serious sex crimes were reported below sensational headlines, but the absence of humour was absolute. The theme of 'victim and offender' was drawn out to the full through the construction of narratives that conjured images not only of 'deviance' and 'normality', but of 'good' and 'evil'. As with press representation of all sex crimes, in the Sunday press or otherwise, offenders were presented as outside what is 'normal' in society. But with the most serious offences, particularly when children are involved, offenders were presented as 'beyond the bounds of existing criminality' (Websdale 1999: 101) – outside even what is 'normal' in crime (Hall *et al* 1978: 31).

The headline 'IRA BANISHED SEX WEIRDO TO SOUTH' illustrates this point (*Sunday World* 26 January 1997: 11). The underlying text catalogued the convicted offender's crimes and conveyed how 'Following the latest alleged sexual assault ... masked gunmen called at [named person's] home ... and told the five feet nothing pervert to get out or be shot'. The fact that the crimes were so abhorrent as to elicit a violent response from another group whose members, at least in the eyes of the law, are themselves 'criminals' emphasised the extreme deviance of the perpetrator. The text of these reports typically called for the harshest measure of the law to be applied, often claiming that the newspaper was instrumental in exposing the 'sex pervert' or 'sex beast'. And readers were congratulated for helping to expose those people whose crimes are seen to represent fundamental ruptures in the social order.

In one edition of the *Sunday World* (5 January 1997), under the general headline 'YOU READ IT HERE FIRST', the newspaper reviewed its achievements 'with the help of the readership' over the previous year: 'Angry parents forced a perverted granddad to give himself up to police'; 'Catholic Sexton [named person] sex pervert exposed by the *Sunday World* was finally exposed in the courts'; 'Paedophile ... was found to be living in a housing estate ... we exposed the sick pervert for what he is'; and, presumably because once was not enough, 'Drug dealers and sex perverts exposed throughout the year – were exposed again'. Through this style of representation, news readers are given a sense of ownership over the criminal justice process. They are empowered actively to participate in the control and punishment of society's deviants.

Related to this, while the majority of sex crime coverage in the dailies was made up of court reporting (53 per cent), courtroom dramas in the Sunday titles appeared significantly less often. Only one sixth (12 out of 73, or 16 per cent) of items in the Sunday newspapers referred to the trial and/or sentencing of sex offenders. The largest single proportion of reports in the Sunday papers (36 per cent) dealt with coverage of the actual event, describing or discussing the offence itself rather than the judicial response to it (compared with 18 per cent in the dailies). The reason for this focus is most probably straightforward business pragmatism. Most of the courtroom action in any given week will have been reported already in the daily press by the time the Sunday papers are being printed. There is little to be gained from essentially reprinting the news unless the 'news' in question is of particular import or interest. And because they are published weekly, Sunday newspapers do not have the same opportunities as the dailies to build a continuing courtroom drama over consecutive days. But there is another (almost certainly unintended but none the less significant) consequence of focusing on events rather than the judicial response to them. The lack of court reporting in the Sunday press provides clear opportunities to frame sex crimes in a particular way.

By focusing on the event rather than the official reaction to it, the Sunday press isolate the crime before it is 'officially' categorised, symbolised and contextualised by the judicial process. In so doing they effectively shift the locus of power in defining the social significance of sex crimes from the judiciary to the press. I am not suggesting that there is any deliberate strategy to avoid court reportage, over and above the requirement not to reproduce old news. But the benefits, however unintended, in terms of contextualising and socially defining sex crime cases are clear. News consumers reading about sex crimes are invited to make their own moral evaluations, but the nature and thrust of these moral evaluations will be influenced by the sources from which the information comes. The omission of the courts from sex crime coverage in the Sunday papers bypasses the principal source from which the social significance of offences is customarily derived. Journalists are freer to proffer their own, or rather their paper's view of the social significance of, and appropriate responses to, sex crimes in accordance with the various agendas to which that paper subscribes. This resultant polemic is almost invariably more punitive than contemporary criminal justice policy.

In five of the ten cases in which the sentencing of convicted offenders was reported it was argued that the punishment had been too lenient or implied that the survivor had been somehow let down by the criminal justice process. The stories headlined 'HORRIFIED BY SENTENCE' (*Sunday Life* 19 January 1997: 2) and 'PERVERT CHEAT CAGED AT LAST' (*Sunday World* 26 January 1997: front page) are two such examples. Both advocated longer jail terms and questioned the current criminal justice response to sex offenders in Northern Ireland. Calls for harsher sentences for convicted sex offenders were not unique to the Sunday press. Daily newspapers sometimes incorporated similar comment when reporting sentences that were perceived as particularly lenient. But the sensational and evocative manner that characterised the Sunday newspapers' articulation of these arguments was largely absent from daily coverage. It was this difference in journalistic style that set newspapers from the two markets apart.

Conclusions

The amount of press attention directed at sex crime escalated substantially between 1985 and 1997. Consistently throughout that period, the abuse of children and young persons was the most frequently reported type of offence. In addition to the increase in the quantity of sex crime reporting in the press, there have been important qualitative changes to the nature of press representations. Some of these are clear and straightforward. Others are subtler and more implicit.

The discussion of wider issues of concern – causes, risks, prevention, the availability of resources for survivors of sex crime, legal issues and debates – has declined considerably. Coverage of wider debates has been replaced by an increasingly narrow focus on the reporting of specific cases of sex crime. What this means is that press representations are becoming ever more impoverished in terms of their informative content. The increasing focus on dramatic event-based reporting in many ways diminishes the usefulness of the news being produced. What is left behind is a news product which aims primarily to shock and frequently, it seems, to entertain, rather than provide useful information and inform open public and political debate.

On the issue of stereotypes, there are a number of ways in which the myth of stranger-danger is reinforced in press discourse. Reports covering the initial offence and investigation of sex crimes most often relate to assaults apparently committed by strangers – though it should also be noted that court reports most often do not. More subtly, though, on the few cases in which advice on prevention and personal safety is included, it almost invariably relates to cases of stranger assault, thus implicitly promoting the stereotype of the 'sex fiend' who may strike again at any time.

There are substantial differences between the construction of sex crime in the daily and Sunday (broadsheet and tabloid) press. The dailies (broadsheets) tend to focus on the more serious examples of sexual offending. The Sundays (tabloids), by contrast, divide their coverage between the most and least heinous examples of sex crime, the latter of which are presented in a frivolous and frequently titillating manner, while the former are geared to maximise the 'shock impact' of the story. Again, then, the primary aim in a significant majority of press representations is to invoke some kind of shock reaction, an aim which would appear to take precedence over the desire to inform in any constructive manner. The next chapter establishes why press attention to sex crime increased so dramatically throughout the 1980s and 1990s.

Notes

1 In 1985, for example, the tribunal established to investigate the systematic abuse of children in public care at the Kincora boys' home (discussed in Chapter 5) accounted for 16 of the 71 (23 per cent) news items that month. In 1995, two cases featured heavily. The ongoing investigation into fresh charges of child sex abuse against the already imprisoned 'paedophile priest' (Moore 1995; Jenkins 1996), Father Brendan Smyth, was reported in 20 items appearing in five newspapers on eight different days, spanning a total of three weeks (see Chapter 5). In addition to this heavily reported scandal, the apparent prison suicide of convicted Gloucester serial killer Fred West, and the ongoing case against his wife regarding her involvement in the Cromwell Road murders, featured in 36 items, printed over a period spanning almost two weeks. Together these cases accounted for more than one third (54 of the 156 news items, or 35 per cent) of the sex crime articles for that period. In 1997, there was no individual case which received comparably high levels of press coverage, but there was a high number of separate incidents involving 'institutional abuse'; that is, the sexual abuse, normally of a child, under the professional care or guidance of the abuser. The year 1990, then, was the only time period that did not record a proliferation of separate incidents of institutional abuse, or a single case that received sustained media attention. This might partly explain the comparatively small amount of press attention to sex crime throughout that period.

2 The number of offences recorded and cleared by the RUC within each sample month are January 1985 – 47 offences recorded, 28 cleared; January 1990 – 99 recorded, 58 cleared; January 1997 – 154 recorded, 105 cleared; January 1997 – 201 recorded, 104 cleared (data provided by RUC Central Statistics Unit).

3 The *Sunday Life* was not launched until 1989 by the Thomson Group, then owner of Belfast Telegraph Newspapers (see Bromley 1997). Even if the *Sunday World*'s coverage for 1985 is excluded, the overall yield is still considerably larger than the *Sunday Life*'s (30 cases and 48 items).

4 See also Appendix I.

5 When ascertaining the proportion of court reporting accounted for by stranger assaults, the issue arises as to what constitutes a 'stranger'. Although no pre-existing relationship may be stated explicitly in a press report, if 'consent' is cited as the key issue (which it frequently is) the victim and offender must have been known to each other, if only in the most casual sense. If a woman is walked home and then assaulted by someone she has

met in a bar that night, for example, there is some sort of pre-existing relationship, but they may reasonably still be thought of as relative strangers. In the context of this analysis, stranger assaults are taken to be those cases in which the victims were – or so it seemed from the report – sexually assaulted by individuals with whom they had no apparent previous relationship or contact.

6 It is not inconceivable that the wild-eyed appearance displayed in at least some of these photographs may be an expression of surprise at the sudden appearance of a lurking photographer.

7 One in ten items overall, decreasing from 14 per cent of items in 1985 (versus 15 per cent in the overall archive) to 6 per cent in 1997 (compared with 7 per cent in the overall archive).

Chapter 5

Commercialism, conflict and culture

Introduction

In the last chapter I mapped the changing contours of press representations of sex crime between 1985 and 1997, related the increase in press attention to the changing official picture, explored the range, context, composition and focus of coverage and noted some of the major shifts which took place during that period. The aim of this chapter is explanation; that is, I want to try to shed some light on why press attention to sex crime in Northern Ireland increased so dramatically throughout the 1980s and 1990s. Five key influences form the basis of discussion. These are, first, changes in the nature and structure of the information marketplace; second, the impact on social awareness of certain high-profile cases; third, changes in the political situation in Northern Ireland; fourth, the activities of various groups, institutions, organisations and movements, both as news sources and in the wider public sphere; and, fifth, broader changes in the cultural sensibilities of news producers and consumers. Considered together, these influences constitute an environment in which the problem of sex crime has found an increasingly expansive space to resonate.

Commercial Exigencies and Industry Growth

'The journalism industry, taken as a whole, is a dynamic, growing sector of the economy in Britain, and in every other advanced capitalist society' (McNair 1999: 19). There are considerable pressures on news agencies to generate additional revenue through advertising in order to remain competitive in an ever-expanding and increasingly aggressive market (see also Barwise and Gordon 1998; Sparks 2000). The need to stimulate profits by attracting advertisers has forced an increase in newspaper size in order to accommodate this additional material (Curran 1986). Furthermore, in order to stay ahead of the competition, or at least on level par, newspapers have been forced to include more content in the form of additional news stories, longer feature articles and bigger and brighter photographs, precipitating still further physical growth. In the case of the English press market, for example, many have responded by including supplements and pull out sections; by 1992 *The Sunday Times* comprised ten sections. The titles considered in this study have not responded to quite the same extent, but their growth has been substantial none the less.

Assessed here in terms of increases in pagination per newspaper between 1985 and 1997, the physical growth of the sample titles was fairly uniform. On average, each increased in size by a little more than 50 per cent.[1] To take just two examples, the *Belfast Telegraph* averaged 22 pages per edition in 1985, but by 1997 its average pagination had increased to 36 pages. And the *Irish News*, which averaged 13 pages per edition in 1985, had grown to 22 pages by 1997. It might be suggested, then, that the increase in sex crime coverage is merely a function of the overall expansion in newspaper size; that all aspects of news coverage, not just crime or, more specifically, sex crime, received a greater amount of space as a result.

It is not possible here to determine the extent to which sex crime coverage increased relative to the coverage of other issues. However, while the physical growth of the sample newspapers may be a contributory factor it cannot account for the dramatic and disproportionate increase in newsprint media discourse about sex crime. Had press attention risen as a function of increasing newspaper sizes, then in 1997 a body of coverage around one-and-a-half times the size of that in 1985 would be expected, even if we overlook the fact that advertising and promotions accounted for much of this growth. The actual amount of sex crime coverage in 1997 far exceeds this approximation, representing an increase that is more than three times that which appeared in 1985. The bulk of explanation for this increase, therefore, lies elsewhere.

The Tabloidisation of the Press

Notwithstanding any influence that newspapers' physical growth may have had, the level of increase in sex crime coverage – by far exceeding the increase in recorded offences – indicates that the issue is considered more important, at least in news terms, than it was two decades ago. There is no question, however, that the increased reporting of sex crime correlates exclusively with a concerted effort by news agencies to promote social awareness about the issue. Sex and crime are routinely manipulated for commercial gain. McNair writes of British tabloid journalism in response to increasing competition: 'in the 1970s and 1980s the form broke qualitatively new ground, sinking to new depths of prurience and sensationalism' (1999: 168). He goes on to locate this growth in 'yellow journalism' within a commercial context: 'From the outset, sex was chosen as the terrain on which the circulation war would be fought' (1999: 168).

For centuries the boundaries between the 'criminal' and the 'kinky' have been blurred in press discourse (Frayling 1986; Caputi 1987; Walkowitz 1992). Soothill and Walby (1991: 22) observe that throughout the 1970s, when sex crimes began to feature regularly as headline news, 'many newspapers were increasingly using the soft pornography of rape, and reports of other sex crimes, as a mechanism to sell newspapers'. And in the 1980s and 1990s, sex crime narratives have been consistently characterised by high levels of sales-orientated sensationalism, and not just in the tabloid press (see, *inter alia*, Nelson 1987; Schlesinger and Tumber 1994; Kitzinger and Skidmore 1995; Lees 1995; Grover and Soothill 1995; Goddard 1996). It is important, therefore, to juxtapose the press's role as principled, educative institutions concerned with advancing social awareness against their role as profit-led organisations in the business of 'selling news' (Brownstein 1991).

A significant consequence of increasing competition in the press market has been the conflation of information and entertainment into a cultural form some call 'infotainment' (Franklin 1997). In effect, news journalism – which for many is supposed to disseminate objective information about important issues to a mass audience and provide a forum for rational-critical debate – is increasingly becoming part of the entertainment industry. The result has been the tabloidisation of large sections of the news media. In such a market, many have observed that the struggle for commercial success has led to a 'dumbing down' of journalism to the level of the lowest common denominator (Bourdieu 1998; Bromley 1998). McNair (1999: 44–5) describes the argument as follows: 'News becomes less concerned with the weighty matters of party politics, economic policy and foreign affairs, and more with frivolous topics of presidential affairs (sexual rather than political), celebrity lifestyle and other staples of the tabloid agenda.' From this perspective, 'quality' media – print, broadcast and radio – have been forced to go 'downmarket' in an effort to win market popularity. With respect to public affairs coverage, most commentators acknowledge a growing polarisation between popular and quality outlets, with the former including more and more entertainment and the in-depth reporting of public affairs rapidly becoming the exclusive preserve of the latter. Overall, however, even the broadsheets have succumbed to market pressures. As Bromley (1998: 35) notes, 'the confusion between "broadsheet subjects and tabloid subjects" has led to fears that broadsheet journalism and tabloid journalism will become indistinguishable'. Jim McDowell, Editor for the *Sunday World*, was convinced that tabloid and broadsheet journalism is converging. He said of the differences between the quality and popular press in the current market, 'There's none. All papers now, whether it is the *Financial Times*, the *Times*, the *Guardian*, the *Daily Telegraph* to a certain extent, they are all "broadloids"' (see also Peak and Fisher 1996).

Some have queried if the trend towards infotainment is necessarily a bad thing, as so many commentators suggest. For McNair (1998: 121), the critique of current mass media trends could be interpreted as 'intellectual elitism which ignores the realities of the contemporary mass media audience'. And in a later polemic he questions the very definition of 'quality' journalism, asking precisely what is it, and who decides (1999: 47): 'From this point of view, the separation of reality into weighty or trivial, serious or flippant, is largely arbitrary; an elite-intellectual response to the democratic advances of the twentieth century, which have threatened that elite's monopoly on defining what counts as "good taste"'. It may be the case, then, that the widespread tabloidisation of the press has had some positive effects. But the increased manipulation of sex crime and the blurring of social reality for commercial gain is not one of them.

All the major English broadsheet and tabloid newspapers are widely available in Northern Ireland. The daily and weekly titles sampled in this study must therefore compete not only with each other, but also with those national titles based overseas. Commenting on the Northern Ireland market, Rosie Uffindel, Social Affairs Correspondent for the *Irish News*, said, 'I think that it is the most competitive newspaper market in the UK'. The *Sunday World*'s Editor accorded: 'It is, yeah. On a daily basis we have got something like 14 titles coming in, and on a Sunday basis we have got 17 titles.' This being so, the press in Northern Ireland are subject to the same commercial pressures to produce 'infotainment' and 'dumb down' in order to stay competitive and win market popularity. Soothill and Walby (1991) and others have pointed out that sex crime coverage can be an effective mechanism for selling copy. Given the highly competitive nature of the market in Northern Ireland, the newspapers considered here would be no more immune to the temptation to manipulate the phenomenon for its marketability than are news agencies elsewhere.

The commercial potency of sex crime

It is no great revelation to suggest that certain 'types' of sex crime sell newspapers: 'Anything involving sex is immensely newsworthy, as is crime, and the combination of the two in a particular event is doubly newsworthy' (McNair 1998: 78). Precisely which types are 'best for business' and why, and the extent to which different outlets might capitalise on their selection and presentation, are discussed below. For present purposes, though, Chris Thornton, Security Correspondent for the *Belfast Telegraph,* supported this general finding and ventured an explanation:

> My general feeling is that newspapers would be more attracted to sex crime stories than to ordinary crime stories. I think that that has a bit to do with the tabloidisation of the press in general which has probably gone on over the last thirty years, I don't know for sure because I wasn't around to see it all happen. A lot of that, I'm sure, is down to the sexual nature of the crime, the fact that sex of some sort is involved.

The *News Letter*'s Editor, Geoff Martin, confirmed that certain newspapers are prone to manipulating the sex crime issue. He went on to stress (and in so doing conjured the liberal pluralist reading of news production) that the level of manipulation is to a significant extent determined by what the target audience is assumed to want: 'I think there are newspapers that have identified that there is a large percentage of the public that buy newspapers for frivolity and titillation and people who clearly market their newspapers towards that readership. So yes, it does sell in certain areas to certain people.' The thrust of these comments is directed in no uncertain terms at newspapers other than the *News Letter*. Stephen Dempster is a *News Letter* news editor. His account of the commercial potency of sex crimes both in other newspapers and within his own was more candid:

> Without a doubt sex crime sells newspapers. I mean, you only have to look at the *Sunday World*s and the *Sunday Life*s of this [world] ... and even our own newspaper. I mean, the *News Letter* is

> a politics-based paper, mainly for Unionism, and the amount of front pages we have on politics is, you know, around two thirds. But even then, over the last six months, I as a news editor certainly would have dealt, you know, with a dozen stories of that sex crime nature ... Don't get me wrong, but if a sex crime story lands on your desk and a political story lands on your desk, unless the political story is that David Trimble's [leader of the Ulster Unionist Party and First Minister of the Northern Ireland Assembly] been molesting somebody in the toilet, or unless its 'Peace Tomorrow', the sex crime story sells, and that's the truth of the matter.

It is clear, that journalists consider sex crimes to be highly newsworthy and extremely potent commercially. This is one key factor in understanding their prevalence in the press. But, as I have already suggested, that is no great revelation. The aim here is to explain the *increase* in the prevalence of sex crime *over time* – to establish if its commercial potency has changed and if the growth in sex crime coverage throughout the 1980s and 1990s can be understood, at least partly, on that basis. Gavin Mairs, of the *Belfast Telegraph*, was convinced that the market considerations are central to understanding the escalation in press attention to sex crime in recent decades. Echoing the above references to the tabloidisation of the media, for him press attention has increased to such an extent, 'Quite simply because the newspaper industry as a whole is fighting a battle to keep its readership'. He went on to suggest why:

> A number of reasons ... change of lifestyle, people have more leisure time, there's more media, satellite, digital, computers ... the whole newspaper industry is gradually contracting slowly. Now basically newspaper editors have to a) try and stop this and b) fight for a bigger share of a smaller market, which leads to 'dumbing down'. A hundred years ago you didn't have television, you didn't have radio ... you had your paper ... everybody bought the paper to find out what was going on. As the proliferation of media occurs, different media outlets ... are all eating into [the market] ... A newspaper market has to fight to get its attention, and one of the best ways to do that is selling sex.

'Sex' and 'sex crime' are, of course, not the same thing, and it is crucial to bear that distinction in mind. But the representation of sex crimes in a highly sexualised manner has been demonstrated repeatedly across mass media markets (Goddard 1996; Naylor 2001) and in Northern

Ireland, as elsewhere, journalists are of the view that sex crimes sell. More than that, however, it would seem that with the ongoing tabloidisation of the news media in an increasingly competitive market, the commercial potency of sex crime has actually increased.

Locating the construction of sex crime narratives within the context of a changing information marketplace helps to make sense of the disproportionate increase in their prevalence, but two important distinctions need to be reiterated here.

First, while it is important to counterbalance the press's role as key providers of public information with their role as profit-led businesses subject to the commercial exigencies of extreme competition, it is equally important not to tar all news agencies with the same lascivious 'yellow press' brush. The fact that more sex crime cases are being reported in the press does not necessarily mean that they are (all) being reported in a salacious or sensational manner. Earlier chapters demonstrated that the news product comes in a range of forms and flavours, can be shaped in a variety of moulds, and caters to an array of different tastes. And Chapter 4 illustrated, more specifically, the differences in the styles of sex crime coverage between the daily and Sunday press. It is important, therefore, not to lose sight of the colourful variation in reporting styles that make up the full spectrum of newsprint media discourse(s) today.

Secondly, as noted in Chapter 3, the term 'sex crime' describes an enormous variety of behaviours (West 2000b). When constructed as press narratives, different forms of sexual offending inevitably evoke different reactions. Some read as more violent, heart-rending, moving, titillating, shocking and, in some examples of Sunday press coverage, apparently amusing than others. The importance of both these qualifiers – and the kind of reductionist argument that would inevitably result from their oversight – becomes clearer when we consider journalists' and practitioners' views about the representation and manipulation of different types of sex crime in the press.

Qualifying the commercial potency of sex crime

The question is not whether the press manipulate sex crime in order to sell copy; they clearly do. The question is to what extent does this happen? What particular forms of sex crime are manipulated the most? And what are the techniques of representation employed? Dominica McGowan, Director of the Nexus Institute, gave her impression of the extent to which sex crimes can be used to stimulate sales. In so doing she echoed the distinction made above, stressing the importance of differentiating between particular types of offence and the corresponding manner in which they are portrayed in the print media:

> Yes, I do [think that sex sells,] but let me qualify what I am saying here; I don't think that child abuse or rape are sex, but I think it can be presented sexually. And if it is skewed in that way, I think that it will absolutely sell papers, of course it will, and I think that that is why people do it ... But ... I don't know that child sex abuse is sold as 'sexy', sold 'sexually'. It's not sold in the way that adult rape is sold.

Soothill and Walby (1991: 35) suggest that 'The construction of the sex fiend helps to sell newspapers, for the sex beast does attract a certain sort of interest'. The nature and extent of this interest will vary from reader to reader and, no doubt for some, will involve titillation, moral outrage, shock, fascination or a combination of all these factors and others. Assessing empirically the precise appeal of adult rape and sexual assault cases is not straightforward, and speculation about the inner workings of news readers' psyches is best avoided in the absence of any substantive evidence here. But whatever the reasons for public interest in adult sex crimes, there is little doubt, as both practitioners and journalists agreed, that offences involving adults and those involving children are reported and received differently.

Irish News Editor Noel Doran acknowledged that 'There would have to be, to a certain extent, a salacious interest in rape cases. That's inevitable'. And salacious interest is hardly likely to be damaging to sales. But he went on to add an important caveat, stressing that 'it would be wrong for us not to report those cases simply because we thought there was some element of titillation in them, because they are important cases and they have to be reported'. Paul Connelly, News Editor for the *Belfast Telegraph*, made a similar point with respect to child sex abuse cases: 'I don't think that just because this is an uncomfortable aspect of society ... that we should ignore it.' When asked about the 'saleability' of sexual offences against children, he was adamant: 'I would argue that child sex abuse does not sell papers ... I would challenge any notion that child sex cases sell newspapers. A couple of the sensational ones like Brendan Smyth [see below], but outside that ... very few papers would splash with a [child] sex case.' Chris Thornton, from the same newspaper, suggested, 'editors know that on the whole people find these crimes very distasteful ... it's not the sort of thing you generally like to read about over breakfast'. These statements suggest that the problem of child sex abuse is repellent to news readers, that there is something about it which makes them feel uneasy, awkward or uncomfortable. And evidence presented throughout this book suggests that this is indeed the case (see also Kitzinger and Skidmore 1995; Kitzinger 1999b). But the fact that an issue is emotionally and intellectually 'difficult' or 'challenging', the fact that it is uncomfortable, disquieting or even upsetting does not necessarily make its representation bad for sales. Indeed, *Sunday World* Editor Jim McDowell's interpretation of the saleability of sex crimes against children was quite different. He insisted that 'child sex abuse is a marketable product', and explained why:

> Everybody who has a child, every parent's worst nightmare is that their child will be abused ... murdered number one, but abused number two. And for that reason it has got an almost fatal fascination for people out there, for anybody who ... [thinks] 'See if that bastard did that to my child, I'd kill him myself, I'd kill him with my own hands'. That's where particularly tabloid papers sell, it's an emotive thing.

In this view, it is the capacity to 'shock', the intense emotional content, the highly resonant concern that one's own children may fall victim to such an atrocity, that makes these cases so eminently reportable. Sales performance is related to reporting issues that people either want to know more about or feel they should know more about – issues that people are interested in, for whatever reason. If there were no public interest in the issue of child sex abuse, if people did not *want* to read the reports, they would not be reported so relentlessly in the press. As the co-ordinator of the RUC Child Abuse and Rape Enquiry (CARE) unit pointed out, 'they wouldn't print these stories if they didn't sell papers'. And *Sunday Life* Editor Martin Lindsay, explained, 'I don't think they like them, but I think they read them'. Thus, the proposition that there is no link between the reporting of child sex abuse cases and newspaper sales seems disingenuous. *Irish News* reporter Rosie Uffindel's explanation of the increase in press attention to sex crime further develops this point:

> I think that the press are responding to people's concerns. Generally there is a greater awareness ... there was a really common or garden piece I had to do about traffic problems with kids getting to school and all these parents were driving their kids to school – why? because they didn't trust them out to walk to school by themselves or to go by bus and so on. They wanted to know that they could get from 'A' to 'B' safely. And the general

> public perception out there is that child abuse is a big problem and it could happen to my child, therefore I want to see that the newspapers are doing their jobs and reporting the cases and I think that newspapers are responding to that. They know that people are interested, they know that it's a story.

I am not suggesting that most news readers are titillated by stories of child sex abuse – though some clearly are. Nor am I proposing that most journalists report child sex-abuse cases with titillation in mind – though some clearly do. But for as long as an issue conjures the requisite news values ('dramatisation', 'proximity', 'personalisation', 'immediacy', 'novelty' and so on), it will be newsworthy and, as such, marketable as a news product. Furthermore, it will be more likely to feature in newsprint media discourse than other issues which do not satisfy, or which satisfy to a lesser extent, those same criteria of newsworthiness. Sex crime cases – including (perhaps even especially) those involving children – however distasteful they may be to the majority of readers, are extremely newsworthy and, on that basis, they are highly marketable. The reluctance of some journalists to acknowledge this is perhaps a reflection of the prevailing taboos around child sex abuse – a fear that any admission that such cases are marketable amounts to a confession that they are in some sense arousing; it does not. Further evidence that the reporting of child sex abuse is influenced by sales concerns derives from considering a phenomenon called 'child abuse fatigue'.

Child abuse fatigue

Media attention to the issue of child sex abuse has been such that examinations of press coverage elsewhere have evidenced a phenomenon generically referred as 'social problem fatigue' (Finkelhor 1994), but in the present context more specifically known as 'child abuse fatigue' (Goddard 1996). The term refers to a level of journalistic 'overkill' on child sex abuse stories, to the point where editors and reporters become frustrated with continually producing reports on the same phenomenon, and concerned that readers will grow weary of reading them. One journalist interviewed by Skidmore (1995: 94) explained that, as a result, he or she was 'always trying to think of how I can still report on something that is incredibly important without it being "boring" '. The suggestion is that issues can be reported so much that audiences becomes saturated and, for a range of possible reasons, do not want to or cannot digest any more.

Yet this finding is far from universal. Research in other social orders has questioned how widespread the existence of child abuse fatigue is (see, for example, Goddard 1996). There is no evidence in the present study of a decrease in press attention to child sex abuse between 1985 and 1997. Quite the contrary. Despite the constant pressure to find the most extraordinary examples of social phenomena in order to shock news readers, child sex cases remained by far the most prevalent form of abuse in the archive. In fact, more than half the sex crimes that featured on the front pages (15 out of 29, or 51 per cent) involved offences against children. The greatest concentration came in 1997, when all but one of the front-page sex crime narratives reported child sex abuse (the other featuring rape). If anything, this suggests the increasing newsworthiness of the phenomenon. So if notions of 'child abuse fatigue' did reverberate through the corridors of Northern Irish news agencies before 1997, they had not reached the levels evidenced in some other studies.

The commercial elements of sex crime reporting are clearly important. They cannot, however, carry the full burden of explanation, for to reduce press discourse purely to economic concerns is to understate the complexity of the role it plays in public life. As Thompson (2000: 241) points out, the idea that the media are 'relinquishing their autonomy as a cultural institution and orientating themselves increasingly towards the maximisation of sales in a highly competitive field' may be part of the picture, 'but it is not everything'. Journalists interviewed in this study were clear about – even proud of – their perceived roles as purveyors of public knowledge and facilitators of open public debate (even though there are considerable constraints on their capacity to perform these functions). The increase in press attention to sex crime must also be understood in the wider context of shifts in the social, cultural and political sensibilities both of those who produce the news and those who consume it. It is these wider shifts that are discussed next.

Social Awareness

Journalists rarely discussed the commercial potency of sex crime unless asked specifically to do so. Given the sensitive nature of the subject and the reluctance of some to admit that certain types of offence might be good for sales, this is not entirely surprising. But on other issues – at least of equal importance – that may have contributed to the increase in press attention to sex crime, journalists were more forthcoming. Most prevalent among these was the issue of increasing social awareness. Many journalists suggested that for a long time there existed a widespread reluctance to accept that sex crime, and child sex abuse in particular, was a serious problem in Northern Ireland. *Irish News* Editor, Noel Doran, put it well when he offered his explanation for their increased prevalence in media discourse:

> There is probably more awareness. I would guess that a lot of that would involve offences against young people and children which were always there, but which were to a certain extent under-reported. People would say, 'That's too … I can't even think about that'. They were too offensive, too difficult to come to terms with. Maybe a feeling that this was almost taboo. It was happening, but these cases are so extreme that it must be very, very rare, when in fact it became clear that they weren't rare at all, they were in fact very common.

Undoubtedly, there is a link between the intellectual and emotional 'difficulty' in thinking about child sex abuse and the sustained reluctance to accept that it is a real and widespread problem. And this, in turn, has continued to militate against open public debate on the issue. It will be important to say more on the implications of this sense of unease at a later stage. More relevant to the immediate discussion, though, Paul Connelly, News Editor for the *Belfast Telegraph*, highlighted the change in public and media perceptions in Northern Ireland:

> In Northern Ireland, in the seventies and possibly the sixties, there was probably a view that sex crimes didn't really happen here. And we now know the uncomfortable truth, in fact, that we are slightly more prone to it, possibly because we have tied up communities and larger family structures. I'm not quite sure what the sociological reasons would be, but I think that this sort of smug feeling that there are places like London where all these rapes and cases happen and that there are none here. I think that that realisation has now been made. And I think that the media has a role in admitting that.

It is certainly plausible that the tight-knit family structures which are characteristic of Northern Ireland (McLaughlin 1993; McShane and Pinkerton 1996) made the open discussions around child sex abuse even more taboo in that social order than in others. Developing this position, the *Belfast Telegraph*'s Chris Thornton suggested that when the problem was finally established on the social and political agenda (in Northern Ireland in the 1980s), the consequences for both media discourse and the sensibilities of the wider news reading publics were profound:

> The increase, I would say, is down to the idea that this sort of thing has been brushed under the carpet for such a long time. There has probably been a feeling that there has been an injustice to the victims in the sense that what has happened to them hasn't been recognised widely enough. I think there is a social conscience thing.

Journalists, thus, were overwhelmingly of the view that social awareness about sex crime – and in particular about the problem of child sex abuse – has grown substantially in recent decades and that this is a major factor in explaining its increasing prevalence in press discourse. But what was the catalyst that precipitated this growing awareness? What were the key events that forced the problem of (child) sex offences on to the social and political agenda? On this issue, both journalists and practitioners were in agreement. Two cases dominated their accounts – the Kincora scandal and the Father Brendan Smyth affair.

The Kincora scandal

The Kincora scandal was originally exposed in 1980. It brought to light for the first time the problem of institutional child sex abuse in Northern Ireland. The case involved the systematic abuse of children by staff at the Kincora boys' home, situated in the largely Protestant area of East Belfast (Moore 1996). In addition to the scale of the abuse, in terms of both the number of victims and the length of time for which it continued, the scandal was highly politicised. Senior political figures, social services and the Protestant Church were each implicated for failing to respond to alleged complaints dating back 'at least five years before the scandal became public' (*News Letter* 12 January 1985: 7), and perhaps as much as a decade (Moore 1996). Furthermore, claims were advanced that an institutional cover-up had been initiated deliberately because the main instigator of the abuse, William McGrath, was under the control of British Intelligence (Campbell 1990).

William McGrath was head or 'housefather' of Kincora and the leader of the evangelical Protestant extremist group Tara. There is evidence to suggest that 'the intelligence services used their knowledge of the homosexual abuses at the home to blackmail and thus control leading protestant figures' (Campbell 1990: 195). McGrath was allegedly one such leading figure. Moreover, the British state has been openly accused of obstructing police inquiries into Kincora for its own political ends (Moore 1996). In short, the Kincora affair shook the establishment. It was awash with rumours of political scandal, intrigue and cover-up, and its aftermath sent tremors across Northern Ireland, arousing public concern which, for some, has yet to settle (Moore 1996). Since the exposure of Kincora, child sex abuse – especially when positions of authority or trust are abused within an institutional context – has maintained a high prevalence in newsprint media discourse.

The Father Brendan Smyth affair

Even more prevalent in participants' accounts was the Father Brendan Smyth affair – though the fact that this case is more recent is probably significant. Father Brendan Smyth, a Norbertine priest, was convicted in 1994 of sex offences against children in four different countries, committed over a period exceeding thirty years (Moore 1995; Jenkins 1996). Like the Kincora scandal more than a decade before, the implications of the Brendan Smyth affair reached far beyond the immediate context of the abuse and penetrated to the very heart of the state, this time in the Irish Republic. The investigation revealed that both the Catholic Church and the Irish government had been aware of Smyth's activities for a number of years and had signally failed to act (Moore 1995).

Exposed by Belfast journalist Chris Moore, the case resulted directly in the collapse of the Irish Fianna Fail government under then Taoiseach Albert Reynolds. This case more than any other aroused concerns about the perceived menace of the Catholic clergy in Ireland. As a result, the issue of clergy abuse became headline news across Northern Ireland and the Republic, providing a new angle for media representations of child sex abuse and ensuring its continued prevalence in the media. In its wake, a plethora of cases and fresh allegations about Smyth and other members of the clergy (both Protestant and Catholic) received unprecedented attention in press discourse. As Jenkins (1996: 190) notes, the 'sudden upsurge in cases produced an impression of a systematic crisis in the Irish Church'.[2] The story broke in the autumn of 1994, and Smyth was sentenced to four years' imprisonment for seventeen charges of sex offences against children in June of that year (Moore 1995). He died in prison in 1998. Both the Father Brendan Smyth affair and the Kincora scandal were still receiving coverage in the Northern Ireland regional press in 1997.

The impact of Kincora and the Father Brendan Smyth affair

Journalists and practitioners consistently cited these cases as central in establishing and consolidating child sex abuse as an issue for concern in Northern Ireland. Both involved the systematic abuse of children over a period of several decades by men in positions of trust and authority. Both were linked to alleged attempts at cover-up by major institutions.

And both had far-reaching political implications that shook the establishment, with the Brendan Smyth affair literally bringing a government it to its knees. The *Sunday Life* Editor, Martin Lindsay, stressed the impact on social awareness of Kincora:

> I think that with sex crime in particular, I think that people in this country are wakening up to sex crime … We have known for years that in areas like the Shankill there was a lot of incest and child abuse by parents and uncles and friends of families. Kincora brought it home. I really think that kind of brought it home to people.

Jim McDowell, Editor of the *Sunday World*, also placed both cases at the heart of the increase in press attention to sex crime. For him:

> [It was] because of Chris Moore. [It was] Kincora and Brendan Smyth. Chris Moore is the only hack in living memory, in my living memory, who has brought down a government. Chris Moore brought down Albert Reynolds's Fianna Fail government. Moore … raised the profile of paedophilia. There was a syndrome in this country for an awful lot of years, and Chris lifted the lid.

This view was reinforced by a number of other journalists. Some stressed that the high-profile coverage which each case attracted sensitised news readers to the problem of institutional child sex abuse. Others commented that a previously taboo issue being linked with political scandal made for an explosive concoction. As one reporter put it:

> Kincora and the Brendan Smyth case would make people aware of it and I suppose it would whet their appetites. That might be the wrong term, but basically give them an interest, or arouse their interest or make them familiar with that sort of crime … Kincora and then the Brendan Smyth thing kept it very much on the boil didn't it? His [Smyth's] crimes spanned the length and breadth of the country and America as well if I remember rightly. Smyth's crimes had far-reaching implications which, to my mind, brought down a government.

These accounts offer some indication of the impact that sexual-political scandals can have on establishment institutions and wider society. Thompson (2000: 234) is quick to dismiss any suggestion that 'beyond the entertainment value and temporary inconvenience they may cause, scandals have no lasting significance and tell us nothing of any enduring value about social and political life'. The point is illustrated primarily with reference to the Watergate affair in the USA, leading to the conclusion that scandals can indeed have 'consequences which spread beyond the lives of the individuals concerned, weakening or even undermining the institutions or policies with which they are or have been linked' (Thompson 2000: 235). Thompson usefully highlights that media exposure of institutional wrongdoing, especially if that wrongdoing has been unsuccessfully covered up, can have serious consequences. To the various sexual-political scandals he discusses can be added the Kincora and Father Brendan Smyth affairs, the latter having a political impact that surely ranks alongside the collapse of the US Nixon administration in the 1970s following the exposure of the Watergate break-ins and cover-up.

There were important social as well as political consequences resulting from these cases. One journalist pointed to the role that their exposure played in convincing survivors they are not alone: 'The Brendan Smyth case was a real turning point in Northern Ireland. It encouraged the public to realise that child sex abuse is a real problem. That case had a huge impact in encouraging people to come forward.' On the same issue, *Irish News* Editor, Noel Doran, remarked:

> Clearly the Smyth case acted as a catalyst and because of that case many more people came forward, not just over Smyth, but over other individuals. Those sorts of testimonies then had much more credibility, and it became clear that there was a problem there … a fairly deep-rooted and widespread problem.

And Geoff Martin, Editor of the *News Letter*, commented, 'when these cases are reported, then other people are encouraged to come forward, the snowball effect'.

The insights provided by survivors themselves are of special relevance here. Christine (not her real name), an adult survivor of child sex abuse, referred directly to the Father Brendan Smyth affair when explaining her reasons for eventually reporting her abuser to the police:

> It was the Fred West and Rosemary West trials that brought it up in my mind. The Fred West trial was so publicised, and so was the Brendan Smyth case, that it made me aware that I wasn't the only one. I mean, I knew I wasn't because it happened to my two sisters. But because those victims were willing to come forward and have these people prosecuted, it made me feel that I had nothing to be ashamed of.

And David (not his real name), also an adult survivor of child sex abuse, stated that, 'Until everything started with the Brendan Smyth case, nobody knew about it [child sex abuse] and nobody wanted to know about it'.

Thus journalists and practitioners accorded that it was these cases – Kincora and the Father Brendan Smyth affair – that did most to establish and sustain the issue of child sex abuse on the social and political agenda in Northern Ireland. And survivors of abuse referred to the Brendan Smyth case in particular as a key turning point in the wider realisation that the culture of denial in Northern Ireland could not continue. The collective impact of the media exposure of these cases was to increase social awareness and to transform sex crime, and child sex abuse in particular, from an issue of private to public concern. The subsequent impact on levels of press attention to sex crime was enormous.

The floodgates opened: representations of institutional abuse

Noel Doran, Editor of the *Irish News*, in acknowledging the prevalence of clergy abuse cases, suggested that accepting the nature and extent of the problem was another bridge that people in Northern Ireland took time to cross:

> The priest thing has been a phenomenon of the last few years, the number of priests who have found themselves in court ... which just never happened before. It took a long time for people to come to terms with that. It's probably the case that the *Irish News* had to come to terms with it as well.

By the mid-1990s, the notion of 'institutional abuse' had extended from the children's home and the Church to the youth club and the school, and now included youth leaders, school caretakers, teachers and headmasters. Some of the most heavily reported cases related to this phenomenon, and the Kincora scandal and Father Brendan Smyth affair were referred to with alarming frequency.

For example, three of the cases reported in 1997 were mentioned in four newspapers. Two of these involved institutional abuse. The first case – carried in each of the dailies – concerned allegations against a Catholic priest for the sexual abuse of young boys. The story contained a number of elements that made it eminently reportable. First, there was the association with clergy abuse, a dominant theme throughout the archive. Secondly, the charges were contested which presented the opportunity to develop a courtroom drama over a period of days. And thirdly, there was the additional and highly unusual event of the jury being dismissed because 'witnesses mixed with the jury panel' (*Irish Times* 8 January 1997: front page). The ensuing narratives recounted the defence counsel's 'BID TO SCRAP PRIEST'S SEX ABUSE TRIAL', because 'Tuesday's "fatal contact" had ensured any future trial would be "tainted"' (*Irish News* 9 January 1997: 7). The trial was subsequently adjourned, but the story was picked up again some days later when it could be reported that 'an appeal for a stay to be placed on the case was turned down' (*Irish News* 16 January 1997: 9) and the case would proceed the following month.

The second story to be reported in four newspapers (including daily and Sunday titles) involved a self-styled youth leader who, according to the *Sunday Life*, 'used the cover of his Christian beliefs to prey on young boys' (12 January 1997: 4). The offender was given a conditional discharge because, as the judge explained, 'what comes across is the profile of a naïve man, a man who behaved unwisely, but not the profile of a predator or an abuser' (*Irish News* 24 January 1997: 7). This was the 'angle' for several reports, which quoted the judge's summing-up and juxtaposed this with the parents' outrage at the verdict. The headline in the *News Letter* offered one of the more forceful expressions of concern: 'SEX ABUSE CASE CALLED PANTOMIME'. 'SEX ABUSE LEADER ESCAPES JAIL' was the more restrained offering by the *Irish News* (24 January 1997: 7). Two weeks prior to the sentencing, the *Sunday Life* (12 January 1997: 4) had devoted virtually a whole page to three items and a large colour photograph of the offender under the headline 'THE FACE OF A PERVERT'. One of the items, entitled 'BETRAYED AND DEEPLY HURT', described how parents had at first 'remained unconvinced of his guilt' and 'even took to the streets in protest' when Calvert was first charged (12 January 1997: 4). Much was made of the fact that the confidence of the families had been won first, though there was no discussion of the significance of the 'grooming process' in child sex-abuse cases or any issues of detection or prevention. As noted above, the virtual absence of reference to the possible causes, risks and prevention of child sex abuse is a point on which many practitioners criticise the press. In the *Sunday Life* the offender was described as an 'evil child pervert' (12 January 1997: 4) and a 'sex pervert' (*Sunday Life* 26 January 1997: 14). The dailies restricted their descriptions to direct use of the name and position as a youth leader.

Thus the increase in press attention (to all forms of sex crime) can be partly understood in terms of the impact of particular high-profile cases and the shifts they precipitated in media, political and public perceptions about the nature and extent of the problem in Northern Ireland.

These factors, coupled with the changing nature of media markets, form a substantial part of the explanation. For a more comprehensive understanding, however, it is necessary to consider other forms of change, some specific to Northern Ireland and others characteristic of wider transformations in late modernity.

Political Change

The political climate in Northern Ireland changed significantly between the mid-1980s and the late 1990s, and a number of journalists and practitioners related these changes directly to the increase in press attention to sex crime over that period. For the Editor of the *Sunday Life*, Martin Lindsay, prior to the 1980s the press's preoccupation with the Troubles left little room for the coverage of other issues of crime, deviance and control:

> I think that many of these crimes were swept underneath the carpet before. I also think, in fact I'm certain because I worked on the [Belfast] *Telegraph* news desk and I was deputy editor of the *Telegraph* before I came here … During the height of the Troubles, if you had bodies lying in the street, frankly papers didn't have the time, didn't even have the interest in a woman shouting 'Rape'. The complete opposite. We were preoccupied with the Troubles and we were preoccupied with all the political ramifications that that brought about. So I don't think … actually journalists had the time, or possibly the inclination, because I'm thinking back and I was on a news desk then, you know, and you could probably count the number of times on that hand that people actually phoned the news desk and said, 'Look, here's a sex crime'. So we normally never got involved until it came to court, and even then … I mean, the list every day was terrorist crimes.

Since the first IRA cease-fire in 1994, fundamental transformations in the political landscape and, most importantly, the shift from violence to political dialogue have created an hiatus in news coverage that has needed to be filled (Hollywood 1997). Referring to this period, Rape Crisis spokesperson Eileen Calder suggested that 'there has been an increase in the reporting of that sort of thing [sex crime] in the press within Northern Ireland because there hasn't been as much political stuff to concentrate on'. During the earlier stages of this analysis, however, the Troubles were still very much a feature of everyday life. The accelerated increase in press attention to sex crime in the latter stages of this research (especially between 1995 and 1997) might therefore be related to changes in the political environment. But while the 1980s and early 1990s witnessed extreme political violence, they were also characterised by significant (even historic) political advances that helped to establish the foundations for the transition to conflict resolution and lasting peace.

The signing of the Anglo-Irish Agreement, for example, by then British Prime Minister Margaret Thatcher and Irish Taoiseach Garret Fitzgerald in November 1985, established closer working relations between the British and Irish governments and sought to arrest the electoral rise of Sinn Fein, the political wing of the IRA (Bowyer Bell 1993). In 1990, then Northern Ireland Secretary of State, Peter Brooke, made the landmark statement that Britain had 'no selfish, strategic or economic' interests in the Union between Northern Ireland and the rest of the UK. In 1993, Conservative Prime Minister John Major and Taoiseach Albert Reynolds issued the Downing Street Declaration, which signalled for the first time the possibility of a united Ireland being democratically achieved, if that was the will of the people. And, of course, the paramilitary cease-fires of 1994 and 1997 offered a palpable sense that lasting peace could be a reality in Northern Ireland.

It is possible, therefore, that these changes did have an effect on the nature of news coverage in Northern Ireland and, in the process, created more space for the coverage of issues that had been buried beneath the Troubles when they were at their height in the 1970s. As the *Sunday Life* Editor, Martin Lindsay, put it:

> I think that all newspapers, including the *Sunday Life*, we all have a different agenda now because, you know, the Troubles have been decreasing over the last number of years and we do now have time to spend on these crimes, which are ... some of them are quite horrendous.

It might be stretching things too far to suggest that changes in the political climate are a primary factor in explaining the increase in press coverage to sex crime throughout the 1980s and 1990s. Nevertheless, the political situation has undoubtedly contributed to making certain cases more newsworthy in media discourse and, as a result, more resonant in the public imagination. Had the Kincora scandal and the Brendan Smyth affair not been so closely intertwined with the political situations in

Northern Ireland and the Republic, it is doubtful that their level of exposure in the media and their subsequent impact on popular consciousness would have been so great.

Organisational Activism

In general terms, perhaps the most significant contribution to increasing the public visibility of sexual violence has come from the feminist movement (Soothill and Walby 1991; Saraga 2001). Emerging from the New Left in the 1970s, new feminist groups and commentators have profoundly influenced society and politics and, in particular, initiated and framed key debates around the problem of (sexual) violence. Also, it was feminists and Rape Crisis groups that established the first Incest Crisis Line in 1978 (Jenkins 1992). Thompson's comments on the impact of feminism in the USA apply more generally: 'Due largely to the women's movement, there was a growing sensitivity in ... society to certain forms of male behaviour which might have been regarded as normal or acceptable in previous decades' (2000: 147–8).

More specifically in the current context, the Editor of the *Irish News*, Noel Doran, suggested that the activities of regional groups and organisations have been a central mechanism in raising public awareness about sex crime in Northern Ireland: 'Then you would have the whole ... probably just a greater awareness ... organisations would set out to try and inform the public that sex crimes were more widespread than perhaps had been portrayed in the papers and those organisations have had some success in achieving that.' The media activities of practitioners and source organisations are explored fully in the chapters that follow and will not, for that reason, be discussed in any great detail here. It is useful here, though, to draw attention to key points in the development of relevant organisations which can help further to contextualise and, thereby, explain the increasing levels of social awareness about sex crime throughout the 1980s and 1990s, and its increasing prevalence in the press.

It is significant, for example, that both the Belfast Rape Crisis Centre and the Nexus Institute, the two main counselling organisations in Northern Ireland, were established in the early 1980s. Both groups are active in the public arena and both, through a range of media and community initiatives, have been important contributors to increasing social awareness about sex crime.

The efforts of the police and other organisations to publicise improvements in the treatment of sex crime complainants have raised the profile of the problem in Northern Ireland generally and also given it greater currency in public (including media) discourses. The Child Abuse and Rape Enquiry (CARE) unit was established in 1985 to deal exclusively with sex crime cases. Initially, its role was limited to taking statements from victims of sexual abuse since the investigation of sex crime cases was largely dealt with by CID. The CARE unit was made investigative in 1994. The RUC's Chief Information Officer described the situation prior to the unit's creation and the reforms which have been instituted since:

> Most of the police stations did not have the facilities for bringing victims in, so a victim could be brought straight into an enquiry room, with other people there, taken off, interviewed in an interview room which is not the most hospitable or friendly place. What we have done now is moved away completely to a situation where they are brought into an actual 'bungalow', which has a kitchen, a drawing room, a child room – there are toys for the kids if there are kids involved – an easy armchair. And it is still a police investigation office ... and that is all designed to save the victim. They are shocked, they have had a terrible experience, and we have got to be caring about it ... And that is the most effective way to be as well, because the more relaxed the person is, they realise they are being treated with respect, then the more open they are going to be and the more we are going to get out of them to get the information for the investigation.

To give some indication of how these developments have been received, a press statement released by Rape Crisis in 1985 called for 'more sympathetic and compassionate treatment from the police' in cases of rape (*Irish News* 11 January 1985: 2). In the same article, the RUC outlined a new initiative directed at making the reporting of rape less traumatic for survivors, 'to make it more feasible to report rape in the first place'.[3] In 1996, the Belfast Rape Crisis position was markedly different:

> While we are a non-directive counselling service and will never try to force a woman to report her rape to the police, we now feel much happier in encouraging them and supporting them to do so. We know that in the majority of cases they will be treated in a sympathetic and respectful manner by specially trained officers.
> (*Annual Report* 1994–6).

Police reforms – and the CARE unit especially – were praised by all the

Plea to RUC over victims of rape

Belfast: The local Rape Crisis Centre has called on the RUC to follow the lead of Scotland Yard in ensuring that victims get "more sympathetic and compassionate treatment from the police."

While welcoming the move to make the reporting of rape to the police less distressing, the centre stressed that police officers investigating complaints should do so with sympathy and tact."

However an RUC spokesman explained that over 80 policewomen had already had special training to assist them in dealing with victims of sexual assault and that male officers were only involved in follow-up investigations.

He pointed out that the charge of rape was "a very easy one to make, and hard to disporve."

Referring to the fact that Scotland Yard were introducing special "victim examination suites" aimed at reducing women's fears, the RUC spokesman stated that most police stations here were equipped with medical rooms, where rape victims had complete privacy.

The London suites will be painted in sooting shades, with showers and improved interview and medical facilities.

Victims will also be provided with track suits, rather than just the towel which they wear at present while their clothes are being forensically examined.

But the Belfast Rape Crisis Centre said that existing legislation would have to be changed to "make it more feasible for women to report rape in the first place," adding that certain kinds of rape were not recognised by law, such as married women being raped by their husband.

It was conceded that "many women have reported that they were well-treated by the RUC on reporting rape; and we have had discussions with them about ways in which the situation can be improved."

Printed courtesy of the *Irish News*.

practitioners and survivors interviewed for this research.

In addition to the activities of regional organisations, initiatives launched throughout the UK have surely influenced popular consciousness in Northern Ireland. Kitzinger (1996: 319), for example, notes that the problem of child sex abuse 'first gained sustained media attention in 1986, when Esther Rantzen launched ChildLine'. Sustained media attention in Northern Ireland dates back to the exposure of Kincora in 1980, and major events like ChildLine did not pass unnoticed in the regional press. The same can be said of high-profile cases outside Northern Ireland – for example, in Cleveland, Rochdale and the Orkney Islands (Nava 1988; Campbell 1988, 1989; Franklin and Parton 1991). Each of these cases involved disputed allegations of the systematic, organised abuse of children. In each, either the Social Services or local medical practitioners and their methods of intervention came under fire from the media. During the reporting of these cases and their aftermath, the efforts of national organisations to increase social awareness about sex crime across the UK complemented the efforts of regional activists in Northern Ireland. Northern Ireland may be unique in a number of ways, but it is not hermetically sealed off from the rest of the UK.

Cultural Change

The final area of consideration relates to more general and widespread cultural changes which are by no means confined to Northern Ireland. Crime and sex are now much more deeply embedded in the routine structures of everyday life than they were several decades ago. With respect to the former, as noted in previous chapters, high levels of crime and concerns over personal safety form part of daily existence (Bauman 2000; Garland 2000). Regarding the latter, 'sex now continually features in the public domain' (Giddens 1992: 1). Both are ubiquitous in mass media output (Marsh 1991; Presdee 2000; Reiner *et al* 2000b; Ewen 2001). Since the normalisation of crime has been discussed already, it is the increasing visibility of sexual matters in public life that I want to focus on here. Ultimately, though, it is the relationship between the two that forms the crux of the argument that follows.

As a result of the sexual revolution which has taken place over the last forty or fifty years, attitudes to sex and intimacy, and relations between men and women more generally, have changed radically. Two key elements, the women's movement and female claims to sexual autonomy and changing discourses around homosexuality, facilitated 'more unfettered discussion of sexuality than previously was possible' (Giddens 1992: 28; see also Foucault 1979; Bauman 2001). One by-product of these ongoing debates has been the moral, political and legal re-evaluation of certain forms of sexual practice that had previously been considered deviant or even perverse and, correspondingly, had remained largely hidden from public view. In this climate of increased social awareness, if not always increased social tolerance, various activists and organisations – especially those representing the views and interests of homosexuals – emerged to promote sexual diversity and minority sexual tastes. The result was the transformation of sexuality from a subject of private fascination to a fundamental construct of daily social life, an 'everyday phenomenon of thousands of books, articles and other descriptive sources' (Giddens 1992: 23).

Though it began in the 1960s, the increasing public visibility of sex accelerated in the 1980s. The role of sex (in its most voyeuristic and titillating forms) in the tabloid circulation wars of the 1970s and 1980s has been noted above. Television, too, has capitalised on the saleability of sex. In the early 1980s, Channel 4 emerged with a view to catering to tastes left unsatisfied by the three existing channels (BBC1, BBC2 and ITV). In addition to new forms of (popular) cultural programmes, some based on the stated remit to cater specifically for minorities, Channel 4 pushed the boundaries of 'acceptable' television viewing by screening films containing unprecedented levels of explicit, and not infrequently violent, sexual activity.

In the 1990s, satellite television, the Internet and the proliferation of magazine titles have increased still further the availability to mainstream media consumers of sexual images (including the sexualisation of children), in both fictional and (supposedly) factual contexts. US talk shows or, as Presdee (2000: 79) calls them, 'humiliation chat shows' like Ricky Lake and Jerry Springer, and their UK counterparts, Trisha and Vanessa, constitute confessionals in which participants willingly disclose their sexual escapades before live audiences and millions of viewers. Soap operas like *Brookside* and *EastEnders* have attempted to deal more seriously with a diversity of sexual behaviours (legal and illegal). Whether some have been addressed as appropriately as they might merits lengthier debate (Medhurst 1998), but the debate at least has been made public. Survivors have referred directly to soap opera characters when explaining the factors that encouraged them to disclose (Kitzinger 1999a). In short, the taboos around openly discussing the majority of sexual behaviours diminished consistently and significantly throughout the 1980s and 1990s.

The mass media constitute one key terrain on which this transformation has taken place, but there are others. Bauman (2001: 224) points out that there is more to the cultural revolution around sex and sexuality than 'the greed for profit, free competition and the refinement of the advertising media'. Sex has also established a strong presence in the classroom. The current co-ordinator of the RUC CARE unit – as a professional and a parent – developed this point:

> I think that there is a much more liberal attitude now to sexual matters generally, you know, in the early eighties and late seventies, even the idea of having sex education in schools was taboo. And now sex education is included in the national curriculum ... I am only going on my gut feeling here, but I know that I have two children myself and they are young, and they know a lot more about sex than I did when I was their age. The level of awareness in the school playground is frightening. And that comes from watching soap operas. *Neighbours* and *Home and Away* will cover the full range of sexual deviance. It's in there, and that's scary.

Sex became a key issue for educational concern after the AIDS panic of the early 1980s. Margeret Thatcher, then Conservative Prime Minister, had openly espoused a return to Victorian moral values on her way into

10 Downing Street. It is somewhat ironic, then, that her government made sex education a priority in schools, investing millions in the 1986 launch of the largest sex education programme in British history. For the Right, AIDS became a symbol of the fruits of sexual promiscuity. For the Left, it became a reason to educate people about safe sex. Whatever the political position, it is beyond question that children are better informed about sex today than were children in previous generations.

There are clear connections between the increasing visibility of sex and sexuality and crime and violence in public life and the increasing levels of attention to sexual deviance and sex crime in the press. As people have become more sensitised (perhaps in some respects desensitised) to sexual matters, and more used to the notion of sex as a public as well as a private issue, debates around sex crime have taken on a new relevance. Feminists established the issue of sexual violence against women and children on the social and political agenda in the 1970s. Throughout the 1980s and 1990s, however, as a result of their continued activities and all those other inter-related influences described in this chapter (perhaps especially the 'discovery' of child sex abuse), it has become more socially pressing, culturally resonant and (lest it be forgotten) commercially viable for journalists to report deviant, violent, *criminal* sexual behaviours.

Increased social awareness and ongoing discourses have placed pressure on key institutions to take the problem of sex crime seriously and implement real changes in policy and practice (fundamental changes in police procedure are one obvious example). This, in turn, has made it less stigmatising and less daunting for survivors to come forward and disclose their abuse. In the midst of these wider cultural changes – precipitated and sustained by a complex of social, moral, normative, legal and commercial forces – sex crime has taken on an ever-more prevalent position in public discourses. It is in this complex, varied and persistently changing context that we can understand the dramatic and disproportionate increase in the prevalence of sex crime in the press.

Conclusions

In this chapter I have identified and discussed the various factors which explain the dramatic increase in press attention to sex crime in Northern Ireland between 1985 and 1997. These are the tabloidisation of the press and increasing market competition, the impact of high-profile cases, the changing political climate, the campaigning activities of various groups and organisations, and wider shifts in the cultural sensibilities of those who produce and consume press discourse.

The collective impact of these shifts and influences has been the creation of a climate in which sexual deviance, including those forms of sexual deviance which attract the label 'criminal', has taken on an unprecedented significance in popular consciousness. There is a clear and widespread fascination with sex crimes – not necessarily a fascination based on sexual gratification, but one which cuts across moral, cultural, economic and political boundaries. The public and media preoccupation with sex crime exists at the interface between the emotional and commercial potency of sexual deviance, the increasing visibility of sex and crime in public life, the widespread fears and anxieties about personal safety and the perennial threat posed by the 'unknown other'. It is grounded in a growing awareness that sexual violence is a widespread problem which needs to be taken seriously and discussed publicly.

There are both positive and negative outcomes associated with the increased prevalence of sex crime in newsprint media discourse. Journalists, practitioners and survivors espoused a range of different views about the quality and social function of press representations of sex offending in Northern Ireland. In the next chapter, attention turns to key players' often conflicting opinions about how sex crimes are, and how they should be, constructed in the press.

Notes

1 Figures for average pagination, circulation and readership are included in Appendix III.

2 At the time of writing another major scandal was breaking in the USA regarding the alleged shielding by the Catholic Church of priests who have been implicated in complaints of child sex abuse. According to the *Guardian* (15 April 2002), 'Thousands of American priests are suspected of interfering with children, and the Archbishops of Boston and New York, traditionally the two most important jobs in the US Catholic church, are under pressure to resign because of their part in covering up the abuses'.

3 A series of news stories, articles and letters to the editor concerning police reforms, available resources for survivors of sexual abuse and the importance of reporting offences were printed at this time. See, for example: *Irish News*, 'Police Urge Rape Victims to Break Silence on Attacks' (25/01/85: 2); *The Irish Times*, 'Clinic for Rape Victims' (08/01/85: 7), 'Rape a Common Hazard' (12/01/85: 4), 'Treatment for Rape Victims' (30/01/85: 11); *News Letter*, 'Women who Fear to Talk, Rape Victims' Silence' (11/01/85: 6), 'Report all Rapists, Victims Told' (25/01/85: 7).

Chapter 6

Consensus and controversy

Introduction

Journalists hold different views about how sexual offending should be reported or, at the very least, work for newspapers that write to different agendas. Practitioners' views on what are the key issues and how they should be portrayed can constitute an ideological battleground that is fiercely competitive. Survivors, too, have their own views on how the problem of sex crime should be represented in press discourse. This chapter seeks to navigate a path through the field of contested opinion and ideological dispute in order to identify the key areas of consensus and controversy around the construction of sex crime in the press.

Sex Crime and Source Organisations in Northern Ireland

The key players in the construction of sex crime as news – aside from journalists and editors themselves – are the police, the judiciary, the probation service, counselling services, social services and survivors of sexual abuse.[1] The police, the judiciary and the probation service are resource-rich. Counselling services, relatively speaking, tend to be resource-poor. Yet each of these organisations is central in the process of framing sex crime in print discourse and shaping popular consciousness about the nature and extent of the problem.

A key objective for all organisations, regardless of their power and resources, is to be accredited with expert status – to be 'recognised socially to be in the position to know' (Ericson *et al* 1989: 4). For it is through recognition of this type that organisations can elevate their position in the 'hierarchy of credibility' (Becker 1967). And the higher the position in the hierarchy of credibility, the greater the likelihood of successfully accessing the media and having disclosures used by journalists, read by audiences and ultimately accepted as legitimate and true (Loseke 1999: 34–7). Expert status is customarily attained through the command and control of frameworks of elite knowledge – that is, specialised insight, understanding or information derived from research or investigation, professional involvement, a particular moral or political position, or first-hand experience of the issue under the media spotlight. Put simply, source organisations strive to give the impression that they command access to information beyond the realms of most 'regular people' (Chermak 1997) and that their accounts are closest to the 'truth'.

Sources manipulate their elite knowledge in order to construct social conditions in a way that advances their position, status or goals (Kitsuse and Spector 1973; Merton 1976; Spector and Kitsuse 1977; Best, 1995; Mulcahy 1995). To recall Sasson's reference to the work of Edelman (1988: 12, cited in Sasson 1995):

> Problems come into discourse and therefore into existence as reinforcements of ideologies, not simply because they are there or because they are important for wellbeing. They signify who are virtuous and useful and who are dangerous or inadequate, which actions will be rewarded and which penalised. They constitute people as subjects with particular kinds of aspirations, self-concepts and fears, and they create beliefs about the relative importance of events and objects. They are critical in determining who exercise authority and who accept it.

Media outlets constitute sites on which various social groups, institutions and ideologies struggle over the definition and construction of social reality (Gurevitch and Levy 1985; Miller and Holstein 1993). Through what can be highly competitive media strategies organisations endeavour to enhance their profile in the public arena (Jenkins 1992), legitimise their position as part of the 'deviance defining elite' (Chermak 1997), and stimulate the development of resources, credibility and, consequently, political power (Surette 1998). As Gamson and Modigliani (1989: 10) point out, 'making sense of the world requires an effort, and those tools that are developed, spotlighted, and made readily accessible have a higher probability of being used'. If the promotional strategies of a particular organisation are successful they can shape the available tools or resources with which people make sense of a given issue, and in so doing increase the likelihood that popular consciousness will coincide with their own beliefs.

With respect to the problem of sex crime, clearly not all groups will command similar levels of expertise in all areas of media interest. For example, counselling services offer advice and support to survivors of sexual abuse, while probation officers work primarily with offenders. Furthermore, different organisations may seek to promote or foreground different issues in accordance with their own social and political agendas. Counselling services (and most survivors), while accepting the need to work with offenders, are vexed by what they see as the disproportionate allocation of government resources to offender-based treatments and programmes while their own organisations struggle to manage with minimal resources. On the other hand, probation workers, while appreciating that survivors require counselling and support, stress the importance of financing initiatives to better understand sex offenders in order to formulate effective strategies for minimising risk and dealing with abuse.

Thus, perspectives on the problem of sex crime, and interpretations of practitioners' stated and actual roles in addressing that problem, while constructed from a common set of objective social conditions, may differ substantially from one group to the next. These conflicting perspectives may be manifested directly in the strategies employed when dealing – either proactively or reactively – with the media. Eileen Calder explained her mindset when sharing a television debate with Oliver Brannigan, Director of the Northern Ireland Probation Service (PBNI):

> Well, say Noel Thompson [prominent BBC Northern Ireland broadcast journalist] is doing a lunchtime newsbreak and he invites me and Oliver along and we are sitting in the Green Room … Oliver and I will have a fairly reasonable discussion for ten minutes. But when we get in there, we know that we have a minute each and we are talking in soundbites and, you know, you have three important things that you want to say and you are going to say them. No matter what Noel Thompson asks you, you are going to say them … 'That's a very interesting question, Noel, but …' You learn to act like a politician. We are probably more successful at communicating when it is not in public.

This example highlights the political essence of news management and demonstrates that the elite knowledge or ideological 'spin' propounded by one group does not necessarily correlate with that of another (Miller 1998, 1993; Schlesinger and Tumber 1994). It also illustrates the importance of the media as a 'field of contestation' (Skidmore 1995: 101) in which different groups compete to define the issues around sex crime in Northern Ireland. The organisations interviewed for this research espoused fundamentally conflicting views in a range of areas, from the role survivors should play in court, to what should be done with offenders once convicted, to the measures that should be taken to monitor them once released. As we will see, though there was broad consensus on certain issues, there was a diversity of views regarding press representations of sex crime, the nature and extent of the problems that currently prevail and what, if anything, should be done about them.

Contextualising the Discussion

Discussions about press representations of sex crime and their possible impact were seldom conducted in general terms. Rather, practitioners and journalists tended to frame their views on sex crime coverage specifically in terms of the representation of child sex abuse. That is, the term 'sex crime' was taken to be broadly synonymous with the sexual abuse of children. This tacit assumption offers clear insights into what 'sex crime' means to those who are in some way involved in the news production process. As detailed in Chapter 4, child sex offences accounted for half the overall archive of sex crime coverage (233 out of 483 items, or 48 per cent). And in Chapter 5 the impact of the Kincora and Father Brendan Smyth cases on professional and popular consciousness about sex crime in Northern Ireland was discussed in some detail. It is perhaps because of the prevalence of child sex abuse in media discourse, its resonance in popular consciousness and its currency in political and policy debates that this form of deviance was so clearly at the forefront of participants' minds.

Indeed, in the last ten years child sex abuse has provided the dominant focus for much of the research on media representations of sex crime; to an extent, it would seem, at the expense of studying the construction of other forms of sexual offending. The present study explores the press representation of a wide range of sex crimes. But because of the prevalence of child sex offences both in the press archive and in the comments of research participants, consideration of the representation of this form of deviance seems a sensible place to begin. Once the contours of the debate have been delineated in this context, the discussion can be broadened to include the construction of other forms of sex offending.

Practitioners' Views on Press Representations of Child Sex Abuse

For practitioners who participated in this research, the most frequently articulated concern – in line with the research literature (Nelson 1987; Soothill and Walby 1991; Kitzinger and Skidmore 1995; West 1996; Goddard 1996; Kitzinger 1996, 1999b; Thomas 2000) – was that press portrayals *distort* the social reality of sex crime. Some went so far as to suggest that, because press representations are misleading, they are potentially damaging. Though critical of the press in a number of respects, however, several practitioners were quick to point out the contribution that the press have made to increasing social awareness about child sex abuse (see also Goddard 1996; Greer 2001a, 2001b, 2003). Indeed, on certain issues, organisations which differ fundamentally in other areas (Rape Crisis and the Probation Service, for example) were in complete agreement. On others, there was a diversity of views espoused by a range of groups, some of which were diametrically opposed. Not surprisingly, then, there was a wide range of opinion regarding the extent to which the representation of child sex abuse and sex crime more generally needs to change.

Increasing Social Awareness

In the previous chapter it was noted that survivors have cited mediated images of sexual abuse as influential in their decisions to disclose. That point can be usefully developed here. Representatives of a range of different organisations accorded that the media can have a significant impact on the number of survivors coming forward, either to the police or to counselling services. As one detective sergeant with the RUC CARE unit explained:

> What you would normally find, if there has been a court case, or somebody has been charged in relation to an offence and they name him … sometimes you do find other victims coming forward there … in relation to that specific case. However … sometimes if there has been a high-profile documentary or something on [TV], you may find that you would get a few calls the next day, not necessarily in relation to that, but I do find that things go up the next day … I think there is definitely a link there, not to a great degree, but even one or two phone calls is a good increase on what we might get in an evening.

The suggestion here is that the impact of press representations is significant, but moderate. Representatives from the two major counselling services in Northern Ireland, the Belfast Rape Crisis Centre and the Nexus Institute, suggested that the effect of media coverage on the number of survivors coming forward can be profound. As Eileen Calder, Rape Crisis spokesperson, explained:

> If the story is about rape, you would get an increase in calls from women saying they have been raped. And if the story is about male rape, you would get an increased number of calls from men. And after the Brendan Smyth[2] case we got calls from all over Ireland.

Between 1985 and 1997 the number of sexual offences recorded by the RUC more than doubled from 653 to 1,444, representing an increase of 121 per cent. While this increase is dramatic, it does not necessarily represent escalating levels of sexual abuse in Northern Ireland. Rather, it was the view of counsellors and police officers that rising figures were indicative of increasing levels of social awareness and a greater number of survivors reporting offences (see also Finkelhor 1984; Mawby and Walklate 1994; West 1996; Levi 1997). Practitioners suggested that this increase was largely due to improvements in police procedures, the impact of high-profile cases on social awareness, the efforts of both statutory and voluntary organisations to publicise the extent of abuse in Northern Ireland and the availability of advice and support for those who might benefit.[3] As one senior CARE officer explained:

> I don't think that crime has gone up. I think that it has always been there ... I am certain that it has always been there. But I think that there is more of an awareness now and the ability to talk about it. It's the whole perception people have now of sexual abuse ... The media, I suppose, have helped in one aspect of it all, making people more aware of it, and I suppose that education programmes, and different things have also helped. But certainly I think that the crime has always been there ... I don't know if it has risen as such. You know, we only see the tip of the iceberg, and that's an awful lot, you know. It's rampant out there. And I think that it has always been like that. And certainly in rural areas, I think that probably in some rural areas you could almost perceive it to be the norm.

The normalisation of abuse in particular areas has been evidenced in other studies. For example, Hood-Williams and Bush (1995: 11) found in a London housing estate that, 'domestic violence may even be seen as part of ordinary life. The climate of acceptance ensures that few will seek the assistance of statutory agencies'. And Gordon (1988: 7) notes in relation to intrafamilial sexual abuse, 'One of the most striking things about incest, that most extraordinary and heinous of transgressions, is its capacity to be ordinary … In the family violence case records it is a behaviour of very ordinary people' (see also Nelson 1987).

Dominica McGowan, Director of the Nexus Institute, offered some insight into just how few survivors report their abuse to the police; 'Often', she explained, 'people don't want to go forward with the names. I mean, over 80 per cent of the people who we are seeing, or are on the waiting list, have no intention of going to the police.' Eileen Calder suggested that the corresponding figure for the Rape Crisis Centre was:

> about 75 per cent. I think that ours [proportion who do go to the police] is slightly higher because we get quite a few referrals from the police, which would then show up in our statistics. I am thinking of women who come into the centre for counselling. And out of those, a quarter have gone to the police.

This estimate tallies with the corresponding figure cited for the London Rape Crisis Centre between 1976 and 1980 (Temkin 1986). It is also worth noting that both Rape Crisis and the Nexus Institute are 'non-directional' organisations. This means that they do not pressure clients to contact statutory authorities against their will. They will, however, contact social services if they learn through the course of counselling that a child is under risk.

Reinforcing earlier arguments, the Belfast Rape Crisis Centre's Eileen Calder suggested that public awareness of sexual abuse has increased partly through public and political attention being focused through the lens of the media. The media's contribution to destigmatising what it means to be a 'survivor of child sex abuse' featured heavily in her comments:

> I think that the media has been part of raising public awareness. [There is] more awareness and slightly less feeling ashamed than there would have been ten years ago. I think people now … intelligent people know now, at least logically, that people are not to blame for being sexually abused. If they come in here and they still don't feel it, they know it up here [points to head]. So at least there is that kind of logical awareness about it that it was wrong and it wasn't their fault. That doesn't change how they feel

> inside, but it might change whether they are prepared to come forward, because there is a bit more knowledge.

Unpacking the nature and extent of media influence on audience perceptions is complex and problematic (Miller and Philo 1999). Certainly, determining its precise nature lies outside the remit of this book. But that does not mean that certain inferences about the influence of the media cannot be made. There is clear evidence to suggest that media representations of crime and deviance, in general terms, can influence the number of people reporting offences to the police (Maguire 1997). And there was a broad consensus among practitioners that media representations of sex crime can be instrumental in encouraging survivors to disclose. But the most important insights into this issue must come from survivors themselves.

Jennifer (not her real name) was abused by her uncle from the age of six. She did not disclose until she was 23, several years after the abuse had stopped. When asked if media coverage influenced her personally, Jennifer confirmed:

> Yes, most definitely ... because what you tend to do is put it to the back of your mind and try to forget about it. All those years you try to act like it never happened, you try to forget that, and every single time you read an article or see it on the TV it brings it up again. And it might cause you problems because when it brings it up you can have all sorts of depressions and anxiety problems, but at least it is coming up there. And burying it does you absolutely no good. It just stores up problems for later. I think that there is an increasing amount of people, because of the press, that are willing to come forward ... It's because, you know, if they read somebody else's story they think, 'I'm not the only one'.

It is not suggested that media influences are the only, or even the main, reason why survivors decide to come forward. But it is important to recognise the role that media coverage can play in demystifying social problems, like child sex abuse, and contributing to the creation of a climate in which survivors feel less inhibited, ashamed and stigmatised in coming forward. Jennifer explained that a range of factors motivated her finally to break her silence. In particular, concern for the welfare of others, which had featured as a powerful deterrent against disclosing, now acted as a prime incentive:

> Lots of things. My own problems, a suicide attempt ... I just wasn't coping at all. I wasn't coping with life. And also there were no other girl children in my extended family, until near enough the time when I disclosed there were three others born, three girl children born within three years. And I think that it was that that led me up to it as well. So I was worried about them, and also my parents had changed a lot and were a lot more understanding.

Christine explained that concern for others was perhaps her greatest motivation in contacting the police:

> I suppose the real reason that I didn't care then about the parents was the thought of somebody else feeling the way I did. For years I hid the feelings of how disgusted I was at myself and how disgusted I was at what was happening to me, and letting it happen to me, you know. I never thought of that until maybe after I had my own kids. And I looked at the kids and went, 'No. No child should feel the way I feel, and I am not going to let them.'

West (1996) echoes a number of these themes, suggesting that 'Fear of sullied reputation, anticipation of harrowing investigations when criminal justice procedures are invoked, feelings of shame, self-blame and fear of revenge attacks or condemnation by family or sex-partner all discourage disclosure' (1996: 52; see also Morris 1987; Temkin 1986, 1987; Bannister 1992; Heidensohn 2002; Wilson and Silverman 2002; Zedner 2002). Media discourse can be an effective mechanism for addressing at least some of these fears and concerns.

The RUC CARE co-ordinator offered her impression of the positive role that media images can play in encouraging survivors to report their abuse. Her comments closely reflect those made by Christine and Jennifer: 'It does make people realise that they are not alone, they are not the only ones that have ever been sexually abused. It also makes people realise that by coming forward to a court they can prevent other victims from having to go through the same thing.' However, statements about press representations of child sex abuse were not all positive. In addition to the above points on increasing social awareness, practitioners expressed a range of concerns regarding the manner in which child sex abuse is represented to news readers. It is to the criticisms and concerns about sex crime in the press that we turn next.

The Reinforcement of Stereotypical Images

As noted previously, sex offenders cannot be easily identified and 'picked out' of a crowd. There is no consistent model or typology into which they can be accurately placed for the purposes of identification and isolation – and public denunciation. In short, 'it is not possible to describe the "typical" child molester' (Grubin 1998: 14). Yet all those practitioners interviewed for this research – including those who commended the press for their contribution to raising social awareness – maintained that media portrayals often imply that child sex offenders are somehow identifiably different (see also Soothill and Walby 1991; Kitzinger 1996; West 1996; Websdale 1999; Thomas 2000). The Director of the Probation Board for Northern Ireland, Oliver Brannigan, outlined his concerns regarding certain sections of the press:

> Some of the press here completely stereotype offenders by portraying them as 'beasts' and 'monsters', as if they had suddenly descended from a land that none of us know … [T]hen they are faced with the local priest, the local minister, the local headmaster, the local solicitor and suddenly this man who was a paragon of virtue and a protector of young people has suddenly, overnight, become some untouchable beast, where as a matter of fact, he was never a paragon of virtue and he is not an untouchable beast. He is just someone who has transgressed very seriously against the norms of this society and has damaged a lot of people. But he is portrayed as some sort of an alien.

Despite their clear differences on other issues (see above), Eileen Calder, of the Belfast Rape Crisis Centre, shared Oliver Brannigan's assessment of press representations of child sex offenders. She stressed that 'the use of words like "beast" and "monster" … does give people the impression that ordinary men do not commit these crimes. Oliver Brannigan and I would agree on that'. And the Director of the Nexus Institute, Dominica McGowan, was concerned in particular that press coverage promotes the view that the greatest threat to children's safety is posed by strangers rather than by those they know:

> It's more about those beasts out there, those animals who are not like us, so there is an 'us and them' situation, and it creates in people a sense of 'baddies and goodies', and it is very black and white. First of all it creates panic, 'Watch your child, don't let them out of your sight because somebody is going to pounce on it and it

> will look like a big hairy monster'. And then it assuages that panic in some way by saying, 'Oh, we can pick these people out ... because you will see this person coming towards you with his knuckles trailing along the ground'.

It was these two elements of press coverage – the use of emotive language and the suggestion that strangers pose the greatest threat – that practitioners identified as most problematic. Concern about the promotion of stereotypical, reductionist images of child molesters was shared to varying degrees by all those practitioners who participated in this study.

Distinguishing between Markets

Most practitioners drew clear distinctions between representations of child sex abuse in the daily and Sunday newspapers. Some went further, directing their comments at particular newspapers within the daily or weekly markets. Some went so far as to target individual journalists. The PBNI's Oliver Brannigan cautioned that 'you have to distinguish between the broadsheets and the couple of tabloids [the Sunday papers] that we have here'. When asked if the press in Northern Ireland are responsible in their coverage of sex crime, the RUC's Chief Information Officer responded, 'With some exceptions, yes; the exceptions being some of the Sunday newspapers'. Olwyn Lyner, Chief Executive of the Northern Ireland Association for the Care and Resettlement of Offenders (NIACRO), was more critical. She hesitated even to call the contents of Sunday newspapers 'news':

> In general terms there isn't much 'news' [gesturing inverted commas] in the Sundays, so they are just regurgitating what they have read and what's been there during the week. And they are putting whatever class of spin that their readers who buy and pay a pound or whatever want to hear in relation to that. There is less news in it, and there is more rubbish ... in the Sunday papers.

Dominica McGowan, Director of the Nexus Institute, made a clear distinction between market sectors:

> I know that there is some good proactive journalism out there [and] when I went through our press cuttings I was really quite surprised and quite pleased to find that Northern Ireland isn't that bad. Most

> of the responsible ones were done by local [regional] newspapers and I thought, 'That's very good'. The ones that had SEX BEAST CAGED were papers like the *News of the World*, and the Sunday [regional] newspapers as well. The Sunday arm of the [*Belfast*] *Telegraph* [the *Sunday Life*] was terrible in particular. It had one front-page spread about a sex abuse case and it was placed beside something about the Lottery.

And the co-ordinator of the RUC CARE unit offered a similar appraisal:

> The Sundays seem to be obsessed. You never lift a Sunday paper, and I'm talking about a tabloid, without some reference to 'sicko', 'pervert' 'alien sex beast' ... always, always. I read the Sunday tabloids to keep myself up to date with the movement of sex offenders in Northern Ireland.

Thus there was a broadly shared concern across the major organisations – counselling services, police, probation and other criminal justice agencies – concerning the promotion of stereotypical images of the risks and perpetrators of child sex abuse. And there was wide agreement that the Sunday press are more prone to producing such representations than the dailies. On these issues, then, there was a degree of consensus, even between those organisations that conflict on other matters. It was in the evaluation of these issues – the perceived consequences of sensationalist, inaccurate and misleading coverage – that differences of opinion became apparent.

The Consequences of Stereotypical Images

The PBNI's Director, Oliver Brannigan, having criticised the press for portraying stereotypical images of child sex offenders, and stressing the differences between daily and Sunday coverage, went on to offer an overall evaluation of press representations of child sex abuse in Northern Ireland: 'I think that they [the press] are fairly restrained. By and large, I think that if you strip the headlines and alter the vocabulary a bit, even in the tabloids, I think that the tabloids here haven't been too bad.' These comments perhaps err on the side of diplomacy. The implication is that Sunday press coverage would be fine if the headlines were changed and the stories rewritten; that would not leave much of the original item behind. Nevertheless, the general thrust of the statement is clear enough. There are problems with press coverage, but the situation could be worse. Again, the PBNI and the Belfast Rape Crisis Centre were uncharacteristically synchronised on this issue. Spokesperson for the latter, Eileen Calder, proposed:

> If you look at articles that have been written in Northern Ireland over the last two or three years [since 1995], just off the top of my head now, you'll sit down and see those awful headlines, but in the actual body of the article you don't get that. I think that you can criticise them, but I think that they do very well. At the end of the day they do more good than they do harm.

This statement, made in 1998, is at odds with one made two years previously. The Belfast Rape Crisis Annual Report for 1994–6 was highly critical of the press's treatment of sex crime, stating that Northern Ireland 'is a society dominated by tabloid journalism which either trivialises or sensationalises the serious issues of sexual violence' (1996: 3). In terms of the above, though, both Eileen Calder and Oliver Brannigan suggest that it is the headlines that are the problem rather than the nature of the stories below. The implication is that sensational and misleading headlines are of relatively minor importance when compared with the underlying narratives. This is an important contention to which I will return in the next chapter. More pressing here, though, is that other practitioners expressed deep concerns regarding the possible effects of press representations. Some felt that the press compound an already inaccurate view of offenders and reinforce rather than challenge the prevailing misconceptions of danger and risk (see also Kitzinger 1999b). The former co-ordinator of the RUC CARE unit suggested: 'I would say that it is overwhelmingly the press that creates this monster in people's minds. There's no doubt that once the press gets something they will shake it to death and get as much mileage as they can.' And the current co-ordinator of the CARE unit suggested:

> I think that most people think that a sex offender is going to jump out and grab the first child that walks past their gate. And they don't know about the grooming process, the process where sex offenders work on parents and groom parents as well as the child.

This view was shared by Jennifer:

> [E]veryone thinks that it's the stranger on the street hiding behind a bush, and the vast majority of survivors I know, it's not. It's either a family member or a friend of the family. Because, you know,

> strangers don't do it because if you abuse a child and you are a total stranger to that child the child is going to run off and tell their parents. But if you are a friend ... what abusers do is they get to know the children and they get to know the parents, or they are a member of the family because then there is less chance of the child ever telling. If that is a trusted and respected member of the community then the child doesn't want to tell. And they are not stupid, you know, they are very intelligent people.

The Chief Executive of NIACRO, Olwyn Lyner, offered her impression of the problems with representations of child sex abuse in both the daily and the Sunday press (see also Lyner 1998):

> I don't think it is telling the community the truth about where the risks for their children are. If we say that our whole purpose is reducing victimisation, then people need to know where the risk is. And they don't need to have their eye on a ball over there that ... is a minimal risk, as opposed to other risks that they may have the opportunity to gain greater control of. So while the community and parents and families are fed myths about where the dangers are, we are not doing a good enough job in protecting children.

For the co-ordinator of the RUC CARE unit, representations of child sex abuse are narrow and misleading and – reflecting the discussion of news values in Chapter 3 – are driven by the commercial need to sensationalise and shock, rather than the social need to increase knowledge:

> I think that they give the sensationalist story, but don't mop up afterwards with a positive message. They put a spin on a story and give the lurid detail as much as they can without identifying the child, but they don't say at the end of the story, 'In order to prevent this happening to your child, we suggest a, b, c, d and e'. Do you know where they are? Do you know who they're with? What time do they come in at night? Do you ask them have they had a good day? Do you take time to talk to your child? If your child starts to tell you something, do you say 'I'm too busy now, tell me again'? ... that sort of thing. It's very basic.

For some practitioners, then, press representations are not only held to be inaccurate and misleading in terms of the dissemination and consolidation of stereotypical images of the sex offender and the identification of the wrong areas of risk. They also fail to provide sufficient information regarding the measures that might be taken to protect children. Building on her previous comments, the Nexus Director proposed that the reductionist portrayal of child sex offenders in the press might actually undermine preventive measures taken to reduce victimization:

> It is actually contributing to a child's vulnerability because it makes the parents take the wrong steps to protect their children ... Like bringing their child to the school bus and then picking them up from the school bus because they think that somewhere between the school and home some madman will grab them and take them away, whereas what will happen is that ninety per cent of child abusers will target their own child. They don't need to be going out and looking round the schools, all they have to do is go into their living rooms and they will find their own child sitting in front of them.

So while practitioners agreed that there are problems with the manner in which child sex offences are reported, and broadly accorded that the problems are more pronounced in the Sunday than the daily press, they differed significantly in their views on the importance of those problems. What is clear is that different groups and source organisations maintained different standards of what is acceptable and what is unacceptable, what is sensational and what is restrained, what is misleading and potentially damaging and what is informative and helpful.

It is interesting to note that in each of these statements the press are assumed to have a direct responsibility to highlight the correct areas of risk and portray the issue of child sex abuse in a way that reflects the social reality of the problem. Reflecting the liberal pluralist reading of news production, journalists are considered to be autonomous players. The implication is that they can report the reality of child sex abuse, but choose not to. It is also worth pointing out at this stage that none of the practitioners have made reference to their own role and responsibilities in the news production process. The notion of social responsibility as it applies to both journalists and practitioners – particularly in a small jurisdiction like Northern Ireland – is central to understanding the construction of child sex abuse and other forms of sex crime considered in this study. Accordingly, it is discussed further in the next chapter. First, though, some conclusions can be usefully drawn from the above.

Conclusions

Practitioners' views on the construction of sex crime in press discourse, while demonstrating some common ground, also show clear variations and, at times, diametrically opposed stances. Four points can be made by way of summary and conclusion.

First, the majority of practitioners acknowledged that newsprint journalism has contributed to increasing social awareness about child sex abuse in Northern Ireland. There is overwhelming evidence presented here to suggest that media representations of child sex abuse – both factual and fictional – can and do have an impact on the number of survivors breaking their silence and disclosing their abuse, either to counselling organisations or the police. In particular, media representations can reassure survivors that they are not alone, that they are not to blame and that help is available. While praising the role of the press in this capacity, however, practitioners were also concerned about the style and content of sex crime coverage.

Secondly, all practitioners interviewed in this study were critical of the press, though some more than others, for promoting stereotypical images of child sex offenders. In particular, the use of emotive labels – 'monster', 'beast', 'fiend' – that stress the 'otherness' of offenders, and the disproportionate focus on cases of stranger abuse were identified as reinforcing misleading stereotypes. The majority of participants differentiated between the daily and Sunday press, arguing that the problems are more pronounced in the latter. Some, though by no means all, commended the daily press for their sensitive treatment of the sex crime issue. Others did not differentiate between market sectors.

Thirdly, practitioners expressed different views about the degree of sensationalism and stereotyping in the press. Some proposed that the problems are essentially limited to headlines and that the underlying stories are in fact quite restrained. Others insisted that the problems with press representations are more fundamental.

And, finally, practitioners expressed different views about the consequences of press representations of child sex abuse. Some were not overly troubled by what they saw as a generally helpful press that occasionally 'makes mistakes' by using inappropriate headlines or a sensational front-page 'splash'. Others were concerned that highlighting the wrong areas of risk and stereotyping offenders may actually undermine efforts at reducing victimisation, the consequences of which might be extremely serious. The next chapter locates these points of consensus and controversy within an empirical framework.

Notes

1 Interviews and informal conversations were conducted with a range of other groups, organisations and individuals involved in some way with sex crime, including barristers, solicitors and housing executive officers. These latter groups play an important part in various areas related to sex crime, but are less involved with the construction of sex crime as news (see also Chapter 8).
2 For an account of the Brendan Smyth affair, see Chapter 5.
3 Further suggesting the influence of media coverage, the Belfast Rape Crisis Annual Report for 1994–6 states that 'There are more [calls to the centre] when national TV e.g. *Cracker* features rape and publicises our number after the programme' (1996: 7).

Chapter 7

Concerns in context

Introduction

The aim in the last chapter was to identify points of agreement and dispute regarding the construction of sex crime in the press. The aim in this chapter is to try to resolve some key issues by locating practitioners' and journalists' often conflicting claims within an empirical framework. The analysis conducted in Chapter 4 provides the foundations for the following evaluation, which focuses on the language and structure of sex crime narratives, how different types of offence and offender are represented, the promotion of stranger-danger, and the contextualisation of sex crime in press discourse.

The Language of Sex Crime Narratives

The use of sensational and reductionist language in the construction of sex crime narratives was a concern shared by all practitioners. In particular, journalists were criticised for their use of labels like 'beast', 'monster' and 'fiend', which stress the 'otherness' of child molesters and contribute to the generation of an inaccurate and misleading stereotype of offenders. The following sections establish the extent to which these criticisms apply to the daily and Sunday press in Northern Ireland.

The daily press

Sensationalist terms like 'beast', 'monster' and 'fiend' were virtually absent from daily press coverage. In the *Irish News*, for example, of the 30 news items reporting 23 cases of child sex abuse, and the 70 items reporting 43 cases of sex crime overall, none of these terms appeared even once. In fact, their use was virtually negligible in all the daily newspapers. The *Belfast Telegraph*'s Chris Thornton offered his impression of the place of stereotypical labels in press representations of sex crime:

> It would depend on the style of the paper. Tabloids would tend to do more of that sort of stuff ... I would try to take on board about over-sensationalising a story, over-emphasising things. I don't think I have ever used the word 'monster'. I think I have used 'sex fiend' before, but I think I would try to avoid it.

The term 'monster' did not appear in any headlines between 1985 and 1997 – even in the Sunday press, though in the latter it was used liberally in the main text. Other terms such as 'sex fiend' and 'sex beast' were used only rarely, appearing in just five of the 410 headlines in the daily press. It is significant that four of these headlines were printed in the *News Lette*r. 'GIRLS GIVEN SEX FIEND WARNING' (30 January 1985: front page) and 'FURY OVER FREED CHILD SEX BEAST' (25 January 1997: 2) are two such examples (see also *News Letter*, 5 January 1990: 9; 17 January 1990: 8). The other appeared in a *Belfast Telegraph* item entitled 'POLICE HUNT SEX FIEND' (2 January 1997: 5), though this story related to the sexual assault of an adult rather than a child. That these labels appeared in the *News Letter* more often than in the other dailies (four headlines from 43 items reporting child sex offences and 81 sex crime items overall) reflects that newspaper's more tabloid-orientated style. Still, the use of these terms was rare, and they were not incorporated into the main texts of any stories in the daily press.

The Sunday press

The use of stereotypical language was much more evident in the Sunday press than in the dailies, though their use was restricted almost entirely to the *Sunday World*. The terms 'sex beast', 'monster' and 'fiend', for example, did not feature much in the headlines of either Sunday newspaper. But in the main text of *Sunday World* narratives, they appeared as a matter of course. One story – remarkably similar to the police officer's description in the previous chapter – carried the headline 'DON'T DUMP SICKO HERE' and began, 'Evil sex beast [named offender] has been re-housed back in Ulster in a street where children play' (*Sunday World*, 5 January 1997: 7). The imagery throughout was unambiguous. The figure of the sexual predator is clearly established and juxtaposed against that of carefree children playing, oblivious to the dangers they apparently face. His sub-human nature is conveyed in the terms 'sicko' and 'beast'. Significantly, and this was the case with all stories on released sex offenders, there is a clear assumption of recidivism, a taken-for-granted notion that sex offenders *will* reoffend (see also Thomas 2000). This suggestion is reinforced still further by the description of the offender as a predatory 'sex beast', as 'evil' (see also Websdale 1999).

The vocabulary of these narratives gives the clear indication that offenders are aliens and outcasts, rather than friends, relatives and members of the community. The *Sunday World* Editor, Jim McDowell, had clear views on the use of these labels:

> The PBNI used to be in the offices above us, and I used to be carpeted [by them and they would ask me] 'why do you call these people monsters?' And I said, 'That's what the victims call them'. Survivors of sex crime call them fucking monsters, and I said that we are the newspaper that these people come to and if they call them monsters, we'll call them monsters, it's dead simple.

Indeed, Jennifer, a survivor of child sex abuse whose story was reported in the regional press, fully supported this style of language:

> One of the great things that I think they do is they actually call them 'monsters' and all sorts of horrible words, and I think that's great because that's exactly what these people are. I had never thought about [my uncle] like that before. He wasn't a monster, he was my uncle ... he wasn't a monster, he wasn't a fiend. And I hadn't felt any anger before then. I hadn't been able to feel any anger. And that was the first time that I thought, 'Yes, he is a fucking bastard, he is a fucking monster'. And I felt vindicated by the fact that someone had actually acknowledged that what he had done to me was horrific. And I thought that that was absolutely brilliant.

This statement suggests that media coverage can provide a kind of catharsis for those who have suffered abuse. The Belfast Rape Crisis Centre's Eileen Calder explained that going to the press can give survivors 'a sense of power and control over their lives to be able to speak out about the injustices that they have suffered and also to help others'. The individual therapeutic benefits of having one's abuser publicly denounced in the press may be considerable and should not be underestimated, still less overlooked. But on the issue of identifying the correct areas of risk, and thereby trying to reduce further victimisation, the message from practitioners and survivors interviewed for this research was clear. As Peter (not his real name), a survivor of child sex abuse, put it:

> The media need to let the public know an abuser can be the most innocent-looking person in creation. They range from the man next door to your uncle, to a brother or a sister. Priests, of course, lawyers, doctors, anyone ... A sexual abuser has no sign to tell of his intent, none whatsoever. And that needs to come across.

This, then, casts the use of emotive labels in a different light. The use of stereotypical terms, as many have noted (Grubin 1998; Soothill *et al* 1998; Thomas 2000), gives the impression that offenders are clearly distinguishable from 'normal' people.

The use of sensationalist language is not difficult to understand. Eileen Calder, spokesperson for the Belfast Rape Crisis Centre, suggested that 'journalists are just ordinary human beings like anyone else, and most people see it [child sex abuse] as the most foul and disgusting crime that anyone can commit. So I don't think that it is surprising that it is portrayed in that way'. Our sense of what we are derives to an extent from 'pointing to what we are not' (Ericson *et al* 1987: 356). Words like 'monster' and 'beast' emphasise (albeit inaccurately) the social distance between news readers and the deviants they read about. In this sense, as noted in Chapter 2, the demonisation of child sex offenders serves to consolidate moral boundaries and promote social solidarity. Moreover, sensationalist terms imbue press narratives with a strong sense of moral outrage. They are emphatic expressions of feeling and emotion which seek to invoke a reciprocal reaction (including the all-important element of shock) within the reader. Garland (2000: 352) observes that 'Outrage and anger are the culture's antidotes to fear and anxiety, and the open expression of these emotions is part of the consolation and therapy it offers' (see also Katz 1988). Few issues are as emotive, or provoke as much outrage and anger, as child sex abuse.

The 'danger to children from sex offenders has become a matter of obsessive public concern' (West 1996: 52). The intense and undifferentiated public fear and loathing of child molesters is clear from the public reaction to their re-housing in the community (MacVean 2000, Thompson 2000; Wilson and Silverman 2002; see also *Observer* 6 August 2000). Media representations are central in generating and sustaining the sensibilities that underpin such volatile reactions. As West (1996: 52) points out:

> Sexually motivated child abductions and murders are extremely rare but receive massive media attention when they occur. In reality, young children are far more often killed by their parents or step-parents than by outsiders and are far more at risk of death from traffic accidents than from sexual predators.

Media representations 'give shape and emotional inflection to our experience of crime, but do so in a way that is largely dictated by the structure and values of the media rather than the phenomena it represents' (Garland 2000: 363). In the Sunday press the emphasis is on shock, even more so than in the dailies. The demonisation of child sex offenders simultaneously taps into and reinforces popular fear and loathing. However (emotionally) understandable this style of press coverage may seem, the typification of child molesters obfuscates the social reality – it misleads, misinterprets, misrepresents and misinforms. And in such a climate, a number of practitioners argued that it may undermine efforts targeted at prevention and protection.

The Conflation of Offenders and Offences

Also striking is how and in what context sensationalist language was used. In the dailies, as noted, the use of terms like 'beast' and 'monster' was rare, restricted to a few headlines describing cases of child sex abuse. The stories that appeared below the headlines were, as journalists contended, 'relatively conservative'. In the Sundays, however, and again mainly in the *Sunday World*, these labels headlined stories that differed enormously. This point is illustrated well by the following examples.

The headline 'Y-FRONT AFFRONT' introduced a story beginning, 'An Ulster sex fiend – who gets his kicks from stealing underwear from clotheslines – leaves a trademark behind …' (*Sunday World* 29 January 1995: 21). And in another item the headline, 'GAYS IGNORE CAMERAS TO HAVE SEX IN TOILETS' began a story which used identical terminology: 'Gay sex fiends are hopping off busses and having it off in a public loo' (*Sunday World* 26 January 1997: 13).

The point is that virtually the same terminology was used in each of these cases, and in cases of child sex abuse, to describe behaviours that varied enormously in terms of deviance, dangerousness and the levels of harm done. The indiscriminate use of these stereotypical labels makes explicit a reductionist sentiment underpinning the majority of sex crime stories in the *Sunday World* and the *Sunday Life*, though to a lesser extent in the latter. Predatory child sex abusers, people who steal underwear from clothes-lines and consenting adult homosexuals who engage in sexual acts in a public place are the same – they are all 'sex beasts', 'sex fiends' and 'sickos'.

This is precisely the style of reporting that practitioners were so critical of. Using the same terms to describe sexually deviant acts that differ enormously in both their perceived and actual levels of harmfulness conflates the vast diversity of behaviours variously deemed criminal into one problem. The distinction between those behaviours is blurred and, as a result, so too is the distinction between the perpetrators, who are categorised into a single homogeneous criminal 'type'. This lack of differentiation reinforces the myth that all sex offenders are equally dangerous, that they all pose an equivalent threat and that they are all to be reviled with the same emotional intensity. The former co-ordinator of the RUC CARE unit suggested that this is the prevailing sentiment in local communities: 'It's the paedophile bandwagon, everybody goes on about paedophiles but in actual fact they are talking about anybody, any sex offender ... Those people who are looking those people out of their area, they don't see the difference between a sex offender and a paedophile. It's all one group.' And the Director of the Northern Ireland Probation Service, Oliver Brannigan, remarked that, 'sex offenders are seen as this group of people who are all the same'. The homogenisation of sex offenders through the indiscriminate use of stereotypical and sensationalist labels contributes to both generating and sustaining this perception by implicitly re-inforcing its validity in the public imagination.

It was not just practitioners who expressed concern over the language and imagery used in the Sunday tabloid press. Noel Doran, Editor for the *Irish News*, agreed that the Sunday papers are capable of sensationalism in the extreme:

> There's no doubt about that. You would have to accept that they are coming out on a Sunday, they have a lot of space, they have their own agenda so they are inevitably going to concentrate on the more sensational aspects of it. Sometimes you pick up one of the two tabloids, the *Sunday Life* or the *Sunday World*, and you would wince a little at some of their covers.

The picture here is very different from that portrayed by the daily press. Sensationalist coverage and stereotypical and highly reductionist language are commonplace. However, some practitioners suggested that notwithstanding customarily emotive and shocking headlines the actual text of stories tends to be reasonably sober. The suggestion is that headlines are only of secondary significance. The above evidence clearly demonstrates that sensationalist vocabulary proliferated throughout Sunday press narratives, but this contention still merits some further consideration.

The Importance of Headlines: Framing the Narrative

Ericson *et al* (1987: 153) note the conventional wisdom among journalists that the only two parts of news stories people read are the first and the last sentences. One senior reporter interviewed for this research suggested that, for some news readers, even this may be an overstatement:

> I have a brother and a son who both read every word and there is a class of people who do that, but generally if the headline is dull and the intro is dull I don't read it because there are all sorts of other things I could be doing.

This being so, headlines are the first and sometimes the only description of sex crimes and their perpetrators that people read. The headline is fundamental in signifying the intended meaning of the narrative. As Hall *et al* (1978: 84) point out, headlines 'are frequently an accurate, if simple, guide to the themes implicit in a story which the newspapers consider represent its most "newsworthy" angle'. They place a particular inflection on the narrative, priming the reader for what is to follow and quite deliberately encouraging his or her sensibilities along a particular path (Barthes 1977). In so doing, headlines 'provide an ideological direction to … reporting' (Jenkins 1996: 59). It is the headline that must first draw attention through the suggestion of shock, scandal or drama, indicating why the story is important and, most importantly, why the reader should read on. In their research on audience reception, Miller and Philo (1999: 29) find that 'some participants could accurately reproduce the language of headlines over a year after they had seen them'. Headlines cannot be dismissed as of only secondary impact or ancillary concern.

Significantly, though, the journalists who write the stories do not generally write the headlines too. Headlines are the responsibility of sub-editors, along with page design and layouts. The *Belfast Telegraph*'s Chris Thornton explained, 'One of the areas where a reporter has the least control is the headlines which go on a story … in fact, no control except in unusual circumstances, and actually that's where we get a lot of grief'. With respect to the Sunday press, the Belfast Rape Crisis spokesperson, Eileen Calder, confirmed, 'Well, the excuse that I get from those ones round the corner [the *Sunday World*] is that Dublin writes the headlines'. But while Chris Thornton accepted that journalistic control over headlines is limited, he was not convinced that reporters can wash their hands of the responsibility altogether:

> Yeah, it's a journalistic cliché that reporters always blame sub-editors for things that go wrong ... Whenever someone rings up they complain to the reporter ... yeah ... subs are an easy scapegoat in that respect. [But] reporters know that they can steer a story a certain way toward the sub-editor, with a headline and that sort of stuff, because of the way they would ... write the introduction for a story.

So there is little to stop journalists from suggesting headlines or possible appropriate wordings through the introduction to the story. A first sentence that reads 'evil child sex beast ...' is likely to encourage a similarly evocative headline. There is, however, another more complicated issue here relating to journalistic autonomy in the news production process.

The idea that journalists can structure stories in accordance with their own journalistic preferences, over and above the form and flavour of the newspaper for which they write, is problematic. Journalists working for tabloid newspapers habitually produce tabloid copy, just as those writing for broadsheets produce broadsheet copy. Consistent editorial influence and the occupational socialisation and professional adaptation of journalists into a particular newsroom culture do much to ensure that the production of sex crime narratives remains in keeping with the overall style of that newspaper. Changing, or at least moderating, the nature of the language used is not, therefore, a matter solely for individual journalists – reporters have insufficient autonomy in that respect. Rather, it is a matter primarily for senior editorial staff. This point is returned to later on.

The Promotion of 'Stranger-danger'

Child sex abuse is most often committed within a context of close social familiarity and is frequently intrafamilial in nature (Nelson 1987; Grubin 1998; NSPCC 1995, cited by Lyner 1998). Yet the research literature consistently demonstrates that cases of 'stranger-danger' attract disproportionately high levels of media attention (Soothill and Walby 1991; Benedict 1992; Jenkins 1992; West 1996; Grubin 1998; Kitzinger 1996, 1999b; Websdale 1999). A number of practitioners criticised the press for portraying child sex abusers as outsiders and strangers – fortifying this image through the use of stereotypical language – and argued that this obscures the reality of the phenomenon and highlights the wrong areas of risk. It is this concern that is evaluated next.

Notions of dangerousness and fear of strangers

Though certainly not the only source of information about the dangers of child sex abuse, press discourse is one cultural form which has devoted an enormous amount of attention to the problem in recent years. The suggestion that media portrayals of child sex offenders can have a direct impact on popular consciousness about risk and danger has been made already. Though the relationship is complex and mediated by a range of factors including personal experience, age, gender, race and national identity (Kitzinger 1999a), it seems absurd to suggest that media images do not influence public attitudes and beliefs (Meyers 1997; Miller and Philo 1999). They may be even more influential where large sections of the public have few if any empirical referents (Young 1981), such as with the 'hidden' problem of child sex abuse.

Kitzinger and Skidmore (1995: 9) find in their study of news production and audience reception that 'although the majority of research participants "knew" a child was more likely to be sexually abused by someone they knew, their fear focused on strangers'. This finding raises important questions about the acceptance of and resistance to various types of information about child sex abuse, and social problems more generally (see also Philo 1999). In particular, it highlights the possibility that news readers may not always organise crime avoidance and preventive measures in accordance with what they 'know' to be the 'real' sources of danger, but may target such measures at the source of their 'fear' – in this case strangers. The association of 'dangerousness' with strangers is reinforced on at least two levels.

First, Bauman (2000: 39) observes that notions of risk and dangerousness tend to sharpen on the 'ambivalent and unpredictable image of the Stranger' (see also Hale 1996). Instead of helping us to 'overcome primitive fears of otherness, contemporary trends encourage us to redefine and dread the Other' (Lianos with Douglas 2000: 103). Faced with the ontological insecurities of everyday life (Giddens 1990), a place of safety from the perceived dangers 'outside' is a crucial part of social existence (Bauman 1998) – and what better place than the home (see also Loader *et al* 1998).

The association of risk and dangerousness with the unknown 'other' tends to be discussed in relation to societies where 'high crime rates are accepted as a normal social fact and crime-avoidance becomes an organising principle of everyday life' (Garland and Sparks 2000: 16). But it also applies more generally. A number of scholars have highlighted the, at best, extremely tenuous links between fear of crime and actual crime rates (Marsh 1991; O'Connell and Whelan 1996; O'Mahony *et al* 2000). People make sense of their social world in accordance with the ideational resources available to them (Gamson and Modigliani 1989; Gamson *et al* 1992), which might typically include 'popular wisdom, personal experiences and bits of media discourse' (Sasson 1995: 9). This is especially significant in Northern Ireland, where, as O'Mahony *et al* (2000) point out, crime rates are low (see also Geary *et al* 2000). There is little to suggest that the image of the stranger will be any less potent in a small jurisdiction like Northern Ireland than it will in social orders characterised by higher levels of crime.

The second point relates to the intellectual and emotional difficulty attached to child sex abuse. People find it is easier to 'make sense' of the phenomenon if it is perceived as something which happens in the public sphere and can therefore be shut out (Kitzinger and Skidmore 1995; Kitzinger 1996). It is harder to conceptualise child sex abuse as something that infiltrates and violates the perceived 'safety' of the home (Smart 1989), that haven from the dangers outside. Suspicious strangers constitute a threat which, although fearsome, is more practicable than the reality; that most sexual assaults are committed by acquaintances, friends and relatives.[1] Journalists described both a general reluctance in Northern Ireland to accept that child sex abuse is a widespread problem, and a resistance to the notion that abuse most often happens in a domestic context. This parallels findings in other research, which journalists – themselves parents and citizens – find it difficult even to think about, still less write about the social context within which the vast majority of abuse takes place (Smart 1989; see also Grubin 1998).

The aggregate impact of these two factors – the general fear of strangers and the reluctance to think about child sex abuse as a domestic problem – tapped into and consolidated by parallel images in the press – reinforces misconceptions about where the risks of child sex abuse lie.

The daily press

There was a marked change in the proportion of cases involving notions of 'stranger-danger' over the period 1985 to 1997. In 1985, 64 per cent of cases (7 from 11) indicated that the alleged abuse had been committed by a stranger. In 1990,[2] the figure had fallen to 33 per cent (5 from 15). By

1995 it had fallen still further to 23 per cent (3 from 13) and 1997 provided the smallest figure of 10 per cent (3 from 30 cases). Estimates regarding the actual levels of child sex abuse by strangers have varied considerably with some surveys indicating that the proportion may be as low as 4 per cent (NSPCC 1995, cited by Lyner 1998). Grubin (1998: 15), in his review of the research literature, concludes that 'the majority of child molesters sexually assault children they know. Most studies find this to be the case three-quarters of the time with up to 80% of abuse taking place in either the home of the offender or the home of the victim' (Bradford *et al* 1988).[3] That means that up to 25 per cent of abuse could be committed by strangers. Should this latter estimate be more accurate, the proportion of cases of stranger-danger reported in the daily press in 1997 (10 per cent) would not in fact be an over-representation, but a substantial understatement.

Most significant, though, is the considerable decrease in the promotion of images of 'stranger-danger' in the dailies between 1985 and 1997. The figures are small and perhaps therefore limiting, but the trend seems consistent none the less. The fall in the number of cases of stranger-danger can be explained at least in part by the corresponding increase in press coverage of institutional abuse – discussed previously – in which the offender and survivor are by definition known to each other. The number of cases of this form of child sex abuse rose in the daily press from four in 1995 (31 per cent of child sex abuse cases) to 18 in 1997 (64 per cent).

The Sunday press

The number of child sex abuse cases reported in the Sunday press was much smaller than that in the dailies (18 cases and 35 items in total). One third of child sex offence cases, (6 out of 18, or 33 per cent) described incidents in which there was no suggestion of a prior relationship between survivor and perpetrator. This is higher than the majority of estimates in the research literature (Grubin 1998), but lower than in some studies (Kelly *et al* 1991). More significant is the fact that five of the six cases were concentrated in 1995 and 1997. Whereas press attention to cases of stranger-danger in the daily press decreased over time, coverage of these types of offence in the Sunday press substantially increased.

All the items reporting cases of stranger-danger appeared in the *Sunday World*. I have already suggested that, the language used in the weekly newspapers was far more sensational and inflammatory than that employed in the dailies. This was especially the case in representations of stranger assaults where the notion of the 'sex beast' could be played out to the full. 'EVIL SEX BEASTS COPPED BY RUC' (*Sunday World* 1 January 1995: 7) headlined one story of an attempted abduction of a child from a local supermarket.[4] Another reported that 'notorious Larne sex beast [named offender] absconded from a bail hostel and went on the run' (*Sunday World* 5 January 1997: 14).

The relative infrequency of child sex abuse stories in the Sunday press is partly attributable to the different case types reported in those newspapers. The bifurcated coverage, polarised between the most and least serious examples of sexual offending, meant that 'trivial' offences accounted for a substantial proportion of reportage (see also Chapter 4). Yet, one form of child sex abuse, which research suggests is highly prevalent (Finkelhor 1984; Parton 1985; Smart 1989; Grubin 1998), was virtually absent from coverage in both the daily and the Sunday press. The following section considers the press representation of incest.

Reporting Incest

A victim survey carried out in 1995 by the National Society for the Prevention of Cruelty to Children (NSPCC) found that 31 per cent of the survivors who took part had been abused by a close relative. Grubin (1998: 8) proposes, on the basis of his review of the existing research, that intrafamilial abuse may account for 'up to a half of the abuse experienced by girls', though no corresponding figure is offered for boys. Baker and Duncan (1985), in collaboration with the polling agency MORI, estimate that 14 per cent of child sex abuse is incestuous in nature (cited in Grubin 1998). And Eileen Calder, spokesperson for the Belfast Rape Crisis Centre, cited that organisation's statistics:

> We have the people who come to us as a result of sexual abuse in childhood and when you look at them as a separate population from the ones who have been raped as adults, almost 50 per cent have been abused by fathers. One year the step-fathers beat the fathers at it, but it's usually fathers, and then step-fathers [and] uncles.

There is thus some considerable room for debate in the proportion of child sex abuse that is incestuous. Even if the most conservative estimates are the more accurate, however, the coverage of this form of sex crime in both the daily and Sunday press was much smaller still, accounting for only 5 per cent of cases and 5 per cent of items reporting child sex offences (5 cases from 93 and 12 out of 233 items).

The daily press

In the daily press incest accounted for only 6 per cent of child sex-abuse cases (4 cases out of 67).[5] No cases were reported in 1985 or 1990, one was reported in 1995 and the remaining three appeared in 1997, perhaps indicating a growing awareness of the problem and an increasing willingness to talk about it. In only one headline was the nature of the offence specified directly – 'INCEST VICTIM PICKS UP THE PIECES' (*Belfast Telegraph* 11 January 1997: 13). This story quoted an incest survivor directly: 'It's hard to believe that anybody could deliberately and consciously hurt a child, but that is what incest and sex abuse is all about.' The piece was different from most examples of sex crime reporting in that it sought to communicate the emotional and physical damage that can be caused by intrafamilial abuse, rather than simply focusing on the 'facts' of the case. In addition, it usefully outlined the launch of a new programme for survivors, providing an element of wider discussion which was extremely rare overall. The term 'incest' appeared in only one other item, in either the headline or the text of the narrative (*Irish Times* 18 January 1997: 4). There are several possible reasons for the under-representation of incest cases in the press.

One common argument journalists advanced against specifying child sex abuse as incestuous was that to do so risks revealing the survivor's identity through 'jigsaw identification'. What this means is that if one newspaper names the full charge of incest and another names the offender but blurs the charge the two pieces of information can be combined and the child's identity discovered. Readership and circulation figures indicate that more than four fifths of people in Northern Ireland read only one of the daily newspapers.[6] As might be expected, there is a larger overlap between the daily and weekly press. But bearing in mind that only a very few sex crime cases were reported in both daily and Sunday newspapers, the chances of jigsaw identification actually happening would appear to be slight. Of course, any possibility that the survivor of child sex abuse might be put through further anguish, however slight, must be taken seriously. But there are ways around this potential problem, as Geoff Martin, Editor for the *News Letter*, explained:

> [M]edia editors talk to each other all the time and it's very, very easy for the media to decide what they are going to do. But the judges very often take that ability away from us by saying that we can't identify this man because it was his niece who was abused. Well then you simply leave out the fact that it was his niece who

was abused and if all the media do that then the link can't be made.

While this is undoubtedly true, it somewhat misses the point of portraying the social reality of sex crime and indicates the importance of identifying the alleged perpetrator wherever possible, thus conjuring the news value of 'personalisation' ('individual pathology') and adding to the drama of a sex crime narrative. Printing the name of an offender and excluding the nature of the crime decontextualise the offence by disregarding the relationship between the survivor and the offender, thus obscuring the true nature of a large proportion of child sex abuse. By contrast, excluding the name, identifying the abuse as incestuous and establishing the close social proximity between survivor and offender would help to disseminate the social reality of the problem. It seems a simple enough point to make, but the Press Complaints Commission Code of Practice 1995, under the heading 'Children in Sex Cases', states the following in relation to reporting child sex abuse (cited in Stephenson and Bromley 1998: 174):

> The press should not, even where the law does not prohibit it, identify children under the age of 16 who are involved in cases concerning sexual offences, whether as victims or as witnesses or defendants. In any press report of a case involving a sexual offence against a child:
>
> - the adult should be identified
> - the term 'incest', where applicable, should not be used
> - the offence should be described as 'serious offences against young children' or similar appropriate wording
> - the child should not be identified
> - care should be taken that nothing in the report implies the relationship between the accused and the child.

So it is not just a journalistic preference, but a formal code of practice to obscure the fact that much child sex abuse is intrafamilial. No journalists referred to the Code of Practice directly in their comments, but Rosie Uffindel, Social Affairs Correspondent for the *Irish News*, alluded to similar constraints when she described the complications in contextualising child sex abuse at both organisational and individual levels:

> Because we are constrained by the legal side of reporting incest most newspapers go down the line of 'you print the name of the accused and blur the charge', you know, just say sex abuse or whatever, but don't say incest because obviously then you identify the child. That's unless the case is such that the editors get together and say that they are going to name the full charge. But that is a lot of effort to go to for every story. So we are constrained by the legal side of things, and wanting to protect the child's identity in which case you avoid saying that it is incest, in which case people reading the paper wouldn't have a clue that in the majority of cases that is what we are dealing with. Perhaps to get the reality across the editors should get together and decide to stop naming the offenders and talk about the actual offences, because that is the only way we are going to get this across.

This is a good example of forward thinking, but it was a minority view among reporters and editors. The fundamentals of journalism dictate that if a name is available, and there is no legal restriction against using it, the name will be printed. In the words of one daily reporter, 'As my old tutor in journalism school said, "Name the bastard!"' For this reason, promoting the reality of child sex abuse – and sex crime more generally – should not be left to journalists alone.

The Sunday press

Only one case and four news items in the Sunday press specified the offence of incest, all of which appeared in the same edition of the *Sunday Life* (19 January 1997: 2). Beneath the headline 'RUC MAN'S EVIL SECRET SEX PAST REVEALED BY THE SISTERS HE ABUSED', the story of the sexual abuse of two sisters unfolded, relating the abuses to which they had been subjected throughout their childhood. 'Tests revealed that the girls' grandfather – now deceased – had also been their father' (*Sunday Life* 19 January 1997: 2). The adjacent report entitled 'THEY THOUGHT WE WERE THEIR SISTERS' explained that the girls had also been raped by their brother, a full-time reserve in the RUC. They had each given birth to healthy children, though for thirty years they did not 'find out which of the two abusers had fathered those children', and 'had to allow their daughters to be brought up as their sisters'. Another item headlined 'HORRIFIED BY SENTENCE' reported that 'the 12-month suspended sentence handed down to an RUC officer for indecent assault has horrified the sisters he abused' (19 January 1997: 2).

The story contained all the news values required for a compelling, dramatic and, above all, shocking sex crime narrative. 'Human tragedy' and 'negative consequences' were obvious from the nature of the offences being described. That one of the perpetrators was an RUC officer conjured not only the news values of 'personalisation' and, more specifically, 'individual pathology', but also linked the abuse with notable or high-status individuals. The passing of a 12-month suspended sentence was an 'unexpected outcome', which contributed further to the 'human tragedy' of the story by foregrounding the lack of justice for the survivors who had the courage to proceed through the courts. The text was set around a half-page photograph, in silhouette, of the two sisters standing side by side. The caption read, 'SHARING A TERRIBLE PAST: abused and raped during their childhood, sisters ... have had to live with the terrible life-long consequences of incest'.

This story, penned by the *Sunday Life*'s Stephanie Bell, starkly conveyed the psychological and emotional harm suffered by the survivors which long outlasted any physical damage. One of the sisters explained that 'I've managed to bury all the feelings and emotion but I know one day it will have to come flooding out'. Another item related that, for one sister, 'her early experience had tragically meant that she would never know the joy of a close personal relationship'.

Survivors interviewed for this research made similar statements about the difficulties of coming to terms with abuse and its long-term effects (see also Maguire and Corbett 1987; Morris 1987; Bannister 1992; Morgan and Zedner 1992; Finkelhor, 1997). And the Belfast Rape Crisis Centre's Annual Report for 1994–6 suggests that, 'Unlike adult women who may have had positive sexual experiences before their attack, survivors of sexual abuse may feel that this will never be possible for them' (1996: 30). Yet this was one of only three reports in the entire archive to include discussion of these factors.

In addition to conveying the lasting emotional trauma experienced by survivors of child sex abuse, the importance of seeking help was communicated in the statement that one survivor 'could never have found the courage to talk about her abuse without the help of counselling'. And fears about reporting abuse to the authorities – a particularly sensitive issue in Northern Ireland – were assuaged by the claim that 'Cathy was full of praise for the RUC officers at the CARE unit who were in charge of the investigation'. This statement was made all the more resonant by the fact that one of her abusers was himself a police officer. In addition, the use of language was moderate when compared with other reports in the Sunday press. Much criticised terms like 'beast' and 'monster' did not feature; the abusers were identified in terms of their relationship to the abused – as father, brother and grandfather. Most often they were simply called 'abusers'. The contextualisation of the abuse was unambiguous and the absence of sensationalism was marked.

This story illustrated how the social reality of child sex abuse can be represented within a framework that is both compelling and dramatic – and therefore highly newsworthy – without being sensationalist or prurient. Unlike much of the coverage in the Sunday press, it demonstrated how narratives can communicate a clear and, most importantly, useful message about child sex abuse. More could have been done. For example, numbers for telephone help lines could have been provided along with contact details for counselling organisations. Direct pleas by RUC CARE officers for survivors to come forward and report their abuse could have been incorporated into the narrative, or formed the basis of an adjacent item. Such pleas were relatively frequent in 1985, but became increasingly infrequent in subsequent time periods.

Ultimately, regardless of how insightful the story may have been, it was the only example of such coverage in the entire archive. As such, it is unlikely to have much impact on wider perceptions of child sex abuse in Northern Ireland.

The Inclusion of Detail

A final issue which merits some attention here is the amount of detail included in sex crime narratives. Some practitioners were concerned about this aspect of press coverage. One suggested that journalists will 'give the lurid detail as much as they can without identifying the child'. But the complaint was far from universal. Eileen Calder, spokesperson for the Belfast Rape Crisis Centre, outlined her experiences of both the daily and Sunday newspapers:

> I have sat with countless survivors while they have talked to journalists in the *Sunday Life* [*Belfast*], *Telegraph*, *Sunday World*, and they have told the most graphic detail and most of it has been left out at the discretion of the reporter writing the article ... reporters do a difficult job.

As in other areas, then, there were conflicting views about the amount of detail included in the coverage of child sex-abuse cases.

The daily press

Consideration of the archive provides clear evidence that the graphic description of child sex offences (or indeed any offences) in the daily press was rare. Only a few cases, either in or out of the courtroom, included the reporting of details over and above the legal classification of sex crimes (such as indecent assault, rape or sexual assault) or the nature of the charges (for example, two counts of gross indecency). On this issue, the *Irish News*' Editor, Noel Doran, said:

> The term 'conservative' would probably apply to the *Irish News*. We certainly would always be very cautious about the amount of detail in a case. Sometimes it's inevitable, it just has to be covered, but we would be fairly sensitive to the amount of detail in those types of cases. We would be very conscious of the fact that we regard ourselves as having a family readership, and whilst there's some things which can't be spared, particularly in sex abuse cases, we would generally avoid trying to be too graphic.

Similar claims were made about sex crime coverage in the *News Letter*. The Editor, Geoff Martin, explained:

> When you report on sex crime in courts, we have a responsibility to record only the court proceedings. Often when we do that we do get readers complaining that we have been salacious or sensationalist, but if the detail of the court reporting at times becomes salacious and maybe sensationalist, well then that is bound to be reflected in the coverage. All I would say about that is that we try to rise above the most basic instincts in our reporting of court cases. We try to be clear and factual and not get bogged down in the detail, but by their very nature you can't report a murder without reporting some gruesome details.

And *Belfast Telegraph* News Editor, Paul Connelly, insisted that 'we will remove any gruesome details from court reports'. More than it being simply a matter of journalistic discretion, this news editor indicated that the minimising of salacious detail amounts to an unwritten editorial policy: 'Oh yeah, absolutely. If it was particularly salacious copy we would [remove it] unless it had to be [included] … there was no way round it.' This begged the obvious question:

> How could there be no way round it? Well, for example, all newspapers would do this … for the sake of argument some guy grabs a woman and forces her to give oral sex to him. You will never see that in a newspaper, you will see '… forced to perform a sexual act'. Now some of the really downmarket newspapers like the *Sunday Sport* might do things like that, but basically newspapers … right across the spectrum … will not do that … particularly with children.

The implication is that the graphic description of sex offences, especially in the coverage of child sex abuse cases, amounts to poor journalism. So daily journalists broadly accorded that representations of sex crime in the daily press in Northern Ireland are relatively restrained in the amount of detail they would include, or would even wish to include. These claims are borne out by evidence in the archive.[7]

The Sunday press

The level of detail included in Sunday press narratives was similar to that in the dailies and requires little further comment here. It is perhaps worth noting, however, that since the specific details regarding the nature of offences most often come to light during the court case, the Sunday press lack of courtroom narratives may account in part for the lack of graphic descriptions of sex crimes. But as with the examination of daily press items above, the charge that the press will include as much detail as is legally permissible seems misplaced. It is not so much the amount of detail included in Sunday reports that is striking. Rather – as the above sections have illustrated – it is the selection of stories in the first instance, the language used in the construction of headlines and the main text and the highly polemical, editorialised nature of much of the reporting that set the two markets apart.

Research in other jurisdictions has found that sensationalist and prurient coverage – particularly of adult sex crimes – has been the norm (Soothill and Walby 1991; Jenkins 1992; Lees 1995). In the context of Northern Ireland, the inclusion of graphic detail is clearly the exception. Soothill and Walby (1991: 68; see also Grover and Soothill 1995) point out that newspapers can present rape trials as 'soft porn' describing the acts 'with such vivid detail as they occurred'. But they find that 'there was little or no sexual titillation employed' during the reporting of trials involving children (1991: 54). Evidence in this study reflects this finding. It is important to be clear, however, that a certain level of detail is necessary if the trauma and sometimes extremely violent nature of sex crimes are to be communicated. On this issue, the comments of Belfast Rape Crisis Centre spokesperson, Eileen Calder, are instructive:

> I remember ... reading in the *Daily Mirror* about a soldier who had committed a number of sexual offences against a woman and they weren't able to charge him with rape because he hadn't penetrated her. The maximum sentence would have been two years and he had actually put his fist inside her. Now you may say that that was terrible for them to describe that in such graphic detail, but it was actually necessary. It was necessary for them to do that to say, 'Right, this is what indecent assault is, indecent assault can be someone touching your breast in a bar that you don't want to, or it can be someone raping you with a broken bottle'. So at times it is perfectly legitimate and necessary to go into graphic detail, although possibly they were not doing it for the right reasons.

Thus journalists and practitioners espoused a range of different views regarding the level of detail which is necessary or appropriate in the representation of sex crimes. Some maintained that 'too much' graphic detail should be removed from press reports because they do nothing to advance the story. Others argued that a certain amount of detail is necessary if the full impact and true nature of sex crime are to be effectively communicated to the news reading audience. The question, then, is 'how much is too much?' The answer may be influenced by a wide range of factors including professional standards/ethics, organisational policy, individual morality, market environment and cultural context. It will always be a value judgement and, as such, will always be contestable. The view taken here is that provided the story is constructed in clinical rather than titillating language, the detailed description of sexual victimisation can be an extremely effective means of communicating the horrors of sexual abuse (see also Benedict 1992). It is not so much the amount of detail, but how that detail is portrayed that is paramount in determining the overall impression given.

Conclusions

On the basis of the evidence presented in this chapter, a number of proposals can be advanced about the nature of representations of child sex abuse, and sex crime coverage more generally, in the Northern Ireland press.

The stereotypical labelling of child sex offenders in the daily press was rare. In fact, the terms of which practitioners were so critical – 'beast', 'monster', 'fiend' and so on – were virtually absent from daily press representations. They were used comparatively frequently in the Sunday press, and proliferated in press narratives in the *Sunday World*. It was in this latter newspaper that the sensational stereotype of the child sex abuser featured most heavily. Crucially, in addition to the stereotypical representation of child sex offenders, the indiscriminate use of these terms serves to homogenise sex crime and sex offenders into a highly inaccurate and misleading deviant 'type', obscuring the full nature and range of sex crimes throughout society.

Images of stranger-danger are reinforced in the press in a number of ways. Quantitatively, however, narratives of stranger assaults were not as prevalent as many practitioners suggested. It is perhaps significant, that participants were asked to give their impressions of sex crime coverage 'from cold'. That is, they did not review press reports before the interviews took place and were, therefore, speaking about press representations from their own professional *and general* knowledge. The police and both counselling organisations keep press archives, and others may do the same. And practitioners are undoubtedly more sensitised than most to the issues of stereotyping, case selection, contextualisation and so on. But the answers they gave in a professional capacity cannot be disconnected entirely from their experiences as news consumers and citizens. It has been suggested already that media images of predatory strangers are more potent than those of offenders known to the victim. Such images may be more enduring for practitioners also. It is perhaps not the steady drip of sex crime coverage in the press, but the occasional downpour that results from high-profile and sensational cases that shapes news readers' (including practitioners') impressions. In short, those cases that employ the stereotypical descriptive labels and promote the potent and culturally resonant image of the dangerous and predatory stranger may be more likely to stick in the mind.

In the daily press, images of stranger-danger featured most heavily in 1985 and 1990, but decreased substantially to a much smaller proportion in 1997. In the *Sunday Life*, the explicit suggestion that strangers pose the greatest threat to children barely featured at all. It was only in the *Sunday World* that cases of stranger-danger increased in prevalence over time. These representations were constructed using the sensationalist and highly emotive language and imagery typical of that newspaper.

The suggestion that the problems with press representations of child sex abuse are limited to the headlines is not borne out by the evidence presented here. As noted, daily representations are relatively conservative in their use of language. This conservatism applies to both the headlines and the text. The same can be said of the *Sunday Life*, albeit to a lesser extent. Again, however, the *Sunday World* is characterised by sensationalism and stereotyping from the initial selection of cases, to the construction of headlines, through the main text to the captions below the photographs. In fact, most of the concerns voiced by practitioners – either collectively or individually – were evident in the *Sunday World*'s representation of child sex abuse and other types of sex crime.

On this last issue, comments must remain speculative, but some tentative propositions can still be made. In the high-crime societies of late modernity, fear of crime focuses on the image of the stranger. There is little doubt that media representations have contributed to the generation of this climate of mistrust and suspicion of 'otherness'. The press are not the only, or even necessarily the most important source, of information about child sex abuse. But as the research described in this chapter indicates, it would be absurd to suggest that media representations are inconsequential. Reinforced by a strong cultural resistance to thinking about child sex abuse as a domestic problem, images of stranger-abuse are highly potent – even though they constitute the minority picture overall. As such, they may indeed, as a number of practitioners proposed, misdirect preventive measures taken to protect children.

In terms of case-based coverage the picture of child sex abuse being portrayed in the press improved at least in some respects in most newspapers throughout period 1985 to 1997. What is known of the social reality of the phenomenon was reflected more closely in the archive for 1997 than in that for 1985. At the same time, however, as indicated in Chapter 4, other problems – like the lack of depth and contextualisation in sex crime coverage, and the decreasing prevalence of discussions of wider issues such as causes, risks and prevention – have worsened.

Thus there have been clear improvements in the representation of child sex abuse over time, and an undeniable increase in social awareness throughout wider society which is without doubt partly attributable to media discourse. But in line with the views of many practitioners, there are still clear problems. The next chapter seeks to locate the changing representations of child sex abuse – and the representation of sex crime more generally – within a wider context. Having suggested the reasons for the increase in press attention to sex crime in Chapter 5, the task now is to explain the nature of sex crime coverage in the press.

Notes

1 This would appear to be a type of displacement. For a discussion from a psychoanalytic perspective of the role of anxiety and, in particular, its displacement in fear of crime, see Jefferson and Hollway (2000).

2 Though the overall number of sex crime cases decreased in 1990, the number of child sex-abuse cases increased.

3 Grubin (1998: 15) goes on to note that community surveys tend to demonstrate higher rates of extrafamilial abuse than offender studies. Kelly *et al* (1991), for example, in a survey of 1,200 16- to 21-year-olds, find that of those who reported some form of sexually abusive experience as children, 44 per cent involved offences by strangers. If examples of 'flashing' are excluded, however, the figure drops substantially to 18 per cent. This latter estimate is more in keeping with the rest of the research literature. These disparities make clear the variance that can occur depending on the definition of abuse used in studies.

4 This case involved the attempted abduction of a child from a supermarket. The assailants were caught on closed circuit television cameras (CCTV), like in the abduction and murder of the young child James Bulger from a shopping facility in 1993, and parallels were made with the Bulger case throughout. The linkages to the Bulger case automatically added drama to the narrative because what happened to the young boy is so well known (see, for example, Cumberbatch 1998). Here, though, the abductors were adults. The deviance of the assailants was stressed still further by the suggestion that 'recently, *Sunday World* revealed that one of the duo may be posing as a transvestite – a man dressed as a woman'.

5 These four cases were reported in seven news items, appearing in *The Irish Times* (19/01/95: 3, 17/01/97: 6, 18/01/97: 4, 25/01/97: front page, 25/01/97: 3); the *Belfast Telegraph* (11/01/97: 13); and the *News Letter* (25/01/97: 9).

6 Readership figures for the sample newspapers are included in Appendix III.

7 In only one case in the daily press could this stance be questioned. In 1995, all three daily newspapers carried the story of a former headmaster accused of molesting his pupils. Compared with how most other cases were reported, both the *News Letter* and the *Belfast Telegraph* were explicit in their attention to detail. The *Belfast Telegraph* (31/01/95: 6) item entitled 'TEACHER ABUSED US, WOMAN TELLS COURT' reported that the accused had 'put the zip of his trousers down and placed her [the defendant's] hand inside his trousers'. The *News Letter* (31/01/95: 3) story headlined 'EX-HEAD DENIES SEXUAL ASSAULTS' quoted one survivor's testimony: 'He would prise your legs open and push himself into you. He would push his penis against my vagina.' In these narratives it could be argued that the inclusion of explicitly sexual descriptions – though entirely factual and taken directly from the

courtroom – did little to advance the story, but may have had a certain salacious interest for a certain type of reader. Still, the coverage of this case was the only potential challenge to the above statement that journalists will 'try not to get bogged down in the detail of cases ... particularly with children'.

Chapter 8

Responsibility and management

Introduction

This chapter seeks to explain why press representations of sex crime in Northern Ireland take on the form and style that they do. A number of issues need to be addressed in light of the preceding discussion. First, the importance of social context is revisited and considered specifically in terms of its impact on news production in a small jurisdiction like Northern Ireland. Secondly, how journalists perceive their own roles in the construction of sex crime is explored, focusing especially on the influences that shape journalistic activities, the level of control they have over those influences and their perceptions of how practitioners can, do and should contribute to the news production process. Thirdly, a similar analysis is applied to practitioners. Here I want explore how they perceive both their own and journalists' roles in the construction of sex crime, the media strategies employed by different groups and how wider cultural sensibilities may affect the way in which different organisations approach media discourse.

News Agendas and the Construction of Sex Crime

Most straightforwardly, the style and content of sex crime coverage can be understood in terms of the news agendas to which the daily and Sunday press subscribe. The daily newspapers considered here are essentially broadsheet in nature. Notwithstanding the progressive influence of tabloidisation on the press more generally, the representations of sex crime in those papers would be expected to reflect that style of journalism. The relatively conservative coverage in the three daily broadsheets, the *Belfast Telegraph*, *The Irish News* and the *Irish Times*, reflects the style characteristic of those papers. And the more sensationalist representations in the *News Letter* equally reflect that paper's more sensationalist style. Indeed, given the mid-market audiences at which the dailies are targeted, it would be surprising if their coverage was not, in the main, reasonably conservative and restrained.

The Sunday papers, by contrast, are underpinned by tabloid values and interests. It is no great surprise, then, that the representation of sex crime in those papers reflects that style of journalism. The most extreme examples of sensationalist and stereotypical coverage appeared in the tabloids. That they were less concentrated in the *Sunday Life* than the *Sunday World* reflects the fact that the former paper is a mid-market tabloid, while the latter could be reasonably described as more downmarket. The prevailing style of 'shock-horror' journalism, particularly in the *Sunday World*, reflects qualities that are typical of contemporary tabloid culture.

So the news agendas that the Northern Ireland press – and indeed the press anywhere – subscribe to are key determinants of the style of sex crime coverage they produce. That much is obvious. But it is by no means the complete picture. Examples of overt sensationalism comprise only one (albeit highly visible) constituent of sex crime coverage. Other problems were evidenced more widely. The subtler, but equally serious problems in both the daily and Sunday press – including the substantial decline in discussions of general issues of concern, the often implicit promotion of images of stranger-danger and the increasing decontextualisation of sex crime narratives – cannot be so easily explained in terms of underpinning news values. There are deeper influences at work here, relating to the wider economic, political, social, organisational and cultural contexts in which the news is produced, which affect fundamentally the activities of both journalists and their sources and the resultant construction of sex crime in Northern Ireland. Identifying and explaining these influences is the objective in the remainder of this chapter.

The Influence of Social Context in a Small Jurisdiction

Geoff Martin, Editor for the *News Letter*, suggested that the social context within which the news is produced has an important influence on how journalists approach their work and, consequently, on the form and flavour of the news product:

> I think that this is where the regional newspapers differ from the [London-based] red-top tabloids, to the extent that we are part of the community that we operate in. You are part of the community and you tend to take a more responsible or sensitive line towards things that are potentially contentious ... You don't go out of your way to titillate readers, you don't go out of your way to be sensationalist.

In this view, which represents that of most daily journalists, the production of news in a small jurisdiction carries with it a certain sense of social responsibility that serves to restrain the representation of sex crime. Certainly, sex crime narratives in the daily press tap into and reinforce the moral consensus around the collective demonisation of sex offenders in Northern Ireland (see Chapter 2). They help to express prevailing popular (punitive) sentiments. But they avoid mining those sentiments too deeply. A certain emotional distance is maintained. The underpinning journalistic imperative of objectivity is diluted, but still apparent. The aim is to inform and frequently to shock (see Chapter 3); but not in a way that incites hysteria or causes panic – not through unmitigated sensationalism.

Journalists writing for the Sunday press similarly highlighted their roles as members of the community. Representations of sex crime here, however, suggest a very different interpretation of what this means. Here, the notion of social responsibility is inflected in a way that means adopting a populist punitive voice and mining the emotions of the readership as deeply as possible. Like daily newspapers, the Sunday press tap into and reinforce the moral consensus around the collective demonisation of sex offenders, but they do so in a campaigning style characterised by unrestrained emotion which explicitly promotes popular fear and loathing. Again, the aim is to inform and, to an even greater extent than in the dailies, to shock; but in the Sunday press this is often done in a highly sensationalist style seemingly geared precisely to incite hysteria and cause panic. As the *Sunday World* Editor, Jim McDowell, declared, 'I live in this community ... Objectivity is not an issue. Impartiality is not an issue. I object to it'.

The point is that journalists' sense of social responsibility within a small jurisdiction like Northern Ireland may have a profound influence on the way in which sex crimes are constructed. But the nature of that influence may vary enormously, depending on how journalists interpret what it means to be part of the community, and how that resonates with their perceptions of what it means to be a journalist (and often a parent) within that social context. With this in mind, it is instructive to consider more closely how journalists and practitioners perceived their and each other's roles in the construction of sex crime in the Northern Ireland press.

Journalists' Roles in the Construction of Sex Crime

Social responsibility and the construction of sex crime

Criticisms of press coverage did not just come from practitioners. Journalists, too, expressed dissatisfaction with their own treatment of the issue (both individually and as a profession), and were forthright in pointing out the factors and forces that prevent them from covering stories in the way they would prefer. The majority of journalists were committed to the view that they have a clear responsibility to provide accurate and useful information about the problem of sex crime. That is not to suggest, of course, that the views they expressed represent the views of all journalists. As Chapter 4 illustrated, there are those who would argue that it is not the press's job to educate the public, and the notion of social responsibility may differ from paper to paper, and person to person. There are undoubtedly journalists who see the sensationalist aspect of sex crimes and little else besides. But in line with the views of a substantial majority of research participants, the argument proffered here is that both journalists and practitioners do have a responsibility – an important responsibility – to inform news audiences about the social reality of sex crime in Northern Ireland.[1] The problem for journalists is that there are forces in the current market – both internal and external to news agencies – which militate against the in-depth discussion of sex crime in the press and, by consequence, the dissemination of the social reality.

Organisational constraints and the construction of sex crime

In previous chapters, journalists identified a number of organisational factors that influence the manner in which sex crimes are reported. For example, the limitation of resources – financial, temporal and human – influences how they represent important social issues. It is not difficult to see how these constraints impact directly on the press construction of sex crime. One daily journalist complained that the restrictions imposed by the time constraints of news production make it difficult to cover sex crimes in sufficient depth:

> I think that we generally fall very short of what would be well intentioned and that's probably down to the pressure of getting a story out, you know. In our case we're a daily news operation and it's bang, bang, get a story out, and it doesn't necessarily get the reflection it would deserve.

Another placed the emphasis on the growing tension between the role of newspapers as profit-making enterprises and their role as providers of public information:

> It is a reporter's job to report, but a newspaper is also a business, and more and more and more this last fifteen years the role of the accountant has become more prominent and the accountant now would be on a par with the editor. Whereas before it was just someone who balanced the books, now the accountant sets the budgets. The accountant should not have any editorial input as to the line of the paper. But he can affect it to the extent that if the budget's too tight you are not going to be able to employ as many reporters as you need to cover important issues as thoroughly as they should be.

Evidence of these changes – regarding in particular the depth of coverage and the location of sex crimes within a wider context – is apparent from the analysis in Chapter 4. Here we saw that the proportion of news items discussing issues of wider concern – such as causes, risks and prevention, legal debates and resources for survivors – fell steeply throughout the 1980s and 1990s. It is clear why, for a variety of organisational and commercial reasons, events and individuals tend to be favoured over debates and issues. But for some journalists, though market conditions place clear pressures on the process of making news, those pressures should not be allowed to compromise the integrity and usefulness of the reportage being produced:

> As a business we have a responsibility to sell newspapers, but we are imparting information to the public and we have a responsibility to make sure that that information is accurate. And not just in specific stories. I think that we also have a responsibility to provide an overall impression, and that is something I don't think newspapers have even started to think about.

This statement makes direct reference to one of the clearest problems identified in this book – the lack of context in sex crime cases. The journalist making the statement, however, like many of those who expressed concern with the manner in which sex crimes are reported, occupies a less senior position within the news agency. This is significant because, in line with the radical reading of news production, the extent to which less senior journalists can influence the ultimate nature of the news product is limited. The issue of journalistic autonomy, therefore, and its influence on the construction of sex crime is addressed next.

Journalistic autonomy and the construction of sex crime

Chapter 2 demonstrated that journalists are constrained by a range of influences that safeguard the reproduction of the particular style and content of news journalism. Reporters do, of course, have their own personal values, views and experiences and these will inevitably, colour their reporting (to an extent). But on a routine basis, due to all those influences discussed previously – editorial influence, occupational socialisation, professional adaptation, career aspirations – there is little room within which those personal characteristics can find resonance. These influences shape all aspects of the news production process, including the representation of sex crime.

Reporters who expressed concern about the construction of sex crime in the press tended also to express frustration at their lack of influence and, thus, their lack of ability to bring about change. Of course certain issues – time constraints, for one – are beyond the control even of editors and owners. But on the allocation of resources, it is senior managers, not general reporters or correspondents, who make the decisions. So too is it senior staff who decide which stories are run and which are dropped, which are leads and which are fillers, which are cut and which are printed in full. With this hierarchy in mind, one daily journalist argued that any changes in the news production process that might address the current problems will come from news agencies' senior ranks:

> I think that senior management have an overall responsibility to look at the paper and say, 'Well, what are we saying about this offence if we put it on the front page?'. But I don't think that we go anywhere near educating people about that. Just through the conversations I have had with journalists over the year I get the impression that sometimes editors aren't even that fussed about the overall context, you know, they have a good story here and they want to use it … And in most newspapers on a local level you just

> have a bunch of staff who have been told to go out on a particular story and it is not down to them to think of the wider picture, because that's not their job. So the ultimate responsibility isn't with the reporter, it's with the senior staff.

Laying the blame for the problems with sex crime coverage – as some practitioners did – squarely and evenly at the foot of 'journalists' fails to acknowledge the hierarchy within newsrooms and the constraints on individual reporters to reproduce the style of coverage deemed appropriate within that working environment. The involvement of senior staff – and editors in particular – would be fundamental to any process of change aimed at addressing the problems that currently prevail.

It needs also to be acknowledged, however, that the responsibility for developing accurate and informative sex crime coverage does not lie with the press alone. Journalists were critical of the limitation of resources available to cover stories in sufficient depth. And reporters were critical of their senior management for not doing enough to bring about change. But nearly all journalists – senior staff included – were vexed and sometimes angered by what they see as highly critical practitioners who do little themselves to contribute to the construction of sex crime in the press. It is perhaps precisely because of the increasing limitation of resources that many journalists stressed the centrality of practitioners playing a more (pro)active role in the news production process.

Practitioners' Roles in the Construction of Sex Crime

The role of sources, as noted, is fundamental to the manufacture of the news product. The majority of practitioners were well aware of this, and many stressed the importance of engaging proactively as sources in the press construction of sex crime. Yet from the evidence in the archive and, perhaps most significantly, from journalists' comments, it would appear that while practitioners' advocacy of proactive news management was clear and unambiguous, the extent to which different organisations put this recommendation into practice differs enormously.

The prevalence of source organisations in the archive

More than half the items in the archive (52 per cent, or 251 out of 483 items) included a direct quotation from a group, organisation or individual. In 74 of the 483 items, direct quotations from court proceedings (whether by the alleged victim or offender, the police, or legal practitioners) were incorporated into the text. Police quotations appeared in 30 of the 483 items. Care organisations appeared as accredited sources in 23 news items, comprising: Social Services (3),[2] the Belfast Rape Crisis Centre (7), the Nexus Institute (1), and others (2).[3] Comment from the Northern Ireland Probation Service featured in one item in the archive, and NIACRO was neither quoted nor mentioned in any items. Alleged offenders and survivors were quoted in 18 and 27 news items respectively, though in the majority of these instances, their involvement may not have been through choice. Other sources included politicians (13 items), religious practitioners (in a professional capacity, not as offenders or victims – 4 items), academics (1 item) and a range of other activists and interested parties who secured press exposure for a single report or story.

What emerges from this picture is, as many journalists argued, a distinct lack of involvement of key agencies in the construction of press narratives about of sex crime. Others have illustrated source organisations actively competing in the media to promote their own values and interest, and rebut those of others (Beckett 1994; Sasson 1995; Miller 1998). The intention, as noted in Chapter 6, is to increase credibility and legitimacy in the public arena, stimulate resources and, ultimately, maximise definitional power and political influence. With respect to the construction of sex crime in Northern Ireland, however, the competition between organisations for media access was some distance from the frenetic field of contestation portrayed elsewhere. In fact, in the context of this research, the most striking characteristic of certain organisations' approach to news management is what appears to be media apathy.

Social responsibility and the construction of sex crime

Dominica McGowan, Director of the Nexus Institute, recognised that practitioners have an important role to play in the construction of sex crime in the press. 'As far as the press is concerned', she proposed, 'I think that we have a responsibility because we have the real information at the coalface to give to journalists.' She went on to argue, however, that the press 'have the responsibility to make space to report that [information], which they don't'. Thus both journalists and practitioners stressed that the responsibility to promote the reality of sex crime in the press is shared between news agencies and source organisations. As one reporter put it:

> I think that a lot of journalists would say that educating people about the reality isn't necessarily a job for journalists to do in the first place. That is the thing that the institutions should be doing … But we are a focus for that education, we are a channel for them to actually educate people.

Regardless of journalists' intentions and beliefs about their own role in the process, the media's potential as an educational resource is rendered effectively impotent if those institutions and organisations that might take the debate forward (which, with respect to sex crime, seems to me to be a pressing requirement) are not forthcoming. On this issue, Dominica McGowan acknowledged that the Nexus Institute should put more effort into engaging proactively in the news production process:

> I think that that is the bit that we probably fall down on. I think that we should probably be more proactive about inviting the press in to do proper stories, to do profiles of situations and people, including ourselves. To be fair to us, all of our time is actually tied up doing the work and we forget that there is this other bit to it.

Here too, then, the lack of resources is cited as a key obstacle against the promotion of in-depth coverage and debate around the problem of sex crime. The difficulties of managing a limited budget and allocating funds to deal simultaneously with operational, educational and public relations issues should not be understated. And organisational constraints do partly explain why the Nexus Institute appeared only once in the archive and seldom featured in the comments of reporters and editors. What is more striking, however, is the fact that comparatively resource-rich organisations appeared equally infrequently.

The vast majority of police comments were printed at the initial offence and investigation stage of coverage. In this context, they almost invariably involved issuing descriptions of offenders and requesting those with information to come forward. When police officers did issue advice on, for example, personal safety and crime prevention, it normally related to stranger assaults and was underpinned by the strong suggestion that the attacker could strike again – thus reinforcing the myth that strangers pose the greatest threat. On only two occasions[4] (both in 1985 and both urging rape survivors to report their abuse) did the police shift beyond the bounds of a specific investigation and offer advice on wider issues of concern. The current CARE co-ordinator accepted that, 'really the statutory agencies could sell the story better than they do, but the media could pick it up better than they do'. Again, then, the notion of shared responsibility is clear.

The Social Services appeared only three times in the archive as an accredited source, the Probation Service appeared only once and NIACRO did not appear at all.[5] Each of these organisations is well funded. Yet their contributions to media discourse were few and far between. It may be the case that organisations made contributions, perhaps as off-the-record disclosures, which went unattributed. But since one function of news management is to raise the profile of those providing information, this is unlikely. It seems that these organisations seldom appear in the press because of their approach to press discourse. On that basis, the Director of the Probation Service, Oliver Brannigan, was asked if he thought the PBNI should be more proactive in dealing with the press:

> Well, the answer is yes, but that is an 'apple pie and motherhood' answer. I think that we have to be very careful because the public get tired very quickly of non-sensational sex crime. And a message about sex crime, we should all work on that, but I think that's only … I think that the only way to get people to understand about sex crime will not be done through stories about sex offenders, it will be done through stories about sex crimes, criminality and about how sex offenders work. The BBC, ITV and most of the newspapers would have my home phone number. We don't get quoted that often. We get a fairly easy time from the press.

It certainly seems reasonable to suggest that one of the most effective means of disseminating the social reality of sex crime is to construct stories about 'crimes, criminality and about how sex offenders work'. And the call to produce more stories discussing issues of wider concern is timely, given that the prevalence of these items fell so dramatically from the 1980s to the 1990s (see Chapter 4). But surely, then, it is incumbent upon those organisations that are best placed to lead the discussion to take the initiative and actively promote those kinds of story in public discourse. The suggestion that organisations are 'getting an easy time' if they are seldom contacted or quoted misses completely the point of proactively using the media to communicate the social reality of sex crime to a wide audience. It might be suggested that it is precisely this type of media apathy that militates against portraying a fuller and more informative picture of sex crime in the press.

Cultural sensibilities and perceptions of survivor and offender groups

There is, however, another explanation, relating to social context and cultural change, which sheds some further light on why certain organisations featured so infrequently in the press. In recent decades there has been a clear shift in how the public and politicians view the problem of crime and, in particular, those who commit crime (Garland 2000; Lianos with Douglas 2000). As high crime rates have become an everyday 'social fact' in many jurisdictions, there has been a marked reduction in society's tolerance of offenders (Bauman 2000). As Garland and Sparks (2000: 17) note:

> Sections of the public [have] become less willing to countenance sympathy for the offender, more impatient with criminal justice policies that are experienced as failing, and more viscerally identified with the victim. The posture of understanding the offender was always a demanding and difficult attitude, more readily attained by liberal elites unaffected by crime or else by professional groups who make their living out of it. This posture increasingly gives way to that of *condemning* criminals and demanding that they be punished and controlled.

Thus, public tolerance of 'ordinary decent criminals' has diminished significantly and given way to a widely held punitive sentiment – articulated in and reinforced by, among others, the mass media. Sex crime, however, is neither viewed nor responded to as 'ordinary decent crime'. No other examples of deviance stimulate the same intensity of public revulsion and condemnation, especially when children are the victims (Thomas 2000; West 2000a, 2000b). Yet, as a number of practitioners pointed out and as the public reaction to the re-housing of released offenders clearly shows (Wilson and Silverman 2002), there is little differentiation between different types of sex offender in the public imagination. This problem is reinforced by the tendency of sections of the press to portray all sex offenders – child sex abusers, consensual homosexual offenders, flashers, rapists – as if they are the same (see Chapters 4 and 7). The sensationalist and stereotypical construction of sex crime serves to group different classifications of sex offender into one homogeneous criminal 'type'.

The mixture between the moral and emotional intensity with which the public revile (homogenised) sex offenders and the wider changes in cultural sensibilities towards crime and criminals more generally produce a highly volatile concoction. As noted in Chapter 2, a strong moral consensus, which transcends party politics and social conflict in Northern Ireland, has been built around the demonisation of the sex offender. In this highly charged climate, any comments that might be perceived – however inaccurately – as placing offenders' interests before those of survivors may face wide condemnation and, ultimately, do more harm than good for the source from which they issued. This, in turn, may have profound implications for some organisations' levels of engagement in press discourse.

Garland (2000: 351) remarks that, 'whoever speaks on behalf of the victim, speaks on behalf of us all'. The Probation Service and NIACRO, however, work primarily with offenders. NIACRO Chief Executive, Olwyn Lyner, argued that the public perception of organisations that work with offenders militates against their proactive involvement in press discourse about sex crime. It is simply bad PR to discuss offender issues in the press:

> Why do any of us work with offenders? The bottom line is that we work with offenders to reduce crime. But if you try to put forward a view that in any way seems to represent ... that there may be a more appropriate way to treat offenders than sensationalising their crime in the media, it is seen then that there is some balancing act that you are doing in favour of the offender that is against the victim. And it is almost impossible to be heard that the reason why we are actually in the business is actually to reduce victimisation. So when you put your head up, particularly if you are proactive in doing that, you are seen as if you are actually speaking on the rights of the offender.

This tension goes some way to explaining why NIACRO did not appear in any of the items in the archive, or in reporters' and editors' comments regarding the role of sources in the news production process. It may also be a significant factor in the Probation Services' lack of presence, though this was not clear from the Director's comments. Offender organisations may be less inclined to engage proactively with the press because of the resentment that their perceived position on sex offenders attracts. Similarly, journalists may be more inclined to contact survivor organisations because of the centrality of victims and victim issues in contemporary criminal justice discourses, and in media representations of crime and deviance (Chermak 1995; Garland 2000). Martin Lindsay, Editor of the *Sunday Life*, for example, noted that, 'all our stories would be victim-driven'.

So in terms of securing positive media exposure and, thus, a platform from which to challenge the prevailing myths around sex crime and sex offenders, it would seem that the chips are stacked firmly against those groups and organisations that are seen to represent offenders' interests. But it is precisely because of the current climate of fear and anxiety, the inaccuracy of media representations and the homogenisation of sex offenders in press discourse that the media contributions of experts on both survivor and offender issues are so vital.

Resource-poor Organisations and Media Activism

The lack of press input by the resource-rich Probation Service, NIACRO, the police and the Social Services becomes even more conspicuous when we consider the activities of the Belfast Rape Crisis Centre, the most under-funded organisation considered in this research. Despite its resource-poor status, the Belfast Rape Crisis Centre maintained a comparatively strong presence in the archive and was virtually ubiquitous in journalists' comments about the role that different groups play in the news production process. Given the resonance of images of the victim in popular and political consciousness, there is no doubt that survivor groups are better placed publicly to disseminate their views, and are likely to receive a more sympathetic hearing when they do so. As one journalist explained, the Rape Crisis spokesperson, Eileen Calder, 'embraces the press because, I mean, she has nothing really to lose. She wants to get the story out, she wants to get attention for the problems … and the press aren't going to turn on her'.

The moral high ground that survivor groups occupy in the public (and to an extent the press's) mind undoubtedly gives them an advantage in securing positive press exposure. However, the Nexus Institute is a survivor group, and its presence both in the archive and in journalists' comments was almost negligible. The Social Services, too, represent survivors' interests, and is extremely well funded relative to both Rape Crisis and the Nexus Institute. Yet this organisation featured infrequently in the archive and was absent entirely from journalists' comments on the roles of different organisations in the news production process. There is another key difference between the Rape Crisis Centre's approach to news management and that of other organisations: the Rape Crisis Centre is highly proactive.

Redressing the Balance of Resources

Normally, resource-poor organisations need to work harder in order to secure media access (Miller, D. 1993; Miller, L. 1993; Manning 2001). Resource-rich groups, by contrast – whose status as credible, legitimate and authoritative tends to be well established – may need to engage with the media only when their status, values or interests come under threat. Miller (1998: 71) notes that resource-poor groups 'are unlikely to be able to gain sustained positive media coverage in the face of strong competition from resource-rich organisations'. He also points out, however, that, 'resource-rich organisations do not always devote the main part of their efforts to managing the media' (1998: 70). This appears to be the case with the Probation Service, the Social Services and NIACRO, at least in terms of their involvement in the construction of sex crime in the press. When competition for media exposure on a given issue is limited (for whatever reason), resource-poor groups – like the Belfast Rape Crisis Centre – may find it easier to influence the debate, advance their status as accredited experts and increase their credibility, legitimacy and definitional power in the public arena.

Nevertheless, organisations with limited resources need to be skilful, adaptable and imaginative in order to secure sustained media coverage (Miller and Williams 1993). As Eileen Calder put it:

> If you want press coverage, you have to, to some level play, their game. And I think that that is something that we have learnt to do, and learnt to do in a very different way from the way probation do it. They probably have more money devoted to presenting their public profile than we have to run this whole centre here, and still they are constantly losing the battle. That's why they absolutely hate us, that is why they like to portray us as mad feminist women who have no sense of justice and law ... and that is not the case at all.

Setting aside for now these organisations' ideological differences, there are a number of ways in which the Rape Crisis Centre 'plays the game' in order to secure positive media coverage and promote victim issues in press discourse. One, as *News Letter* News Editor Steven Dempster pointed out, is providing an angle that will stimulate journalists' and news readers' interest: 'People want to read about personal experiences, they want the human angle ... Eileen Calder will get you somebody who's been through, say, Rohypnol [so-called 'date rape' drug]. And one Eileen Calder story on Rohypnol is going to get across a strong message.'

It could be suggested that there is a fine line between survivors willingly helping to communicate a message and survivors being exploited because they feel obliged – because of the counselling they have received – to go to the press to advance an organisation's interests. Organisations that refuse to provide 'a human angle' in this way should not be criticised, for the interests of the survivor must in every case come first, and undoubtedly those interests are not always best served by going to the press. However, Eileen Calder noted that the Rape Crisis policy on this issue has changed since the centre's opening in 1982:

> At the start, it would have been against our policy even to ask someone if they would be interested in speaking to the press, obviously because people feel a certain loyalty towards you or a certain gratefulness, which they don't need to feel. But they do tend to do that, and they may not have the power to say 'no'.

The softening of the position now was explained in terms of wider changes in social awareness about sex crime and the partial destigmatisation of being a survivor, and the increased understanding and expertise of some journalists who work with the centre on a regular basis. Also, that survivors of sex crime have been through a terrible ordeal does not mean that they are incapable of making a rational and informed decision – with the guidance of counsellors – about speaking to the press. Anonymity is always guaranteed, and survivors are only named if they specifically request to be so. It is crucial that survivors receive adequate care and support, but it is also crucial that they are not patronised. And it is worth noting that, should a survivor resolve to talk to the press, there is little a counsellor will be able to do about it. In such a situation, providing advice and support may be the only viable option.

Another (perhaps less controversial) and more routinely employed strategy is providing information to news agencies 'fit to print'. A substantial amount of the material that the press receives from the Rape Crisis Centre is pre-written in plain, straightforward language and frequently backed up with statistics. That the centre provides pre-packaged news items containing 'hard facts' in an appropriate journalistic format makes them more attractive to news editors seeking to fill pages and meet deadlines. This strategy is not unique to the Belfast Rape Crisis Centre. Catering to the needs of journalists is standard practice for all organisations that wish to maintain a profile in the public arena (McNair 1999). Dominica McGowan, for example, noted that the Nexus Institute engages in similar practice: 'Well we release most of our information through press releases, on a fairly regular basis but not like,

"Oh, it's time to do it again". And certainly if they were doing stories they would ring us up and ask us for a comment, or do an interview.' I am not suggesting that the Belfast Rape Crisis Centre is the only organisation that engages regularly and proactively with the press. The point is that, despite that organisation's resource-poor status, its media presence in the archive eclipsed all those other organisations considered in this research barring the courts and the police; that is, except for those institutions around which the press actively organise their crime news production and upon which journalists rely for routine access to information. A further insight into the very different levels of media activism demonstrated by source organisations can be gleaned from the comments of journalists themselves. As one daily reporter explained: 'I never hear from probation … I will now know a lot of the major players, but Nexus only came across about three weeks ago and I got this massive pack from them, I think it was their annual report or something.' And the Editor of the *Sunday World* maintained that, 'I have never met anybody from Nexus, and the only time I have ever heard from the Probation Board is when Breige [Gadd – former Director] or Oliver [Brannigan – current Director] want to carpet me over something'.

So in addition to the archival evidence of media activism, journalists, when asked about the role different organisations play in the news production process, almost invariably foregrounded the activities of the Belfast Rape Crisis Centre. *News Letter* Editor Geoff Martin, for example, described his newspaper's communication with other agencies:

> Well most organisations have annual reports which would usually generate press interest. We would usually get involved at that time. But certainly I know that we have done features in which the Rape Crisis Centre have helped us, and we have gone to them in order to get a responsible overview of the situation.

And a daily journalist confirmed, 'We do a lot of work with Eileen Calder'. It is standard practice for organisations to publish annual reports. And inasmuch as generating press interest around an annual report contributes to disseminating the social reality of sex crime, most organisations contribute to the process. But in terms of engaging proactively with the press on a regular basis in order to challenge the myths that currently prevail, an undertaking that all practitioners agreed is important, it is clear that some organisations are more (pro)active than others.

Proactive and Reactive Media Strategies

It is not my intention to be unduly critical of the Probation Service, the Nexus Institute, NIACRO, the police or the Social Services. Each organisation carries out important work and each makes invaluable contributions to addressing the problem of sex crime in Northern Ireland. Nor should it be forgotten that, for those organisations that might be perceived as representing offenders' interests, engaging with the press is a difficult undertaking and, in terms of public relations, may even be potentially counter-productive. Nevertheless, most journalists were committed to the view that it is essential to develop ongoing relations with sources who might assist them in better communicating accurate and useful information about sex crime. In this context, some practitioners' lack of activism was a source of considerable irritation and frustration. As one reporter put it:

> I get pissed off with these organisations that just send you the odd press release and think that that is the story. And they are not building up relationships with individual reporters, which really is crucial, because if you have a relationship with a particular reporter and say, 'Yeah, I like what you wrote there' and actually try and work with someone over a period of time, then I think that it starts to pay dividends and you get a reporter that knows what they are talking about. But if you are just going to react to the worst stories, or even worse, not react at all and just keep a low profile, then you can't blame the press for just going on what they think is a story because no one else is telling them any different.

The criticism of organisations that prefer to 'keep a low profile' is especially pertinent in light of the PBNI Director's above comments on the question of adopting a more proactive stance towards news management. In large part, though, the concern over developing positive journalist–source relations over time was also shared by practitioners. Dominica McGowan, Director of the Nexus Institute, for example, readily accepted that, 'we should be more responsible about building a relationship', and again added the caveat that the responsibility is a shared one: 'I don't see why they can't educate themselves so they don't just send any journalist out, they send a journalist out who has a clue about what is actually happening.'

Shared Responsibility and Partnership

It is a question, therefore, of establishing partnerships between practitioners and journalists at the individual-personal level, as well as the organisational-professional level. The most productive and reciprocal journalist–source relations are built around trust (Reiss 1984; Ericson *et al* 1989; Schlesinger and Tumber 1994). Levels of trust between journalists and practitioners, however, can vary enormously. Most practitioners had clear notions of where the priorities of news agencies lie. Belfast Rape Crisis spokesperson, Eileen Calder, put it plainly: 'I would say that anybody with half a brain knows that a newspaper is a business and it is the business of newspapers to sell papers. And you have to be careful because that is always going to be their number one priority.' But at the same time, the majority of practitioners, including Eileen Calder, accept that this is simply the nature of the media beast. The requirement to be careful when dealing with the press should not – perhaps even cannot (see Chapter 2) – preclude the use of the newspapers either to advance organisational goals and interests or as an educative resource to promote the social reality of sex crime to a mass audience.

Some practitioners were suspicious of newspapers – most often the Sunday titles, where sensationalist and stereotypical coverage is commonplace – regardless of the individual journalist. That suspicion is perhaps often, but not always justified. It was suggested in Chapter 7, for instance, that some of the most insightful, sensitive and informative sex crime narratives appeared in the mid-market tabloid *Sunday Life*. Most often, however, to recall one practitioner's comments, 'it's not about papers, it's about people'. If there are individual journalists who cannot be trusted to report a sensitive issue like sex crime in a sensitive way – and evidence in this book indicates that there clearly are – then those journalists should not be assigned to sex crime stories. But there is a greater body of evidence to suggest that a substantial number of journalists want to improve the nature of sex crime coverage, to challenge the myths, to contribute to the debate and to raise social awareness about the realities of sex crime in Northern Ireland.

It is also clear that the majority of practitioners are keen to develop working relations with individual journalists to contribute to that process. Indeed, some practitioners were well aware that failings on their own part to engage proactively in media discourse somewhat undermined the force of any criticisms they might direct at the press. As the Nexus Director, Dominica McGowan, conceded:

> We can't really say to the press, 'Well what are you doing that for?' when they can rightly come back and say, 'Well, you're not giving us anything else, are you? I mean we have to fill the space with something'. So we certainly intend to follow that up.

Conclusions

In broad terms, press representations of sex crime can be understood as a function of the wider style of the newspaper in which they are produced. Put simply, broadsheet newspapers produce broadsheet coverage, and tabloids produce tabloid coverage. The influence of the underpinning news values helps to explain the use of language and the levels of sensationalism demonstrated in different newspapers, but these are only part of the full picture of sex crime coverage. Other problems are clearly evidenced across tabloid and broadsheet newspapers alike and, therefore, cannot be explained in these terms. In particular, the lack of depth and contextualisation in press representations of sex crime are consequences of the wider environment in which the news is produced and need to be understood in this context.

Some journalists suggested that the social context of news production in a small jurisdiction like Northern Ireland serves to restrain the nature of sex crime coverage because journalists are part of that community. The indication is that it would be inappropriate to report sex crimes in a sensationalist or salacious way, for to do so would be an affront against the community to which journalists themselves belong. The sense of social responsibility and community partnership no doubt does influence the news production process, but that influence may vary considerably depending on how that sense of responsibility is interpreted and inflected. Both broadsheet and tabloid journalists would argue that they are fulfilling their roles within the community, yet the form and flavour of their sex crime coverage and the messages that coverage imparts may differ enormously.

That said, the majority of journalists accorded that the press have a clear responsibility to provide accurate and useful information about sex crime; that is, to contribute to disseminating the social reality of the problem in Northern Ireland. Most readily accepted their own failings in the construction of sex crime, acknowledging that there is insufficient depth of coverage and a lack of contextualisation in what are overwhelmingly case-based narratives. Journalists complained that changes in the nature of the market – in particular an increasing lack of resources which has accompanied increasing competition – prevent the coverage of sex crimes in sufficient depth. But they also stressed – in line with arguments advanced earlier – that most journalists lack the influence to effect significant change. Many were critical, therefore, of the perceived absence of will among senior managers to take steps to address this problem. But journalists also stressed the role that organisations can and should play in the news production process. They identified practitioners' lack of media activism as a key factor militating against the construction of sex crime in a way that challenges the prevailing myths.

The majority of practitioners accepted also that they have a clear responsibility to contribute to the dissemination of the social reality of sex crime. Most conceded that they could put more effort into engaging proactively with the press to achieve that objective and, like journalists, cited a lack of resources as one key factor that militates against greater levels of media activism. That said, the most resource-poor organisation considered in this research manages to engage proactively with the press on a regular basis with the resources available. The Belfast Rape Crisis Centre is highly proactive and occupied a prominent place both in the archive and in the comments of reporters and editors on the role of source organisations in the news production process.

Given current cultural sensibilities towards crime and criminals, and the moral consensus around the demonisation of sex offenders, survivor groups are better placed to promote their interests. Nevertheless, it is beyond doubt that many of those groups in Northern Ireland who were so critical of press representations of sex crime could be doing more to improve the situation. Practitioners, in turn, were critical of the press for not making room to report issues that they deem important. They were also critical of editors for sending ill-informed journalists who do not understand the key issues in the problem of sex crime and need to be educated on the spot.

The aim in the final chapter is to summarise the key points made throughout this book and to offer some tentative suggestions regarding the possible future tangents of the representation of sex crime in the press.

Notes

1 Some journalists were more willing than others to enter into discussion about the problems with the construction of sex crime in the press, and in particular to discuss their own organisations and senior managers. Because of the sensitive nature of the discussions, the possible consequences of criticising one's own organisation, and in order that they might talk freely

and openly, journalists were assured that their comments on these issues would remain anonymous.

2 The Social Services appeared in the press as the subject of investigations about their own misconduct or malpractice three times as often as they appeared as accredited sources (9 times and 3 times respectively). It is only appearances as accredited sources that are considered here. For accounts of the representation of the Social Services in the English press, see Dominelli (1989), Hill (1990), Franklin and Parton (1991) and Jenkins (1992).

3 Surprisingly, neither ChildLine nor Victim Support – both of which provide valuable advice and support to survivors of sex crime – nor the NSPCC, were mentioned in any items in the archive.

4 *News Letter* (25/01/85: 7) and *Irish News* (25/01/85: 2).

5 Social Services – *News Letter* (02/01/90: 8, 04/01/90: 7) and *Irish News* (03/01/90: 3). Probation Service – *Belfast Telegraph* (22/01/97: 4).

Chapter 9

Conclusions

Introduction

In these closing sections, I do not intend to propose any simple answers to the issues and problems which have been identified and explored in this study. For one, I do not feel that any such simple answers exist. More importantly, however, I have attempted to conduct a rigorous analysis of the construction of sex crime in the press and, where others focus on practical policies (Wilson and Silverman 2002), my objective has been to understand and explain sociologically the phenomena under investigation. A number of policy-related issues which arose during the course of this research could be developed here. For example, the possibility of establishing a forum for discourse between journalists, practitioners and other interested parties; developing closer practitioner press relations; and revising journalist training could all be fruitful areas for further investigation.

Briefly, a forum for discourse (or whatever it might be called) would offer those involved the chance to exchange views and concerns and, where appropriate, advance and debate recommendations to improve the present situation. I discussed the idea – first advanced by a Belfast solicitor – with a number of participants in this study. It met with some resistance, mainly from journalists, but also found considerable support. PBNI Director, Oliver Brannigan, for example, insisted, 'Oh it will happen, certainly, and we will help to set that up'. Four years later nothing has been organised. The Chief Executive of NIACRO, Olwyn Lyner, commented: 'Well I certainly haven't been involved and I would assume that we would have had some connection. So I feel quite let down that that didn't happen.'

More realistically, a higher level of media activism among practitioners could contribute to addressing current problems, and at the same time encourage closer working relations between journalists and source organisations. The majority of practitioners I interviewed complained that they require better funding. The shortage of resources, it seems, is a universal problem. But clearly some organisations are better than others at managing that problem and engaging with the press using the resources available. The Belfast Rape Crisis Centre, despite its resource-poor status, maintained a profile in both the archive and journalists' comments which eclipsed that of comparatively resource-rich organisations. This is partly due to the centrality of victim issues in public debate. But it is also due to the way in which staff establish individual relations with journalists and provide material 'fit to print' on a regular basis. Other organisations might usefully follow this example and devote greater energies to engaging proactively with the press.

Yet even with this additional effort, practitioners noted how difficult and frustrating it can be to deal with journalists who are ill-informed about key issues related to sex crime. Journalists, on the other hand, complained that current training courses provide little insight into how sensitive issues like sex crime should be reported. One obvious suggestion would be for practitioners – representing both survivor and offender groups – to give seminars on journalism training courses about the importance of, for example, contextualisation and the use of language in the construction of sex crime narratives. It would be naïve to expect the coverage of sex crimes to become part of the training curriculum, but relevant points could reasonably be addressed in sessions on reporting sensitive issues more generally.

There is little point, however, in practitioners expending resources and journalists taking special training if their contributions never make it to print. It is clear that journalists in less senior positions have little power to influence the form and flavour of the news product. It is also clear that the general constraints on news production have a direct and considerable influence on the construction of sex crime. Addressing the current problems with press representations, therefore, would require change to be initiated by those at the top of the newsroom hierarchy.

The implementation of any one of these suggestions or, still better, all of them, would undoubtedly contribute to improving the current situation. I want to conclude, however, by reinforcing the point that the processes through which sex crimes come to be constructed in newsprint media discourse are multifaceted and highly complex. There are no simple, quick-fix solutions.

Understanding Press Representations of Sex Crime

The press construction of sex crime depends on a diversity of social, cultural, political, organisational and economic factors. Some of these vary from newspaper to newspaper, some remain constant across news outlets in Northern Ireland, and some apply to press markets in late capitalist societies more generally. Chapter 2 sought to highlight the limitations of applying an overly rigid and deterministic explanatory framework to the analysis of news production. It also pointed to the dangers of using generalised models to explain news production across social orders that may differ considerably in political, economic and cultural terms. The framework I have outlined and used throughout this book synthesises elements of the radical and liberal pluralist interpretations and seeks to establish a foundation which is flexible, yet sufficiently sturdy, to support an analysis of the construction of sex crime in the Northern Ireland press.

Understanding press representations of sex crime requires more than a sound knowledge of the organisational constraints on news production and the inclinations and motivations of journalists and sources, for these do not exist independently. They are influenced by career aspirations and newsroom culture, ideological predilections, the wider marketplace, politics, public opinion and a range of other variables. Many of these have changed significantly in recent decades and continue to do so today. Moreover, sources and journalists often express conflicting views regarding how sex crimes should be reported in the press and hold different interpretations of their own roles and responsibilities in that process. Those who expressed a desire to effect change are obstructed by the unequal distribution of power within newsrooms, between journalists and sources, and between competing source organisations. To make the point once more – sex crime is a contested terrain.

Nor is an understanding of current market conditions, characterised by escalating levels of competition, tabloidisation and the increasing requirement to shock, sufficient to elucidate the myriad forces that shape the construction of sex crime. It is beyond doubt that the cultural form of news has changed in recent decades, and this has been due in part to market pressures. Each of the newspapers considered here was quite different in 1997 – in terms of size and structure, the amount of sex crime coverage and, to a significant degree, case selection and style – than it was in 1985. But not all newspapers have been affected by the changing commercial environment in the same way. Different newspapers write for different markets and audiences; they maintain different agendas which are underpinned by different values and beliefs. The press are not monolithic, and neither is the news they produce. Representations of sex crime vary considerably, depending not only on the particular newspaper producing the reportage, but also, and especially in a small jurisdiction like Northern Ireland, on the individual journalist writing the story.

The diverse nature of the subject under investigation complicates matters further. The term 'sex crime' refers to a wide range of behaviours, the seriousness of which differs enormously. Indeed, the criminal status of some of these behaviours – for example, certain consensual homosexual offences and offences around prostitution – was called into question by a number of participants in this study. The representation of sex crime in the press, then, is not some constant, fixed category; it cannot be adequately explained with general observations and statements. There are important differences between how particular types of offence are portrayed, and between the messages that different newspapers impart, and these need to be borne in mind. Yet there are certain themes running through the sex crime narratives produced in Northern Ireland. These broader characteristics offer important insights into the ways that sex offenders, sex crimes, victims of sexual violence and related issues are perceived, both by journalists and sources, and news consumers. This, in turn, helps to define the cultural space that sex crime – and its construction as news – occupies in contemporary life.

The Nature of Press Representations of Sex Crime

Chapters 4 and 7 illustrated that the language used in most of the regional newspapers – that is, the specific words and phrases used in the construction of sex crime narratives – is relatively conservative. Terms like monster, fiend and beast, about which practitioners expressed considerable concern, were virtually absent from five of the titles. In the tabloid *Sunday World*, however, these terms were routinely incorporated into an array of sex crime stories in which both the nature and the seriousness of the offence varied enormously. The indiscriminate use of highly emotive terms in this newspaper gives a clear indication of the impact that the narratives are intended to have. But it also suggests that all sex offenders – from those who engage in consensual homosexual acts in a public place to serial child sexual abusers and sex murderers – are the same. This message was most explicit in Sunday tabloid journalism. But it was evident in subtler forms in all the newspapers.

Despite some considerable variation in the stylistic nature and target audience of the different titles, the rhetoric they employ varies only by degree. In their constant focus on the absolute 'otherness' of sex offenders, none of the newspapers distinguished in any consistent and meaningful way between the perpetrators of different forms of sex crime. The result is the homogenisation of all sex offenders into a single criminal type. This obscures understanding of the full nature and extent of the problem of sex crime and promotes the undifferentiated fear and loathing of sex offenders throughout society. This, in turn, militates against the development of useful discourses about how different types of sex offender might best be dealt with to address their offending behaviour, while minimising the risk they pose to others.

The image of the predatory stranger looms large in press discourse. The indication in all the newspapers is that 'ordinary' people do not commit sex crimes. They do. The impression is that sex offenders are somehow identifiable, somehow visually distinct from 'normal' people. They are not. The proportion of sex crime stories relating directly to cases of stranger-danger decreased in five of the six newspapers between 1985 and 1997 (Chapter 4) – largely, it seems, because of the rise in press attention to cases of institutional abuse in which there is, by definition, some form of pre-existing relationship between victim and offender. Yet it is still stranger assaults that receive the biggest headlines and the most prominent placement in the press.

Fear of crime, as argued in Chapter 6, tends to focus on the image of the stranger. But in relation to sex crime – and child sex abuse in particular – that image is especially potent. It is both disconcerting and in many ways impractical to think that the greatest threat comes from those we know. Journalists, as much as anyone else, continue to experience difficulties in coming to terms with this social fact. Fears and hostilities are displaced – consciously or otherwise – and projected on to deviant stereotypes to which the press, among others, give substance. Presence (lurking in dark alleys or wastelands), personality (manipulative, predatory, evil) and appearance (unkempt, dishevelled, wild-eyed) are all prominent features of the popular stereotype of the sex offender. These latter characteristics are frequently reinforced by the photographs accompanying sex crime stories, though more often (and interestingly) they are challenged. Yet the image of the predatory stranger maintains its potency, even despite the dramatic increase in the media profile of institutional abuse and the less visible but statistically significant presence of intrafamilial abuse.

It would be disingenuous to suggest that the press, or wider mass media, are solely responsible for perpetuating of the myth of stranger-danger. The relationship between media images and news audiences is a complex, dialectical one. There is a certain complicity in the promotion of this myth, reinforced by a palpable reluctance to conceptualise the risk of sexual victimisation in domestic terms. It is the nature of news production to focus on the novel, the unusual, the exception to the rule. Cases of sex crime, as indicated in Chapter 3, are no different in this regard from other social phenomena. And given the fundamental requirement in the construction of sex crime narratives to 'shock', exceptional cases – especially those featuring predatory strangers – will continue to receive the biggest headlines and the most prominent positions. But extraordinary examples of sex crime are presented as if they are ordinary – as if they represent the norm. In this sense, and in others, the construction of sex crime in the press is becoming increasingly decontextualised.

Chapter 4 demonstrated that the vast majority of sex crime coverage (around 90 per cent) is case based. Advice on personal safety and crime prevention, on the few occasions on which it is presented, tends only to be offered in relation to specific cases. Most often these are cases of stranger assaults, with the emphasis on the risk of further attacks. This practice, again common to all the newspapers, further reinforces the impression that it is strangers who pose the greatest threat. What is most significant, however, is that the proportion of items discussing issues of wider concern has decreased substantially since the 1980s, as levels of market competition and tabloidisation have increased. The focus on case-based reporting starves news readers of information relating to causes, risk and prevention, including what might be done to reduce the risk to themselves and others.

Sex Crime and the Press in a Divided Society

I suggested earlier that many of the issues dealt with in this book are generic. The escalating commercial pressures of news production, increasing social awareness about the nature and extent of sex crime, growing identification with victims and decreasing tolerance with offenders, and the normalisation of issues of sex and crime in everyday life are clearly experienced across many late capitalist societies. These broader themes are important and help to explain how and why sex crimes are represented in the Northern Ireland press in the ways illustrated throughout this book. But Northern Ireland is also different from other societies in a number of crucial respects and, in that jurisdiction, the construction of sex crime takes on a special relevance.

Across western liberal democracies social life is increasingly individualised and defined in terms of difference, diversity and division. As Bauman (2001: 159) contends, 'Individuals have been offered (or, rather, cast into) freedom of unprecedented proportions – but at the price of similarly unprecedented insecurity'. The human predicament is characterised by uncertainty and instability – in terms of career and social position, possessions and partnerships, identity and social bonds, neighbourhood and community, and personal safety. Notions of trust and tolerance occupy an ever-shrinking space in this climate of fear and anxiety. People, as noted in Chapter 6, are less tolerant of criminals, and notions of rehabilitation give way to punitive sentiments of punishment and retribution. But sex offenders are different from 'ordinary' criminals; especially those who offend against children. In such cases, the abuse of trust is of the highest order and the tolerance that child sex offenders – and, by association and homogenisation, all sex offenders – receive from the press and wider society is correspondingly low.

Northern Ireland is fractured politically, culturally, socially, economically and geographically, and the changing depth and direction of its many fissures influences profoundly the nature of the news that is produced. It is a fundamentally divided society. This has important implications for the construction of issues of law and order and, more specifically, the press construction of and social response to sex crime and its perpetrators. In more stable social orders, the demonisation of sex offenders provides an emotional outlet, a focus not just for those fears and anxieties precipitated by the risk of sexual victimisation, but perhaps also for the insecurities that have become a part of everyday life. In Northern Ireland, the denunciation of sex offenders creates a space within which a moral consensus can flourish, transcending party politics and religious differences and establishing an enemy against which all normal, decent, reasonable people can unite. In the context of ongoing social and political flux, this space is pivotal.

Related to this issue, it is significant that cases of institutional abuse dominated the archive in the latter stages of the analysis (though it was still the stranger assaults that received the biggest headlines). Offences by members of the clergy were by far the most frequently and heavily reported institutional incidents, and stories of abuse by Catholic priests became a regular feature of press discourse. That these cases were not only reported, but prioritised, in both the Nationalist and Unionist press indicates the newsworthiness of institutional scandal. But it also reinforces the proposition that the construction of sex crime transcends the political and religious divide in Northern Ireland.

The extent of child sex abuse by members of the clergy was for years difficult for many to think about, still less accept and discuss openly. The realisation, it seems, has now been made and, as a result, the floodgates have been opened and the abuse of trust within an institutional context has become a staple of press discourse. Yet what might be thought of as the ultimate abuse of trust – that perpetrated by family members within a domestic setting, that which invades and violates the sanctity and safety of the home – is still virtually absent from the pages of the Northern Ireland press.

Instances of incest eclipse stranger assaults, both in terms of their frequency and, many have suggested, in terms of the long-term effects of abuse (Grubin 1998; West 2000b; Wilson and Silverman 2002). But the reluctance of a number of journalists, and the wider publics for which they write, to think and talk about this reality reflects a powerful emotional and intellectual block to discussing child sex abuse as a domestic problem. That stranger assaults are reported to the police more frequently than cases of incest could be offered up as one reason why they are reported more frequently in the press. And the possibility of 'jigsaw identification' was a commonly cited explanation, though this problem could be easily addressed by specifying the nature of the offence and omitting any names. But the resistance to publicly discussing the problem of incest in Northern Ireland (and elsewhere) is based on more than police statistics and the determinants of newsworthiness. Perhaps it reflects a reluctance to give up one of the last places of 'safety' in an ever more uncertain and insecure world. Perhaps it betrays a fear of jeopardising precious connections with the few in whom it is still (apparently) safe to 'trust'. What is clear is that incest, at present, is a crime too far.

Closing Comments: Future Directions of Press Representations

The representation of sex crime in Northern Ireland changed dramatically throughout the 1980s and 1990s. An increasing focus on sensational and dramatic sex crime 'events' undermines the integrity and, in many ways, the usefulness of the news being produced. It seems that the press representation of sex crime, particularly in the tabloids, is becoming a source of (a certain kind of) entertainment rather than serious information, a cultural form designed to shock rather than educate, reinforcing existing stereotypes rather than facilitating open and progressive debate. At best, representations give an inaccurate and misleading impression of the nature and extent of sex crime in society. At worst, they may actually increase the likelihood of victimisation by focusing attention on the wrong areas of danger and risk, and misdirecting preventive measures taken to increase the personal safety of adults and children. If the press construction of sex crime continues along this same trajectory it risks becoming little more than a mechanism for generating further public fear and loathing, devoid of any serious discussion around those issues that might actually challenge existing stereotypes, encourage serious debate and inform public opinion and criminal justice policy.

Yet all this needs to be balanced against the fact that certain forms of sexual violence, against women, children and men, once hidden, are to an increasing extent being discussed publicly. Escalating levels of press attention to sex crime – however inaccurate or misleading newspaper representations may be – have contributed enormously to increasing social awareness and at least partially reducing the stigma associated with being a survivor of sexual abuse. The press have been key mechanisms in raising the profile of relevant organisations, publicising campaigns for police reforms, reporting those (highly significant) reforms once implemented and in helping to create a climate in which survivors feel less inhibited and ashamed about coming forward and disclosing their abuse.

The challenge lies in finding the balance between the positive and negative aspects of the press representation of sex crime. That would require the concerted and co-operative efforts of journalists and practitioners at the most senior levels. On the part of journalists, a more careful selection, construction and contextualisation of sex crime cases could help to communicate more accurately the areas of risk, and the possible causes of and preventive measures that might be taken to reduce the likelihood of sexual victimisation. On the part of practitioners, a more proactive engagement with the press could help to disseminate useful information about these same issues, at the same time further raising the profile of those organisations involved with the problem of sex crime and actively confronting the myths that currently permeate so much press discourse.

Commercial pressures, organisational constraints, cultural sensibilities, the thrust of public opinion, the suspicion with which many journalists and practitioners view each other, the hierarchical structures within newsrooms – the current direction of all these influences suggests that the problems with press representations of sex crime are unlikely to be addressed in the near future, and may become worse. As one journalist put it, 'I don't think that anything is going to change in practice, with the *Sunday World*s of this world'. How accurate this assessment turns out to be remains to be seen. Yet as the volume of sex crime in the press steadily increases, and the quality of the information being provided steadily deteriorates, can this possibility be left to chance?

Appendix I

Definitions of sex offences

> The strength of a society's commitment to certain core values such as bodily integrity, personal autonomy and gender equality can be measured by the effectiveness with which it outlaws sexual aggression and exploitation, the extent to which it tolerates consensual, non-exploitative sexual relations, and the fairness with which it treats both victims and perpetrators of sexual crime. (O'Malley 1996: 1)

It is now a sociological truism that deviance requires social reaction (Becker 1963; Matza 1964). An act is not inherently deviant in itself. Rather deviance is ascribed to an act through the social reaction it elicits. As deviance is a socially defined phenomenon, the social and moral constructs which determine the definition of an act as such will vary from one culture and one era to another (Ericson *et al* 1987). The aim in this section is to outline the current definitions of one specific form of social deviance: sexual offending.

It is the task of the state to allow its citizens the maximum freedom to seek personal and sexual fulfilment while endeavouring to prevent sexual exploitation and abuse. Definitions of sexual offences can be complex and technical and disagreement is most likely to arise when the boundaries separating appropriate levels of sexual behaviour from sexual victimisation and abuse are disputed. Recent debates in both Ireland and England on the legal age of consent for minors exemplify the difficulties in arriving at universally acceptable boundaries. It is not always necessary for an act to be carried out in the absence of consent, nor is physical contact between parties always required for a sexual offence to be committed. What amounts to a contravention of law will depend on time, location and other circumstances, as standards of decency and tolerance vary from one generation and one culture to another.

The difficulties in finding adequate and universally acceptable definitions of sexual crimes are duly noted. But the current study is not so much concerned with detailed legal and cultural definitions of the full spectrum of sexual offences, but more the derivation of a comprehensive and, most importantly, practical model for their classification and subsequent quantitative and qualitative analysis in press discourse.

The RUC (now the Police Service of Northern Ireland (PSNI)), the Garda Siochana (Republic of Ireland) and the Director of Public Prosecutions (DPP) each implement different models for the recording and classification of sexual offences. None of the above institutions provided sufficiently comprehensive systems of classification for use here. For example, the RUC Chief Constable's annual reports did not address the difference between *sexual assaults* committed against adults and those committed against children and young persons, grouping them together as *indecent assault against a female* or *indecent assault against a male*. The RUC have classified sexual offences against children and young persons separately since April 1998, but statistical literature for the period examined in this research – 1985–97 – did not account for age differences. The DPP did not break down sexual offences any further than the RUC (DPP Statistical Branch) and publications reflected similar ambiguities in offence classification.

Thomas O'Malley, in his 1996 publication *Sexual Offences,* provides a more comprehensive and, for the purposes of this study, more practical guideline for offence classification. Distinction is drawn between heterosexual and homosexual offences and between offences involving adults and those involving children and young persons. Although some legal definitions of sexual offences may vary slightly between Irish, Northern Irish and English criminal law, within the context of this study the differences are sufficiently minor to allow classification using the definitions O'Malley (1996) identifies. The offences recorded from the sample newspapers were therefore grouped into the following categories: rape, sexual assault, sexual abuse of children and young persons, incest, sexual offences against the mentally impaired, (consensual) homosexual offences, indecency, pornography, sexual harassment.

Rape

Rape included any act of intercourse by a man with a woman of or above the prescribed legal age without her consent. The legal age of consent varies from region to region. For example, the legal age of consent in Northern Ireland and the Republic of Ireland is seventeen years. The legal age of consent in England and Wales is sixteen years. These variations were taken into consideration when compiling the database. Related offences, such as *attempted rape* and *aiding and abetting rape*, were also included in this category.

Sexual Assault

Any act of indecent assault on any unrelated male or female above the prescribed age of consent was included in this category. This comprised a wide range of behaviour from unwanted touching to violent sexual attacks. Extremely minor cases of indecent assault may be legally classified as *sexual harassment* (see below). The offence of male rape was also included in this category.

Sexual Abuse of Children and Young Persons

This category included any offences of a sexual nature committed against persons below the prescribed age of consent, excluding cases in which the offender and victim were directly related. Such offences are not always committed against the will of the person on whom the sexual act is performed, but the law does not recognise consent as an issue in dealing with sexual offences against those under the prescribed age. Both homosexual and heterosexual offences against children and young persons were grouped in this category.

Incest

Many offences of rape and child abuse are incestuous. Nevertheless, the offence of incest merits treatment in its own right. Sexual intercourse between persons within specified degrees of consanguinity, constitutes *incest*. Offences of incest are not necessarily committed without the consent of one of the parties, nor do they necessarily involve intercourse with a child or young person. For the purposes of this study the offence of incest was not treated as gender-specific.

Sexual Offences against the Mentally Impaired

Any sexual offences committed against mentally impaired persons above the prescribed age of consent were categorised here. Cases involving offences against mentally impaired persons below the prescribed age of consent were included in the category *sexual abuse of children and young persons*.

Homosexual Offences

This section included only those *homosexual offences* involving physical contact in which two parties were acting in concert. The offence of buggery without consent, or male rape, was included in *sexual assault* above. Acts of *gross indecency* do not require physical contact but it is essential that both men consent.

Indecency Offences

Criminal law contains a multitude of offences relating to indecency and obscenity, although many of them have traditionally been viewed as offences against public order rather than sexual offences (O'Malley 1996). It is essential that the conduct leading to the charge should constitute an outrage to public decency. As discussed above, what amounts to such an outrage will depend on time, location and other circumstances. Indecent exposure, nuisance calling and stripping in a public place are examples of *indecency offences*.

Prostitution

It is not an offence to perform a sexual act with another person for payment provided the act is not otherwise illegal. Prostitutes are constrained, however, by laws that attempt to restrict the public manifestations of their activities:

> The very nature of their work forces most prostitutes to operate at the margins of the law and often in direct contravention of it. Few can afford the facilities which would permit them to remain within its bounds. In effect, therefore, prostitution *is* criminalised and this exacerbates the problems encountered by women for whom it provides a means of livelihood. (O'Malley 1996: 182)

This category includes *soliciting*, *procuration* and other related offences.

Pornography and Sexual Harassment

Pornography – there is a long-standing history of debate around the relationship between pornography and sexual violence. Criminal sanctions against distributors, retailers and others who allow pornography to become available to children are probably the best way of enforcing the principle that such material presents a distorted image of human relationships and gender equality. The impact on adults of non-violent erotic material depicting adult actors does not appear to be sufficiently detrimental or immediate to warrant censorship (O'Malley 1996: 416). The debate continues.

Sexual harassment – means unwarranted conduct of a sexual nature, or other conduct affecting the dignity of women and men at work. Legally, this can include unwelcome but moderate physical, verbal or non-verbal conduct. In the current study, any degree of unwelcome contact was classified as *sexual assault* and only those cases which involved verbal, or otherwise, but no physical abuse were recorded here.

It is fully acknowledged that there are inconsistencies between legal definitions of certain offences throughout the UK and Ireland. Care has been taken to account for these differences where significant. In the context of this study, however, the differences are of a sufficiently minor nature not to confound quantitative results or distort qualitative discourse.

Appendix II

The recording of sex crime reports

Criteria of Recording for Cases

The prerequisite for a case to be recorded was any reference to a sexual act for which the perpetrator could be legally prosecuted. Cases which might have included a sexual element, but which did not include specific reference to a sexual offence within the news item, were excluded from the database. For example, the headline in the *Irish News* (20 January 1995) read, 'TEENAGE GIRL [*sic*] BODY FOUND IN WATER'. Although the motive and method of the murder *may* have been of a sexual nature, no reference was made to this in the text. The case was therefore not classified as a sex crime and not included in the database. Similarly, the hunt for missing schoolgirl Zoe Evans in early 1990 was followed tirelessly by the press. But no mention was made of the possibility of a sexual motive behind the disappearance. Zoe's body was found six months after the search began. Her stepfather had suffocated her. He received a life sentence for murder. Because neither the media nor the police proffered a sexually motivated explanation, the crime was not included for consideration. On several occasions an edition of one of the sample newspapers did not contain any examples of sex crime coverage. In such a case the edition was simply excluded from the database.

Recording and classification of cases

A database was compiled using Microsoft Excel. The spreadsheet comprised cases recorded and classified according to the following 24 criteria: name of paper; type of offence; offender named; religion; issue date; stage; victim quoted; race noted; page number; sentence; offender quoted; description/issues; section; column inches; others quoted; location; author; photographs; key quotes/phrases; case total; headline; victim named; religion noted; copy.

Most of the above criteria are self-explanatory, but some benefit from further clarification.

Section refers to the section of the newspaper in which the story was published, for example News, Features, Editorial, Letters to the editor, In brief (a series of short stories condensed into one page or section of a page).

Type of offence – where the offence was specified in the news item, this classification was entered into the spreadsheet. Where the offence was not specified, most often before a case had come to court, one was entered from the list described in Appendix I.

Stage of coverage – cases were categorised into six different stages of coverage, as follows:

1. Offence and investigation – coverage of the initial offence and the ensuing investigation, including the questioning of suspects and the arrest of an alleged offender.
2. Court – coverage dealing with court proceedings, from initial remand up to, but not including, sentencing. Coverage of appeals is also grouped in this category.
3. Sentencing – coverage of the sentencing of an alleged offender.
4. Prison – coverage of offenders in prison.
5. Release – coverage of offenders' release from prison and reintegration into the community.
6. Other – material relating directly to sex crime but not falling into any of the above categories, for example letters to the editor, features on sentencing policy as the result of a particular case, editorial comment.

Location – the offences were classified as having been committed in Northern Ireland, the Republic of Ireland or Other. The latter category refers to crimes being committed anywhere outside Ireland.

Case total – the total number of cases in that edition of the newspaper.

Copy – indicated whether a hard copy of the item should be requested from library staff for further analysis.

Appendix III

Details of sample newspapers

Availability of Sample Newspapers

1 *Belfast Telegraph* – available throughout Northern Ireland, Dublin, Donegal and by mail subscription.
2 *Irish News* – available throughout Ireland, London, Manchester, Birmingham, Belgium and by mail subscription.
3 *The Irish Times* – available throughout Ireland, London and by mail subscription.
4 *News Letter* – available throughout Northern Ireland.
5 *Sunday World* – available throughout Northern Ireland.[1]
6 *Sunday Life* – available throughout Northern Ireland.

[1]There is a Southern edition of the *Sunday World* available throughout Southern Ireland and current negotiations are investigating the possibility of a Scottish edition. This study deals only with the Northern edition.

Circulation Figures for the Sample Newspapers

	B. Telegraph	*Irish News*	*Irish Times*	*News Letter*	*Sun. World*	*Sun. Life*
Jan–June 1985	151 799	41 383	85 420	N. member	75 000	n.a.
Jan–June 1990	141 310	43 609	93 187	66 183	77 000	53 420
Jan–June 1995	136 714	44 443	95 310	66 363	66 000	98 612
Jan–June 1997	131 829	47 494	105 302	65 478	72 000	103 124

Note: Figures supplied by the Audit Bureau of Circulation (ABC).

Average Pagination Figures for Sample Newspapers

	B. Telegraph	*Irish News*	*Irish Times*	*News Letter*	*Sun. World*	*Sun. Life*
Jan 1985	22	13	n.a.	n.a.	48	n.a.
Jan 1990	28	13	n.a.	32	48	64
Jan 1995	32	21	n.a.	44	56	68
Jan 1997	36	22	n.a.	48	64	80

Note: Figures supplied by ABC.

Readership Figures for Sample Newspapers

Belfast Telegraph

417,000 people in Northern Ireland read the *Belfast Telegraph.*
48,000 of these people also read the *Irish News.*
48,000 read the *News Letter.*
163,000 read the *Sunday Life.*
74,000 read the *Sunday World.*

Irish News

157,000 people in Northern Ireland read the *Irish News.*
12,000 also read the *News Letter.*
62,000 read the *Sunday Life.*
65,000 read the *Sunday World.*

News Letter

103,000 people in Northern Ireland read the *News Letter.*
33,000 also read the *Sunday Life.*
10,000 read the *Sunday World.*

Sunday Life

339,000 people in Northern Ireland read the *Sunday Life.*
96,000 of these people also read the *Sunday World.*

Sunday World

218,000 people in Northern Ireland read the *Sunday World.*

Figures supplied by Belfast Telegraph Newspapers Ltd (sourced from Northern Ireland Target Group Index, 1998).

Appendix IV

List of interviews

23 March 1998	RUC Detective Inspector and former Co-ordinator of CARE unit
14 June 1998	Jennifer (not her real name), adult survivor of child sex abuse
16 October 1998	Chris Thornton, Security Correspondent, *Belfast Telegraph*
18 October 1998	Chris Thornton, Security Correspondent, *Belfast Telegraph*
26 October 1998	Gavin Mairs, General Reporter, *Belfast Telegraph*
29 October 1998	Noel Doran, Editor, *Irish News*
10 November 1998	RUC Detective Sergeant and CARE unit officer
11 November 1998	Paul Connelly, News Editor, *Belfast Telegraph*
18 November 1998	RUC Chief Information Officer, Press Office
25 November 1998	RUC Chief Superintendent and Deputy Chief Information Office, Press Office
26 November 1998	Dominica McGowan, Director, Nexus Institute for Adult Survivors of Sexual Abuse
3 December 1998	Oliver Brannigan, Director, Northern Ireland Probation Service (PBNI)

7 December 1998	Rosie Uffinel, Social Affairs Correspondent, *Irish News*
8 December 1998	Geoff Martin, Editor, *News Letter*
9 December 1998	Lecturer in Newspaper Journalism and Senior Broadsheet Journalist
12 December 1998	Member of the Housing Executive for Northern Ireland
13 January 1999	Eileen Calder, spokesperson, Belfast Rape Crisis and Sexual Abuse Centre
18 January 1999	Eileen Calder, spokesperson, Belfast Rape Crisis and Sexual Abuse Centre
22 January 1999	Eileen Calder, spokesperson, Belfast Rape Crisis and Sexual Abuse Centre
8 April 1999	RUC Chief Information Officer, Press Office
8 June 1999	Eileen Calder, spokesperson, Belfast Rape Crisis and Sexual Abuse Centre
22 June 1999	RUC Detective Sergeant and CARE unit officer
23 June 1999	Catherine (not her real name), adult survivor of child sex abuse
6 July 1999	RUC Detective Chief Inspector and Curren Co-ordinator of CARE unit
14 October 1999	Ronan Henry, Deputy News Editor, *Belfast Telegraph*
6 January 2000	Martin Lindsay, Editor, *Sunday Life*
12 January 2000	Jim McDowell, Editor, *Sunday World*
18 January 2000	Sunday journalist
19 April 2000	David (not his real name), adult survivor of child sex abuse
23 November 2000	Olwyn Lyner, Chief Executive, NIACRO
16 November 2000	Stephen Dempster, News Editor, *News Letter*
17 January 2001	Iain Pratt, Company Secretary, Irish Times Ltd

17 January 2001	Steven Moore, News Editor, *News Letter*
3 April 2001	Chris Thornton, Security Correspondent, *Belfast Telegraph*
3 April 2001	Stephen Dempster, News Editor, *News Letter*
14 April 2001	Noel Doran, Editor, *Irish News*
23 April 2001	Geoff Martin, Editor, *News Letter*

References

Bagdikian, B. (1997) *The Media Monopoly*, fifth edition, Boston, MA: Beacon.

Bailey, S. (1993) 'Fast Forward to Violence: Violence Visual Imaging and Serious Juvenile Crime', *Criminal Justice Matters*, 11: 6–7.

Baker, A. and Duncan, S. (1985) 'Child Sexual Abuse: A Study of Prevalence in Great Britain' in *Child Abuse and Neglect*, 9: 457–67.

Bannister, A. (ed.) (1992) *From Hearing to Healing*, NSPCC, London: Longman.

Barker, M. and Petley, J. (eds) (2001) *Ill Effects: The Media/Violence Debate*, second edition, London: Routledge.

Barthes, R. (1977) 'The Photographic Message', in R. Barthes, *Image-Music-Text: Essays Selected and Translated by Stephen Heath*, London: Fontana Collins.

Barwise, P. and Gordon, D. (1998) 'The Economics of the Media', in A. Briggs and P. Cobley (eds) *The Media: An Introduction*, London: Longman.

Bauman, Z. (1998) *Globalization: The Human Consequences*, Cambridge: Polity Press.

Bauman, Z. (2000) 'Social Uses of Law and Order', in D. Garland and R. Sparks (eds) *Criminology and Social Theory*, Oxford: Oxford University Press.

Bauman, Z. (2001) *The Individualized Society*, Cambridge: Polity Press.

Becker, H. (1963) *Outsiders: Studies in the Sociology of Deviance*, New York, NY: Free Press of Glencoe.

Becker, H. (1967) 'Whose Side are we on?', in J.D. Douglas (ed.) (1970) *The Relevance of Sociology*, New York, NY: Appleton-Century Crofts.

Beckett, K. (1994) 'Setting the Public Agenda: "Street Crime" and Drug use in American Politics', *Social Problems*, 41, 3: 425–47.

Beirne, M. and Greer, C. (1999) *The Agreement and a New Beginning for Policing in Northern Ireland: Conference Report and Human Rights Benchmarks for Change*, Belfast: CAJ.

Belfast Rape Crisis Collective (1990) *Annual Report of the Belfast Rape Crisis and Sexual Abuse Centre 1990*, Belfast: Belfast Rape Crisis Centre.

Belfast Rape Crisis Collective (1996) *Annual Report of the Belfast Rape Crisis and Sexual Abuse Centre 1994–1996*, Belfast: Belfast Rape Crisis Centre.
Benedict, H. (1992) *Virgin or Vamp*, Oxford: Oxford University Press.
Best, J. (1990) *Threatened Children*, Chicago, IL: University of Chicago Press.
Best, J. (1995) *Images of Issues: Typifying Contemporary Social Problems*, second edition, Hawthorne, NY: Aldine de Gruyter.
Bew, P., Gibbon, P. and Patterson, H. (1996) *Northern Ireland, 1921–1996: Political Forces and Social Classes*, London: Serif.
Bew, P. and Gillespie, G. (1993) *Northern Ireland: A Chronology of the Troubles, 1968–1993*, Dublin: Gill & Macmillan.
Blumler, J. and Gurevitch, L. (1995) *The Crisis of Public Communication*, London: Routledge.
Bourdieu, P. (1998) *On Television and Journalism*, London: Pluto.
Bowyer Bell, J. (1993) *The Irish Troubles: A Generation of Violence 1967–1992*, Dublin: Gill & Macmillan.
Bradford, J.M.W., Bloomberg, D. and Bourget, D. (1988) 'The Heterogeneity/Homogeneity of Pedophilia', in *Psychiatric Journal of the University of Ottawa*, 13: 217–26.
Breed, W. (1980) *The Newspapermen, News and Society*, New York, NY: Arno Press.
Briggs, A. and Cobley, P. (eds) (1998) *The Media: An Introduction*, London: Longman.
Bromley, M. (1997) 'Writing Terrorism out of the Story', in A. O'Day (ed.), *Political Violence in Northern Ireland: Conflict and Conflict Resolution*, London: Praeger.
Bromley, M. (1998) 'The "Tabloiding" of Britain: "Quality" Newspapers in the 1990s', in H. Stephenson and M. Bromley (eds) *Sex, Lies and Democracy: The Press and the Public*, London: Longman.
Brownstein, H. (1991) 'The Media and the Construction of Random Drug Violence', *Social Justice*, 18, 4: 85–103.

Cameron, D. and Frazer, E. (1987) *The Lust to Kill: A Feminist Investigation of Sexual Murder*, Cambridge: Polity Press.
Campbell, B. (1988) *Unofficial Secrets: Child Sexual Abuse – The Cleveland Scandal*, London: Virago.
Campbell, B. (1989) 'Cleveland's Dilemma', *New Statesman and Society*, 21 February.
Campbell, D. (1990) 'Still Dark in Paranoia Gulch', in B. Rolston and D. Miller (eds) (1996) *War and Words: The Northern Ireland Media Reader*, Belfast: Beyond the Pale.
Caputi, J. (1987) *The Age of the Sex Crime*, London: The Women's Press.
Carey, S. (1993) 'Mass Media Violence and Aggressive Behaviour', *Criminal Justice Matters*, 11: 8–9.
Carlen, P. (1976) *Magistrates' Justice*, London: Martin Robinson.
Cavender, G. and Mulcahy, A. (1998) 'Trial by Fire: Media Constructions of Corporate Deviance', *Justice Quarterly*, 15, 4: 697–719.
Chadwick, P. (1989) *Media Mates*, Melbourne: Macmillan.

Chermak, S. (1995) *Victims in the News: Crime and the American News Media*, Boulder, CO: Westview Press.

Chermak, S. (1997) 'The Presentation of Drugs in the News Media', *Justice Quarterly*, 14, 4: 687–718.

Chibnall, S. (1977) *Law and Order News*, London: Tavistock.

Chomsky, N. (1989) *Necessary Illusions*, London: Pluto.

Cohen, S. (1980) *Folk Devils and Moral Panics: The Creation of the Mods and Rockers*, Oxford: Oxford University Press.

Cohen, S. and Young, J. (eds) (1981) *The Manufacture of News: Social Problems, Deviance and Mass Media*, London: Constable.

Coleman, C. and Moynihan, J. (1996) *Understanding Crime Rates*, Buckingham: Open University Press.

Collins, R., Curran, J., Garnham, N., Scannell, P., Schlesinger, P. and Sparks, C. (eds) (1986) *Media, Culture and Society: A Critical Reader*, London: Sage.

Corner, J. (1998) 'Why Study Media Form?', in A. Briggs and P. Cobley (eds) *The Media: An Introduction*, London: Longman.

Cuff, E., Sharrock, W. and Francis, D. (1998) *Perspectives in Sociology*, London: Routledge.

Cumberbatch, G. (1989) *A Measure of Uncertainty: The Effects of Mass Media*. Broadcast Standards Council Research Monograph 1, London: John Libbey.

Cumberbatch, G. (1998) 'Media Effects: the Continuing Controversy', in A. Briggs and P. Cobley (eds) *The Media: An Introduction*, London: Longman.

Cumberbatch, G., Woods, S. and Maguire, A. (1995) *Crime in the News: Television, Radio and Newspapers: A Report for BBC Broadcasting Research*, Birmingham: Aston University, Communications Research Group.

Curran, J. (1986) 'The Impact of Advertising on the British Mass Media', in R. Collins *et al* (eds) *Media, Culture and Society: A Critical Reader*, London: Sage.

Curran, J. (1998) 'Newspapers: beyond Political Economy', in A. Briggs and P. Cobley (eds) *The Media: An Introduction*, London: Longman.

Curran, J. (2000) 'Rethinking Media and Democracy', in J. Curran and M. Gurevitch (eds) *Media, Culture and Society*, third edition, London: Arnold.

Curran, J. and Gurevitch, M. (eds) (2000) *Mass Media and Society*, third edition, London: Arnold.

Curran, J. and Seaton, J. (1997) *Power without Responsibility: The Press and Broadcasting in Britain*, fifth edition, London: Routledge.

Davis, R.C., Lurigio, A.J. and Skogan, W. G. (eds) (1997) *Victims of Crime*, second edition, London: Sage.

Dillon, M. (1989) *The Shankill Butchers: A Case Study in Mass Murder*, London: Hutchinson.

Ditton, J. and Duffy, J. (1983) 'Bias in the Newspaper Reporting of Crime', *British Journal of Criminology*, 23, 2: 159–65.

Dobash, R.E. and Dobash, R. (1979) *Violence against Wives*, New York, NY: Free Press.

Dominelli, L. (1989) 'Betrayal of Trust', *British Journal of Social Work*, 19: 291–307.

Dominick, J. (1978) 'Crime and Law Enforcement in the Mass Media', in C. Winick (ed.) *Deviance and Mass Media*, London: Sage.

Downes, D. and Rock, P. (1998) *Understanding Deviance: A Guide to the Sociology of Crime and Rule Breaking*, third edition, Oxford: Oxford University Press.

Durkheim, E. (1964) *The Division of Labour in Society*, New York, NY: Free Press.

Entman, R. (1989) 'How the Media Affect what People Think: an Information Processing Approach', *Journal of Politics*, 51, 2: 347–70.

Epstein, E.J. (1973) *News from Nowhere*, NewYork, NY: Random House.

Ericson, R. (1991) 'Mass Media, Crime, Law and Justice: an Institutional Approach', *British Journal of Criminology*, 31, 3: 219–49.

Ericson, R., Baranek, P. and Chan, J. (1987) *Visualising Deviance: A Study of News Organisation*, Buckingham: Open University Press.

Ericson, R., Baranek, P. and Chan, J. (1989) *Negotiating Control: A Study of News Sources*, Buckingham: Open University Press.

Ericson, R., Baranek, P. and Chan, J. (1991) *Representing Order: Crime, Law and Justice in the News Media*, Buckingham: Open University Press.

Ewen, S. (2001) *Captains of Consciousness: Advertising and the Social Roots of the Consumer Culture – 25th Anniversary Edition*, New York, NY: Basic Books.

Fattah, E. (1997) 'Toward a Victim Policy Aimed at Healing, not Suffering', in R.C. Davis *et al* (eds) *Victims of Crime*, second edition, Thousand Oaks, CA, and London: Sage.

Ferrell, J. (1999) 'Cultural Criminology', *Annual Review of Sociology*, 25: 395–418.

Ferrell, J. and Sanders, C. (1995) *Cultural Criminology*, Boston, MA: Northeastern University Press.

Ferrell, J. and Websdale, N. (eds) (1999) *Making Trouble: Cultural Constructions of Crime, Deviance, and Control*, Hawthorne, NY: Aldine de Gruyter.

Finkelhor, D. (1984) *Child Sexual Abuse: New Theory and Research*, New York, NY: Free Press.

Finkelhor, D. (1994) 'The "Backlash" and the Future of Child Protection Advocacy', in J. Myers (ed.) *The Backlash: Child Protection Under Fire*, London: Sage.

Finkelhor, D. (1997) 'The Victimisation of Children and Youth: Developmental Victimology' in R.C. Davies *et al* (eds) *Victims of Crime*, second edition, London: Sage.

Finkelhor, D. and Yllo, K. (1985) *License to Rape: Sexual Abuse of Wives*, New York, NY: Holt, Rinehart & Winston.

Fishman, M. (1978) 'Crime Waves as Ideology', *Social Problems*, 25: 531–43.

Fishman, M. (1980) *Manufacturing the News*, Austin, TX: University of Texas Press.

Foucault, M. (1979) *The History of Sexuality*, London: Allen Lane.

Franklin, B. (1997) *Newszak and News Media*, London: Arnold.

Franklin, B. and Parton, N. (eds) (1991) *Social Work, the Media and Public Relations*, London: Routledge.

Frayling, C. (1986) 'The House that Jack Built: Some Stereotypes of the Rapist in the History of Popular Culture', in S. Tomaselli and R. Porter (eds) *Rape*, Oxford: Blackwell.

Galtung, J. and Ruge, M. (1970) 'The Structure of Foreign News', in J. Tunstall (ed.) *Media Sociology*, London: Constable.

Gamson, W., Croteau, D., Hoynes, W., and Sasson, T. (1992) 'Media Images and the Social Construction of Reality', *Annual Review of Sociology*, 18: 373–93.

Gamson, W. and Modigliani, A. (1989) 'Media Discourse and Public Opinion on Nuclear Power', *American Journal of Sociology*, 95: 1–37.

Gans, H. (1980) *Deciding What's News*, London: Constable.

Garfinkel, H. (1956) 'Conditions of Successful Degradation Ceremonies', *American Sociological Review*, 61: 420–4.

Garland, D. (2000) 'The Culture of High Crime Societies: some Preconditions of Recent "Law and Order" Politics, *British Journal of Criminology*, 40: 347–75.

Garland, D. and Sparks, R. (eds) (2000) *Criminology and Social Theory*, Oxford: Oxford University Press.

Garnham, N. (1998) 'Media Policy', in A. Briggs and P. Cobley (eds) *The Media: An Introduction*, London: Longman.

Geary, R., McEvoy, K. and Morison, J. (2000) 'Lives Less Ordinary: Crime, Communities and Policing in Northern Ireland', *Irish Journal of Sociology*, 10: 49–75.

Gerbner, G. and Gross, L. (1976) 'Living with Television: the Violence Profile', *Journal of Communication*, 26, 1: 173–99.

Giddens, A. (1990) *The Consequences of Modernity*, Cambridge: Polity Press.

Giddens, A. (1992) *The Transformation of Intimacy: Sexuality, Love and Eroticism in Modern Societies*, Cambridge: Polity Press.

Gieber, W. (1964) 'News is what Newspapermen Make it', in L. Dexter and D. Manning White (eds) *People, Society and Mass Communications*, New York, NY: Free Press.

Gitlin, T. (1980) *The Whole World is Watching*, Berkeley, CA: University of California Press.

Goddard, C. (1996) 'Read All about it: the News about Child Abuse', *Child Abuse Review*, 5, 5: 301–9.

Goldenberg, E. (1975) *Making the Papers: The Access of Resource-Poor Groups to the Metropolitan Press*, Lexington, MA: D.C. Heath.

Golding, P. and Murdock, G. (2000) 'Culture, Communications and Political Economy', in J. Curran and M. Gurevitch (eds) *Media, Culture and Society*, third edition, London: Arnold.

Goode, E. and Ben-Yehuda, N. (1994) *Moral Panics: The Social Construction of Deviance*, Oxford: Blackwell.

Gordon, L. (1988) *Heroes of their own Lives: The Politics and History of Family Violence*, New York, NY: Penguin.

Grabe, M.E., Zhou, S.H. and Barnett, B. (1999) 'Sourcing and Reporting in News Magazine Programs: 60 Minutes versus Hard Copy', *Journalism and Mass Communication Quarterly*, 2: 293–311.

Graber, D. (1980) *Crime, News and the Public*, New York, NY: Praeger.
Grabosky, P. and Wilson, P. (1989) *Journalism and Justice: How Crime is Reported*, Sydney: Pluto Press.
Greenslade, R. (1997)'The Rest is Waffle', *Guardian*, 1 September.
Greer, C. (2001a) 'Risky Business', *Criminal Justice Matters*, 43: 28–9.
Greer, C. (2001b) 'Crime in the Press: a Case Study of Sex Offending in Northern Ireland', unpublished PhD Thesis, The Queen's University of Belfast.
Greer, C. (2003) 'Sex Crime and the Media: Press Representations in Northern Ireland' in P. Mason (ed.) *Criminal Visions: Representations of Crime and Justice*, Cullompton: Willan.
Grover, C. and Soothill, K. (1995) 'The Social Construction of Sex Offenders', *Sociology Review*, 4: 29–33.
Grubin, D. (1998) *Sex Offending against Children: Understanding the Risk. Police Research Series Paper 99, Policing and Reducing Crime Unit*, London: Home Office.
Gubrium, F. (1993) 'For a Cautious Naturalism', in G. Miller and J. Holstein (eds) *Constructionist Controversies*, Hawthorne, NY: Aldine de Gruyter.
Gurevitch, M. and Levy, M.R. (eds) (1985) *Mass Communications Review Yearbook 5*, Beverly Hills, CA: Sage.

Hagell, A. and Newburn, T. (1994) *Young Offenders and the Media*, London: Batsford.
Hale, C. (1996) 'Fear of Crime: a Review of the Literature', *International Review of Victimology*, 4: 79–150.
Hall, R.E. (1985) *Ask any Woman*, Bristol: Falling Wall Press.
Hall, S. (1973) 'The Determinations of News Photographs', in S. Cohen and J. Young (eds) (1981) *The Manufacture of News: Social Problems, Deviance and Mass Media*, London: Constable.
Hall, S. (1981) 'The Social Production of News', in S. Cohen and J. Young (eds) (1981), *The Manufacture of News*, London: Sage.
Hall, S., Critcher, C., Jefferson, T., Clarke, J. and Roberts, B. (1978) *Policing the Crisis: Mugging, the State and Law and Order*, London: Macmillan.
Hallin, D.C. (1986) *'The Uncensored War': The Media and Vietnam*, New York, NY: Oxford University Press.
Hansen, A. (1991) 'The Media and Social Construction of the Environment', *Media, Culture and Society*, 13, 4: 443–58.
Hartley, J. (1982) *Understanding News*, London: Routledge.
Haug, F. (2001) 'Sexual Deregulation or, the Child Abuser as Hero in Neoliberalism', *Feminist Theory*, 2, 1: 55–78.
Hauge, R. (1965) 'Crime in the Press', *Scandinavian Studies in Criminology*, 1: 147–64.
Hearold, S. (1986) 'A Synthesis of 1043 Effects of Television on Social Behaviour', in G. Comstock (ed.) *Public Communications and Behaviour*. Vol. 1, New York, NY: Academic Press.
Heidensohn, F. (2002) 'Gender and Crime', in M. Maguire *et al* (eds) *The Oxford Handbook of Criminology*, third edition, Oxford: Oxford University Press.

Herman, E. and Chomsky, N. (1994) *Manufacturing Consent: The Political Economy of the Mass Media*, New York, NY: Pantheon.

Hetherington, A. (1985) *News, Newspapers and Television*, London: Macmillan.

Hill, M. (1990) 'The Manifest and Latent Lessons of Child Abuse Enquiries', *British Journal of Social Work*, 20: 197–213.

Holland, P. (1998) ' "The Direct Appeal to the Eye"? Photography and the Twentieth–century Press', in A. Briggs and P. Cobley (eds) *The Media: An Introduction*, London: Longman.

Hollywood, B. (1997) 'Dancing in the Dark: Ecstasy, the Dance Culture and Moral Panic in post Ceasefire Northern Ireland', *Critical Criminology*, 8: 62–77.

Hood-Williams, J. and Bush, T. (1995) 'Domestic Violence in a London Housing Estate', in C. Byron (ed.) *Home Office Research Bulletin*, 37.

Hope, T. and Sparks, R. (eds) (2000) *Crime, Risk and Insecurity*, London: Routledge.

Howe, A. (ed.) (1998) *Sexed Crime in the News*, New South Wales: The Federation Press.

Jefferson, T. and Hollway, W. (2000) 'The Role of Anxiety in Fear of Crime', in T. Hope and R. Sparks (eds) *Crime, Risk and Insecurity*, London: Routledge.

Jenkins, P. (1992) *Intimate Enemies: Moral Panics in Contemporary Great Britain*, Hawthorne, NY: Aldine de Gruyter.

Jenkins, P. (1994) *Using Murder: The Social Construction of Serial Homicide*, Hawthorne, NY: Aldine de Gruyter.

Jenkins, P. (1996) *Pedophiles and Priests: Anatomy of a Contemporary Crisis*, New York, NY: Oxford University Press.

Jenkins, P. (1999) 'Fighting Terrorism as if Women Mattered', in J. Ferrell and N. Websdale (eds) *Making Trouble: Cultural Constructions of Crime, Deviance, and Control*, Hawthorne, NY: Aldine de Gruyter.

Katz. J. (1988) 'Seductions and Repulsions of Crime', in E. McLaughlin *et al* (eds) (2003) *Criminological Perspectives: Essential Readings*, second edition, London: Sage.

Kavanagh, D. (2000) *British Politics: Continuities and Change*, fourth edition, Oxford: Oxford University Press.

Kellner, D. (1990) *Television and the Crisis of Democracy*, Boulder, CO: Westview Press.

Kelly, L., Regan, L. and Burton, S. (1991) *An Exploratory Study of the Prevalence of Sexual Abuse in a Sample of 16 to 21 Year Olds*, London: Child Abuse Studies Unit, Polytechnic of North London.

Kidd-Hewitt, D. (1995) 'Crime and the Media: a Criminological Perspective', in D. Kidd-Hewitt and R. Osborne (eds) *Crime and the Media: The Post-Modern Spectacle*, London: Pluto Press.

Kidd-Hewitt, D. and Osborne, R. (eds) (1995) *Crime and the Media: The Post-Modern Spectacle*, London: Pluto Press.

King, R. and Wincup, E. (eds) (2000) *Doing Research on Crime and Criminal Justice*, Oxford: Oxford University Press.

Kitsuse, J. and Spector, M. (1973) 'Toward a Sociology of Social Problems: Social Conditions, Value Judgements and Social Problems', *Social Problems*, 20: 407–19.

Kitzinger, J. (1996) 'Media Constructions of Sexual Abuse Risks', *Child Abuse Review*, 5, 5: 319–33.

Kitzinger, J. (1998) Untitled. Paper presentation at 'Reporting Abuse', conference organised by NIACRO and Barnardos, Belfast, 5 November.

Kitzinger, J. (1999a) 'A Sociology of Media Power: Key Issues in Audience Reception Research', in G. Philo (ed.) *Message Received*, London: Longman.

Kitzinger, J. (1999b) 'The Ultimate Neighbour from Hell? Stranger Danger and the Media Framing of Paedophiles', in B. Franklin (ed.) *Social Policy, the Media and Misrepresentation*, London: Routledge.

Kitzinger, J. and Skidmore, P. (1995) *Child Sexual Abuse and the Media. Summary Report to ESRC*. Award no. R000233675. Report available from Glasgow Media Group.

Koss, S. (1984) *The Rise and Fall of the Political Press in Britain*, London: Hamish Hamilton.

Lees, S. (1995) 'The Media Reporting of Rape: the 1993 British "Date Rape" Controversy', in D. Kidd-Hewitt and R. Osborne (eds) *Crime and the Media: The Post-Modern Spectacle*, London: Pluto Press.

Levi, M. (1997) 'Violent Crime', in M. Maguire *et al* (eds) *The Oxford Handbook of Criminology*, second edition, Oxford: Oxford University Press.

Levitas, R. and Guy, W. (eds) (1996) *Interpreting Official Statistics*, London: Routledge.

Lianos, M. with Douglas, M. (2000) 'Dangerization and the End of Deviance: the Institutional Environment', in D. Garland and R. Sparks (eds) *Criminology and Social Theory*, Oxford: Oxford University Press.

Lichter, S.R., Rothman, S. and Lichter, L.S. (1986) *The Media Elite: America's New Powerbrokers*, Bethesda, MD: Adler & Adler.

Livingstone, S. (1996) 'On the Continuing Problem of Media Effects', in J. Curran and M. Gurevitch (eds) *Mass Media and Society*, London: Arnold.

Loader, I., Girling, E. and Sparks, R. (1998) 'Narratives of Decline: Youth, Dis/order and Community in an English Middletown', *British Journal of Criminology*, 38, 3: 388–403.

Loseke, D. (1999) *Thinking about Social Problems: An Introduction to Constructionist Perspectives*, Hawthorne, NY: Aldine de Gruyter.

Lyner, O. (1998) Untitled. Paper presentation at 'Reporting Abuse', conference organised by NIACRO and Barnardos, Belfast, 5 November.

MacDougall, C. (1968) *Interpretative Reporting*, New York, NY: Macmillan.

MacVean, A. (2000) 'Risk, Policing and the Management of Sex Offenders', *Crime Prevention and Community Safety: An International Journal*, 2, 4: 7–18.

Maguire, M. (1997) 'Crime Statistics, Patterns and Trends: Changing Perceptions and their Implications', in M. Maguire *et al* (eds) *The Oxford Handbook of Criminology*, second edition, Oxford: Oxford University Press.

Maguire, M. and Corbett, C. (1987)*The Effects of Crime and the Work of Victim Support Schemes*, Aldershot: Gower.

Maguire, M., Morgan, R. and Reiner, R. (eds) (1997) *The Oxford Handbook of Criminology*, second edition, Oxford: Oxford University Press.

Maguire, M., Morgan, R. and Reiner, R. (eds) (2002) *The Oxford Handbook of Criminology*, third edition, Oxford: Oxford University Press.

Maguire, M. and Pointing, J. (eds) (1988) *Victims of Crime: A New Deal?*, Buckingham: Open University Press.

Manning, P. (2001) *News and News Sources: A Critical Introduction*, London: Sage.

Marsh, H.L. (1991) 'A Comparative Analysis of Crime Coverage in Newspapers in the United States and other Countries from 1960–1989: a Review of the Literature', *Journal of Criminal Justice*, 19, 1: 67–80.

Mason, P. (ed.) (2003) *Criminal Visions: Representations of Crime and Justice*, Cullompton: Willan.

Matza, D. (1964) *Delinquency and Drift*, New York, NY: Wiley.

Mawby, R. and Walklate, S. (1994) *Critical Victimology*, London: Sage.

McChesney, R.W. (1997) *Corporate Media and the Threat to Democracy*, New York, NY: Seven Stories Press.

McEvoy, K. (1996) 'Newspapers and Crime: Narrative and the Construction of Identity', in J. Morison and C. Bell (eds) *Tall Stories: Reading Law and Literature*, Aldershot: Dartmouth.

McGarry, J. and O'Leary, B. (1995) *Explaining Northern Ireland: Broken Images*, Oxford: Blackwell.

McGregor, J. (1993) *Crime News as Prime News in New Zealand's Metropolitan Press*, Auckland: Legal Research Foundation.

McLaughlin, E. (1993) 'Women and the Family in Northern Ireland: a Review', *Women's Studies International Forum*, 16, 6: 553–68.

McLaughlin, E., Muncie, M. and Hughes, G. (eds) (2003) *Criminological Perspectives: Essential Readings*, second edition, London: Sage.

McNair, B. (1998) *The Sociology of Journalism*, London: Arnold.

McNair, B. (1999) *News and Journalism in the UK: A Text Book*, third edition, London: Routledge.

McShane, E. and Pinkerton, J. (1996) 'The Family in Northern Ireland', *Studies*, 75: 67–176.

McVeigh, R. (1995) *It's Part of Life: Harassment and the Security Forces in Northern Ireland*, Belfast: CAJ.

Medhurst, A. (1998) 'Tracing Desires: Sexuality and Media Texts', in A. Briggs and P. Cobley (eds) *The Media: An Introduction*, London: Longman.

Merton, R.K. (1976) 'The Sociology of Social Problems', in R.K. Merton and R.A. Nisbet (eds) *Contemporary Social Problems*, fourth edition, New York, NY: Harcourt Brace Jovanovich.

Meyers, M. (1997) *News Coverage of Violence against Women: Engendering Blame*, Thousand Oaks, CA, and London: Sage.

Miliband, R. (1973) *The State in Capitalist Society*, London: Quartet.

Miller, D. (1993) 'Official Sources and "Primary Definition": the Case of Northern Ireland', *Media, Culture and Society*, 15: 385–406.

Miller, D. (1998) 'Public Relations and Journalism: Promotional Strategies and Media Power', in A. Briggs and P. Cobley (eds) *The Media: An Introduction*, London: Longman.

Miller, D. and Philo, G. (1999) 'The Effective Media', in G. Philo (ed.) *Message Received*, London: Longman.

Miller, D. and Williams, K. (1993) 'Negotiating HIV/AIDS Information; Agendas, Media Strategies and the News', in Glasgow University Media Group, *Getting the Message: News, Truth and Power*, London: Routledge.

Miller, G. and Holstein, J. (eds) (1993) *Constructionist Controversies: Issues in Social Problems Theory*, Hawthorne, NY: Aldine de Gruyter.

Miller, L. (1993) 'Claims-making from the Underside: Marginalization and Social Problems Analysis', in G. Miller and J. Holstein (eds) *Constructionist Controversies*, Hawthorne, NY: Aldine de Gruyter.

Mirrlees-Black, C., Budd, T., Partridge, S. and Mayhew, P. (1998) *The 1998 British Crime Survey*. Home Office Statistical Bulletin, Issue 21/98, London: Home Office.

Mirrlees-Black, C., Mayhew, P. and Percy, A. (1996) *The 1996 British Crime Survey*. Home Office Statistical Bulletin, Issue 19/96, London: Home Office.

Molotch, H. and Lester, M. (1974) 'News as Purposive Behaviour: on the Strategic Use of Routine Events, Accidents, and Scandals', *American Sociological Review*, 39: 101–12.

Moore, C. (1995) *Betrayal of Trust: The Father Brendan Smyth Affair and the Catholic Church*, Dublin: Marino.

Moore, C. (1996) *The Kincora Scandal: Political Cover-up and Intrigue in Ulster*, Dublin: Marino.

Morgan, J. and Zedner, L. (1992) *Child Victims: Crime, Impact and Criminal Justice*, Oxford: Oxford University Press.

Morris, A. (1987) *Women, Crime and Criminal Justice*, Oxford: Blackwell.

Mulcahy, A. (1995) 'Claimsmaking and the Construction of Legitimacy: Press Coverage of the 1981 Northern Irish Hunger Strike', *Social Problems*, 42, 4: 449–67.

Muncie, M. and McLaughlin, E. (eds) (2001) *The Problem of Crime*, London: Sage.

Murdock, G. (1974) 'Mass Communication and the Construction of Meaning', in N. Armistead (ed.) *Rethinking Social Psychology*, London: Penguin Books.

Murdock, G. (1990) 'Redrawing the Map of Communications Industries; Concentration and Ownership in the Year of Privatisation', in M. Ferguson (ed.) *Public Communication: The New Imperatives*, London: Sage.

Murdock, G. (1991) 'Patrolling the Border: British Broadcasting and the Irish Question in the 1980s', *Journal of Communication*, 41, 4: 104–15.

Murdock, G. (2000) 'Restructuring the Ruined Tower: Contemporary Communications and Questions of Class', in J. Curran and M. Gurevitch (eds) *Media, Culture and Society*, third edition, London: Arnold.

Nava, M. (1988) 'Cleveland and the Press: Outrage and Anxiety in the Reporting of Child Sexual Abuse', *Feminist Review*, 28: 103–21.

Naylor, B. (2001) 'Reporting Violence in the British Print Media: Gendered Stories', *Howard Journal*, 40, 2: 180–94.

Nelson, S. (1987) *Incest Fact and Myth*, Edinburgh: Stranmullion.

NIACRO and Barnardos (1998) *Reporting Abuse: A Conference Held at the Queen's University of Belfast, 5th November, 1998 – Conference Proceedings*, Belfast: NIACRO.

O'Connell, M. and Whelan, J. (1996) 'The Public Perceptions of Crime Prevalence, Newspaper Readership and "Mean World" Attitudes' in *Legal and Criminal Psychology*, 1: 179–95.

O'Mahony, D., Geary, R., McEvoy K. and Morison, J. (2000) *Crime Community and Locale: The Communities Crime Survey in Northern Ireland*, Aldershot: Ashgate.

O'Malley, T. (1996) *Sexual Offences; Law, Policy and Punishment*, Dublin: Round Hall/Sweet & Maxwell.

Paglia, C. (1992) *Sex, Art, and American Culture*, London: Penguin Books.

Palmer, J. (1998) 'News Production: News Values', in A. Briggs and P. Cobley (eds) *The Media: An Introduction*, London: Longman.

Parton, N. (1985) *The Politics of Child Abuse*, London: Macmillan.

Patten, C. (1999) *A New Beginning: Policing in Northern Ireland. The Report of the Independent Commission on Policing in Northern Ireland*, Norwich: HMSO Copyright Unit.

Peak, S. and Fisher, P. (1996) *The Media Guide, 1997*, London: Fourth Estate.

Pearson, G. (1983) *Hooligan: A History of Respectable Fears*, London: Macmillan.

Pfohl, S. (1977) 'The "Discovery" of Child Abuse', *Social Problems*, 24: 310–23.

Philo, G. (1999) *Message Received*, London: Longman.

Presdee, M. (2000) *Cultural Criminology and the Carnival of Crime*, London: Routledge.

Quinney, R. (1973) 'There's a Lot of Folks Grateful to the Lone Ranger: with some Notes on the Rise and Fall of American Criminology', *The Insurgent Sociologist*, 4: 56–64.

Rees, R. (1998) *Ireland 1905–1925: Volume One – Text and Historiography*, Newtownards: Colourprint Books.

Reiner, R. (1996) 'The Case of the Missing Crimes', in R. Levitas and W. Guy (eds) *Interpreting Official Statistics*, London: Routledge.

Reiner, R. (2000a) 'Researching the Police', in R. King and E. Wincup (eds) *Doing Research on Crime and Justice*, Oxford: Oxford University Press.

Reiner, R. (2000b) *The Politics of the Police*, third edition, Oxford: Oxford University Press.

Reiner, R. (2002) 'Media Made Criminality: the Representation of Crime in the Mass Media', in M. Maguire *et al* (eds) *The Oxford Handbook of Criminology*, third edition, Oxford: Oxford University Press.

Reiner, R., Livingstone, S. and Allen, J. (2000a) 'Casino Culture: Media and Crime in a Winner-Loser Society', in K. Stenson and D. Cowell (eds) *Crime, Risk and Justice*. Cullompton: Willan.

Reiner, R., Livingstone, S. and Allen, J. (2000b) 'No More Happy Endings? The Media and Popular Concern about Crime Since the Second World War', in T. Hope and R. Sparks (eds) *Crime, Risk and Insecurity*, London: Routledge.

Reiss, A. (1984) 'Selecting Strategies of Control over Organisational Life', in K. Hawkins and J. Thomas (eds) *Enforcing Regulation*, Boston, MA: Kluwer-Nijhoff.

Rock, P. (1973) 'News as Eternal Recurrence', in S. Cohen and J. Young (eds) *The Manufacture of News: Social Problems, Deviance and the Mass Media*, London: Constable.

Rolston, B. (1991a) 'News Fit to Print: Belfast's Daily Newspapers', in B. Rolston (ed.) *The Media and Northern Ireland: Covering the Troubles*, Basingstoke: Macmillan.

Rolston, B. (ed.) (1991b) *The Media and Northern Ireland: Covering the Troubles*, Basingstoke: Macmillan.

Rolston, B. and Miller, D. (eds) (1996) *War and Words: The Northern Ireland Media Reader*, Belfast: Beyond the Pale.

Roshier, R. (1973) 'The Selection of Crime News by the Press', in S. Cohen and J. Young (eds) *The Manufacture of News*, London: Constable.

Ruane, J. and Todd, J. (1996) *The Dynamics of Conflict in Northern Ireland: Power, Conflict and Emancipation*, Cambridge: Cambridge University Press.

Saraga, E. (2001) 'Dangerous Place: the Family as a Site of Crime', in J. Muincie and E. McLaughlin (eds) *The Problem of Crime*, London: Sage.

Sasson, T. (1995) *Crime Talk: How Citizens Construct Social Problems*, Hawthorne, NY: Aldine de Gruyter.

Schlesinger, P. (1987) *Putting Reality Together*, second edition, London: Methuen.

Schlesinger, P. (1990) 'Rethinking the Sociology of Journalism: Source Strategies and the Limits of Media-centrism', in M. Ferguson (ed.) *Public Communication: The New Imperatives*, London: Sage.

Schlesinger, P., Murdock, G. and Elliott, P. (1983) *Televising Terrorism: Political Violence in Popular Culture*, London: Comedia Publishing Group.

Schlesinger, P. and Tumber, H. (1994) *Reporting Crime: The Media Politics of Criminal Justice*, Oxford: Clarendon Press.

Schlesinger, P., Tumber, H. and Murdock, G. (1991)'The Media Politics of Crime and Criminal Justice', *British Journal of Sociology*, 42, 3: 397–422.

Schudson, M. (2000) 'The Sociology of News Production Revisited (again)', in J. Curran and M. Gurevitch (eds) *Media, Culture and Society*, third edition, London: Arnold.

Sherizen, S. (1978) 'Social Creation of Crime News: All the News Fitted to Print', in C. Winnick (ed.) *Deviance and Mass Media*, Beverly Hills, CA: Sage.
Sigal, L.V. (1973) *Reporters and Officials*, Lexington, MA: Heath.
Skidmore, P. (1995) 'Telling Tales; Media Power, Ideology and the Reporting of Child Sexual Abuse in Britain', in D. Kidd-Hewitt and R. Osborne (eds) *Crime and the Media; The Post-modern Spectacle*, London: Pluto Press.
Smart, C. (1989) *Feminism and the Power of Law*, London: Routledge.
Smith, S. (1984) 'Crime in the News', *British Journal of Criminology*, 24, 3: 289–95.
Soothill, K. (1995) 'Sex Crime News from Abroad', in R. Dobash *et al* (eds) *Gender and Crime*, Cardiff: University of Wales Press.
Soothill, K. and Francis, B. (1998) 'Poisoned Chalice or Just Deserts? The Sex Offenders Act 1997', *Journal of Forensic Psychiatry*, 9, 2: 281–93.
Soothill, K., Francis, B. and Ackereley, E. (1998) 'Paedophilia and Paedophiles', *New Law Journal*, 12 June: 882–3.
Soothill, K. and Jack, A. (1975) 'How Rape is Reported', *New Society*, 32, 663: 702–4.
Soothill, K. and Walby, S. (1991) *Sex Crime in the News*, London: Routledge.
Sparks, C. (2000) 'From Dead Trees to Live Wires: the Internet's Challenge to Traditional Newspapers', in J. Curran and M. Gurevitch (eds) *Mass Media and Society*, third edition, London: Arnold.
Sparks, R. (1992) *Television and the Drama of Crime: Moral Tales and the Place of Crime in Public Life*, Buckingham: Open University Press.
Sparks, R. (1995) 'Entertaining the Crisis: Television and Moral Enterprise', in D. Kidd-Hewitt and R. Osborne (eds) *Crime and the Media; The Post-modern Spectacle*, London: Pluto Press.
Spector, M. and Kitsuse, J. (1977/1987) *Constructing Social Problems*, Hawthorne, NY: Aldine de Gruyter.
Stanko, E. (1990) *Everyday Violence*, London: Unwin Hyman.
Stenson, K. and Cowell, D. (eds) (2000) *Crime, Risk and Justice*. Cullompton: Willan.
Stephenson, H. and Bromley, M. (eds) (1998) *Sex Lies and Democracy: The Press and the Public*, London: Longman.
Stephenson-Burton, A.E. (1995) 'Through the Looking Glass: Public Images of White Collar Crime', in D. Kidd-Hewitt and R. Osborne (eds) *Crime and the Media; The Post-modern Spectacle*, London: Pluto Press.
Sumner, C. (1997) 'Censure, Crime and State', in M. Maguire *et al* (eds) *The Oxford Handbook of Criminology*, second edition, Oxford: Oxford University Press.
Surette, R. (1998) *Media, Crime and Criminal Justice: Images and Realities*, second edition, Belmont, CA: Wadsworth.

Temkin, J. (1986) 'Women, Rape and Law Reform', in S. Tomaselli and R. Porter (eds) *Rape: An Historical and Cultural Enquiry*, Oxford: Blackwell.
Temkin, J. (1987) *Rape and the Legal Process*, London: Sweet & Maxwell.
Thomas, T. (2000) *Sex Crime: Sex Offenders and Society*, Cullompton: Willan.

Thompson, J.B. (1990) *Ideology and Modern Culture*, Cambridge: Polity Press.
Thompson, J.B. (2000) *Political Scandal: Power and Visibility in the Media Age*, Cambridge: Polity Press.
Thompson, K. (1998) *Moral Panics*, London: Routledge.
Tomaselli, S. and Porter, R. (eds) (1986) *Rape: An Historical and Cultural Enquiry*, Oxford: Blackwell.
Tuchman, G. (1978) *Making News: A Study in the Construction of Reality*, New York, NY: Free Press.
Tunstall, J. (1971) *Journalists at Work: Specialist Correspondents, their News Organisations, News Sources and the Competitor-Colleagues*, London: Constable.

Waddington, P.A. (1986) 'Mugging as a Moral Panic: a Question of Proportion', *British Journal of Sociology*, 37, 2: 245–59.
Walkowitz, J. (1992) *City of Dreadful Delight: Narratives of Sexual Danger in Late Victorian London*, London: Virago Press.
Wartella, E. (1995) 'Media and Problem Behaviours in Young People', in M. Rutter and D. Smith (eds) *Psychological Disorders in Young People*, London: Wiley.
Weaver, P. (1975) 'Newspaper News and Television News', in D. Cater and R. Adler (eds) *Television as a Social Force*, New York, NY: Praeger.
Websdale, N. (1999) 'The Social Construction of "Stranger-Danger" in Washington State as a Form of Patriarchal Ideology', in J. Ferrell and N. Websdale (eds) *Making Trouble: Cultural Constructions of Crime, Deviance, and Control*, Hawthorne, NY: Aldine de Gruyter.
West, D. (1996) 'Sexual Molesters', in N. Walker (ed.) *Dangerous People*, London: Blackstone Press.
West, D. (2000a) 'Paedophilia: Plague or Panic', *The Journal of Forensic Psychiatry*, 11, 3: 511–31.
West, D. (2000b) 'The Sex Crime Situation: Deterioration more Apparent than Real', *European Journal on Criminal Policy and Research*, 8: 399–422.
Whale, J. (1977) *The Politics of the Media*, London: Fontana.
White, D.M. (1950) ' "The Gatekeeper": a Case Study in the Selection of News Selection', *Journalist Quarterly*, 27: 383–90.
Wilczynski, A. (1999) 'Moral Panics and the Reporting of Child Sex Abuse', *The Australian and New Zealand Journal of Criminology*, 32, 3: 262–83.
Williams, P. and Dickinson, J. (1993) 'Fear of Crime; Read All about it; the Relationship between Newspaper Crime Reporting and Fear of Crime', *British Journal of Criminology*, 33, 1: 33–56.
Wilson, D. and Silverman, J. (2002) *Innocence Betrayed: Paedophilia, the Media and Society*, Cambridge: Polity Press.

Young, A. (1998) 'Violence as Seduction: Enduring Genres of Rape', in A. Howe (ed.) *Sexed Crime in the News*, Sydney: The Federation Press.
Young, J. (1981) 'Beyond the Consensual Paradigm: a Critique of Left Functionalism in Media Theory', in S. Cohen and J. Young (eds) *The*

Manufacture of News: Social Problems, Deviance and Mass Media, London: Constable.

Young, J. (1988) 'Risk of Crime and Fear of Crime: a Realist Critique of Survey-based Assumptions', in M. Maguire and J. Pointing (eds) *Victims of Crime: A New Deal?*, Buckingham: Open University Press.

Zedner, L. (2002) 'Victims', in M. Maguire *et al* (eds) *The Oxford Handbook of Criminology*, third edition, Oxford: Oxford University Press.

Index